PREGNANCY SICKNESS

Using Your Body's
Natural Defenses
to Protect
Your Baby-to-Be

MARGIE PROFET

Illustrations by Mary Krikorian

Addison-Wesley Publishing Company, Inc.

Reading, Massachusetts   Menlo Park, California   New York
Don Mills, Ontario   Harlow, England   Amsterdam   Bonn
Sydney   Singapore   Tokyo   Madrid   San Juan
Paris   Seoul   Milan   Mexico City   Taipei

This book is meant to educate and should not be used as an alternative to appropriate medical care. The author has exerted every effort to ensure that the information presented is accurate up to the time of publication. However, in light of ongoing research and the constant flow of information it is possible that new findings may invalidate some of the data presented here.

Many of the designations used by manufacturers and sellers to distinguish their products are claimed as trademarks. Where those designations appear in this book and Addison-Wesley was aware of a trademark claim, the designations have been printed in initial capital letters (i.e., Tylenol).

Library of Congress Cataloging-in-Publication Data
Profet, Margie.
    [Protecting your baby-to-be]
    Pregnancy sickness : using your body's natural defenses to protect your baby-to-be / Margie Profet ; illustrations by Mary Krikorian.
        p.   cm.
    Originally published in 1995 under the title: Protecting your baby-to-be.
    Includes bibliographical references and index.
    ISBN 0-201-15492-7
    1. Morning sickness.   2. Pregnancy—Trimester, First.
3. Abnormalities. Human—Prevention.   I. Title.
RG579.P757   1997
618.3'2—dc21   97–7307
                                                              CIP

Cover design by Suzanne Heiser
Text design by Diane Levy
Set in 11-point Simoncini Garamond by G&S Typesetters, Inc., Austin, TX

1 2 3 4 5 6 7 8 9-DOH-00999897
First paperback printing, April 1997

CONTENTS

CONTENTS

PREFACE

TIME AND AGAIN over the last eight years, while riding a subway, hanging out at a cafe, or washing up in a ladies' room, I'd end up in conversation with women from various walks of life about my research on the function of pregnancy sickness (the food aversions, nausea, and vomiting characteristic of the first trimester of pregnancy). What struck me about these women, most of whom were not scientists, was that they were fascinated to learn about the science of their bodies. In fact, they were far more interested in learning *why* their bodies behaved the way they did during pregnancy than they were in simply being told what to do about it. If the "why" was explained in a way that made sense to them—that is, if the science was accessible and interesting—they would often think out loud, excitedly ask questions, analyze their own experiences, and come up with "what if" scenarios. What especially impressed me about the average "woman in the street" was that she so often zeroed in on the key questions that a well-trained biologist would ask, such as, "If pregnancy sickness has a function, why is it so variable among women?" and "If pregnancy sickness is so important, shouldn't my pets get it, too?" When we parted, many of these women would enthusiastically remark, "You should write a book on this." And so I did. Many parts of this book are written in response to their questions.

PREGNANCY SICKNESS

This book is intended primarily for women who are experiencing the first trimester of pregnancy or who are planning to become pregnant. It is also intended for their parenting partners and health care providers. In the course of researching pregnancy sickness, I came to realize that a pregnant woman's understanding of its function has significant practical implications for how she should behave toward food and other substances during the first trimester, and that a lot of the advice given to first-trimester women by authors of popular books on pregnancy is not only seriously misinformed, but potentially dangerous. No book that doles out pregnancy advice has ever taken into account the function of pregnancy sickness—none of them has even seemed to realize that pregnancy sickness is important.

As this book will show, pregnancy sickness helps protect the baby-to-be from birth defects by discouraging the first-trimester woman from eating foods with high levels of naturally occurring toxins. Pregnancy sickness is perhaps the defining characteristic of the first trimester, the period of the baby-to-be's development during which major birth defects can occur, and a first-trimester woman—and her parenting partner—should respect her pregnancy sickness. The goal of pregnancy sickness is to protect the baby-to-be from birth defects, and this book furthers that goal by also including information on how to reduce various kinds of risks that pregnancy sickness does not protect against. I think that a woman can give no greater gift to her baby than a healthy start in life.

In researching the function of pregnancy sickness, I progressed from theory to applications, and that's the order in which I present the information in this book. The first part of the book (Chapters 2 through 5) provides a framework for understanding why the first-trimester woman gets pregnancy sickness and why

Preface

the first-trimester baby-to-be is so vulnerable to harm from so many natural things that an adult, or even a second-trimester baby-to-be, is not vulnerable to. The second part of the book (Chapters 6 through 12) provides practical advice for the first-trimester woman to help her protect her baby-to-be.

Each chapter has one illustration, drawn by artist Mary Krikorian, which is meant to highlight the chapter's main point. The illustrations can be used as a succinct preview of the book, by a woman wondering what the book is about, or as a succinct review of the book, by a woman who has already read it. If, after reading the book, a woman reviews these illustrations and thinks "Oh, how totally obvious," then they will have served their purpose.

Woven into this book are the contributions of various people who over the years have shared their time, ideas, and criticisms with me. Above all, I thank Don Symons, who was a part of the process from start to finish and who edited the entire book manuscript. The book is dedicated to him. Two of my closest colleagues, George Williams and Mark Shigenaga, played at least an indirect role, in that for years we've bounced ideas off each other. While I was in the middle of my academic research on pregnancy sickness, I was fortunate to land a job in the biochemistry laboratory of Bruce Ames at the University of California at Berkeley, who alerted me to some of the key research on toxins and birth defects. More recently, this book benefited from discussions with Sam Wasser, Eugene Weinberg, and Cassandra Henderson. My agents, Katinka Matson and John Brockman, introduced me to Addison-Wesley, and, early on, Katinka Matson gave me some key suggestions about how to focus the book for the audience I was trying to reach. My editors

PREGNANCY SICKNESS

at Addison-Wesley—Liz Perle McKenna during the initial stages of the book and Nancy Miller during the final stages—provided many useful suggestions for making the book accessible to that audience. Mary Krikorian, the illustrator, was a joy to work with, even as she labored over multiple drafts of each illustration. I'd also like to thank the various family members, friends, and others who allowed me to interrogate them about their pregnancy sickness. Some of their experiences have ended up as anecdotes in the book.

The luxury of having the time to write this book was made possible by the generous financial support of two foundations: the Leonard X. Bosack & Bette M. Kruger Foundation of Redmond, Washington; and the John D. & Catherine T. MacArthur Foundation of Chicago, Illinois.

Finally, I'd like to thank the three people in my life who most inspired me to think and explore: my parents, Robert and Karen Profet, and my college philosophy professor Harvey Mansfield.

Chapter One

Introduction

PREGNANCY IS USUALLY VIEWED as a nine-month continuum, divided, for convenience, into three equal parts—the first, second, and third trimesters. This division categorizes the baby-to-be much like a T-shirt—small, medium, or large. But the way that a woman thinks about her pregnancy should reflect its natural, functional organization, not arbitrary divisions. The baby-to-be develops in two distinct stages, and as its needs change, so do the physiology, psychology, and behavior of the mother-to-be.

The different parts of a baby-to-be have to form before they can grow. There are two main stages of prenatal development and pregnancy, which this book refers to as the "formation stage" and the "growth stage." Special terms already exist for the baby-to-be in the early formation stage and the baby-to-be in the growth stage: "embryo" and "fetus." During the formation stage, the embryo's cells multiply very rapidly and differentiate into the various organs and tissues that make up a human body. During the growth stage, the fetus grows from a tiny entity that could easily fit in the palm of the mother's hand to a seven-or-so-pound baby ready for birth. The formation stage spans the period from about two weeks to fourteen weeks after conception. The growth stage spans the period from about fourteen weeks after conception until birth. (Technically, an embryo is referred to as

PREGNANCY SICKNESS

a fetus at eight weeks after conception, the completion of the most critical period of organ formation; but since many of the fetus's organs are still forming during the first few weeks of the fetal period, the formation stage spans both the embryonic period and approximately the first six weeks of the fetal period.) The formation stage happens to coincide with the first trimester, so this book will use the two terms interchangeably. There is an easy way to remember the dividing point between the two stages of pregnancy: if the woman is not yet "showing" her pregnancy

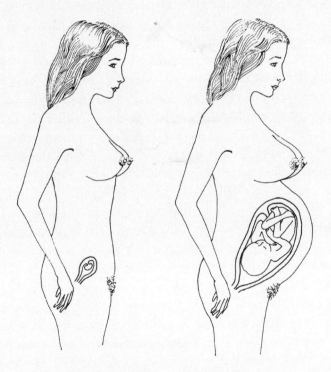

There are two main stages of pregnancy:
the formation stage and the growth stage.

is usually in the formation stage, but once she begins to "show" it is in the growth stage.

The decisions a woman makes that will affect the health of her baby-to-be should be based on an understanding of the natural divisions of pregnancy.* The focus of this book is the formation stage—the stage that is most crucial to the health of the baby-to-be, yet the one that is traditionally ignored in pregnancy books. Pregnancy books written for a lay audience uniformly fail to demarcate these two stages appropriately. As a result, women get a lot of "generic" pregnancy advice that is really appropriate only to the fetus, not the embryo. The fetus does not undergo the kind of metamorphoses that the embryo does and therefore does not need the kind of protection the embryo needs. As this book will show, various changes that women experience during the first trimester, which are routinely regarded as nonfunctional side effects of pregnancy, actually function to protect the embryo. Much of the advice first-trimester women are typically given even runs counter to what nature is telling them.

---

*Throughout this book pregnancy is dated from the *time of conception*. (Normal human gestation—from conception to birth—takes about 266 days, which is 38 weeks, or eight and three-quarter months.) For the sake of convenience, most obstetricians and gynecologists date a pregnancy from the first day of the woman's last menstrual period (LMP), rather than from the day she actually got pregnant, because a woman usually can pinpoint the day she started her last period but not necessarily the day she conceived. The time lag between the LMP and conception, which equals the time lag between the LMP and ovulation (give or take a day or two), is generally about two weeks—but it can vary considerably from woman to woman, depending on the length of her menstrual cycle, and from cycle to cycle in a woman whose cycles are irregular. Dating a pregnancy from the LMP automatically assumes a two-week time lag from the LMP to conception, but this is often less accurate than dating a pregnancy from the estimated date of conception/ovulation, which takes into account not only the LMP, but the length and regularity of an individual woman's menstrual

Anxiety About Birth Defects

Every expectant woman hopes that her baby will be born perfectly healthy. But anxiety about birth defects often accompanies the anticipation of motherhood, motivating many women to undergo prenatal testing in the third, fourth, or fifth month after conception. If serious fetal abnormalities are detected, the pregnant woman faces the sometimes agonizing decision of whether or not to continue the pregnancy. Even if testing does not reveal abnormalities, the woman cannot be assured that her fetus is healthy, because many abnormalities cannot be detected prenatally, and some do not become apparent until well after birth. Thus, although women do have control over whether or not to carry a baby with known birth defects to term, they often feel helpless to prevent birth defects from occurring in the first place.

Pregnancy Sickness:
Natural Protection Against Birth Defects

What pregnant women up until now have not realized, however, is that nature provides a mechanism that is designed to protect embryos from birth defects: pregnancy sickness (commonly, but misleadingly, called "morning sickness"). Pregnancy sickness is a

---

cycle, her memory of when recent sexual intercourse took place, and the results of ovulation kits or other methods of detecting ovulation.

Furthermore, to me it does not make sense to say that a woman is four weeks pregnant when she conceived only two weeks ago. Many women who have already experienced one pregnancy may be used to dating pregnancy from their LMP, but I believe it's important to date pregnancy instead from the date of conception, estimated as accurately as possible. Awareness of the true age of the embryo or fetus is crucial in determining its stage of development and the kind of protection it needs.

Introduction

collection of symptoms, which invariably include food and odor aversions, and often include nausea and vomiting as well. Virtually all women experience pregnancy sickness during the first trimester of pregnancy. Pregnancy sickness protects the embryo from naturally occurring plant and bacterial toxins in the mother's diet that can cause birth defects or miscarriage. It does this by causing the mother to become repulsed by smells and tastes that indicate toxicity. Human pregnancy sickness, like other human physiological mechanisms, evolved over millions of years—long before the invention of agriculture—when our ancestors lived by hunting wild animals and gathering wild plants. The environment of the ancestral hunter-gatherer differed vastly from that of a modern woman living in a technological society. Although the modern embryo is as vulnerable as the ancestral embryo to birth defects, pregnancy sickness is not as fail-safe in the modern environment as it was in the environment in which it evolved. Once women become aware of the purpose of pregnancy sickness and the way it works, they can take specific steps to ensure that their embryos have the protection that pregnancy sickness was designed to give.

Every mechanism in the body was designed to solve some problem in the ancestral environment. The problem that pregnancy sickness solved was the vulnerability of the developing embryo to the natural toxins in the human diet. The natural environment contains a vast spectrum of toxins—probably more than a million—and new ones are always evolving. Plants, which constitute much of the human diet, can't fight, hide from, or flee from animals that want to eat them, so they defend themselves with chemical warfare. As discussed in Chapter 2, every plant, without exception, produces an array of natural toxins to deter its enemies. Natural toxins exist even in seemingly harmless foods that come from plants, such as broccoli, celery, potatoes, nutmeg, sweet basil, and soybeans. Toxins also exist in many meats and other animal products, because the bacteria and molds that commonly infest these products produce toxins. Thus, natural toxins have always been abundant in human diets.

Humans, like other animals, have evolved many defenses against toxins, which is why we can eat many of the toxins in foods without being harmed by them. Such mechanisms include ways to detect and avoid dangerous levels of toxins as well as ways to detoxify and eliminate toxins that have been eaten. Many toxins that in low doses are easily tolerated by adults, however, can harm or even kill an embryo by disrupting the process of organ formation and causing permanent malformations, as discussed in Chapter 3. Because the human body cannot possibly know inherently which *particular* toxins, of the vast spectrum that exist in nature, would cause defects in the embryo's organ formation, pregnancy sickness is designed to recognize *general* cues of toxicity, thereby preventing the embryo from being exposed to high doses of potentially devastating toxins.

Pungent odors and bitter tastes are the main cues of natural toxins. Pregnancy sickness causes the woman to have strong aversions to these cues. Even a woman's most cherished foods can become unpalatable or nauseating. In this way, pregnancy sickness deters the mother from inflicting high levels of toxins on her susceptible embryo. Not all toxins can cause birth defects in humans, but all toxins should be suspected and, in high doses, avoided. This is the goal of pregnancy sickness.

Pregnancy sickness is really just a recalibration of physiological mechanisms that everyone uses all the time, as discussed in Chapter 4. The brain stem (a primitive part of the brain just above the spinal cord) contains a special organ whose function

Introduction

is to monitor the level of toxins in the bloodstream and trigger nausea, vomiting, and food aversions if the level reaches a certain threshold. In early pregnancy this threshold is lowered, so that the brain stem triggers these unpleasant symptoms with less provocation. In addition, during the first trimester, the mother's sense of smell is enhanced, enabling her to detect toxins at lower doses.

Misconceptions About Pregnancy Sickness

Pregnancy sickness does not necessarily imply feeling "sick." Many women who do not vomit or have prolonged bouts of nausea during early pregnancy assume that fate has spared them from pregnancy sickness. But the primary symptoms of pregnancy sickness are food and odor aversions, and first-trimester women who do not feel "sick" are, nevertheless, usually repulsed by certain foods and odors that they previously found attractive. If a first-trimester pregnant woman suddenly finds herself opting for bland foods in lieu of her favorite spicy dishes, she is experiencing pregnancy sickness. She does not even have to be conscious of food aversions to have pregnancy sickness. Virtually all women in the first trimester must alter their diets, consciously or unconsciously, to avoid feeling sick (or sicker, as the case may be).

"Morning sickness" is a misnomer, because it can occur at any time of day. The aversions of early pregnancy occur whenever the woman is exposed to offending foods and odors, and nausea can last throughout the day or even be worse in the evening. But some pregnant women do feel especially sick upon rising in the morning, as discussed in Chapter 5, hence the reference to "morning" in the English and many Western European terms for the syndrome. Most non-Western languages, however, do not refer to "morning" in their terms for pregnancy sickness. In

Russian, for example, the term, literally translated, is "pregnancy indisposition"; in Cantonese it is "pregnancy response"; and in Korean it is "fake vomiting."

Pregnancy Sickness Is Universal

There is a myth that in some cultures women don't experience pregnancy sickness. But pregnancy sickness has no cultural or historical boundaries. As discussed in Chapter 5, women everywhere get it, whether they live in industrialized or nonindustrialized societies (and at least some other animals appear to get it, too). The African !Kung San women who live by hunting and gathering wild foods, much as our preagricultural ancestors did, even recognize pregnancy sickness as one of the first signs of pregnancy. The earliest written account of pregnancy sickness is a description on papyrus from about 2000 B.C. Hippocrates, the famed Greek physician who lived about 400 B.C., regarded pregnancy sickness as a sign of pregnancy: "When in a woman who is suffering from neither rigors nor fever, menstruation is suppressed and she suffers from nausea, she is pregnant."

Some women claim that they didn't experience pregnancy sickness during their pregnancies. But in all probability they did, even if they weren't aware of it or don't remember it. Many women in industrialized countries try hard to maintain an image of superwoman, able to cope smoothly with the often conflicting demands of pregnancy, family, and career. Feeling nauseated and throwing up without being "sick" may seem to be signs of weakness. It's not uncommon to hear women say things like, "Oh, being pregnant is a breeze. I haven't had any pregnancy sickness so far. . . . Well, O.K., I did throw up the other day when I made coffee for the first time in two months"; or "I've felt perfectly fine

Introduction

the entire pregnancy. I had no pregnancy sickness at all. I could eat anything I wanted, . . . Well, just not Chinese food or anything else spicy."

Some women simply forget about their pregnancy sickness soon after it goes away. A year or so after her second child was born, my sister Julie insisted, "Oh, I had such an easy pregnancy. I never had any kind of pregnancy sickness. I felt just fine the whole time." I reminded her of a ski trip we took together when she was eight weeks pregnant: at one restaurant she couldn't stand the garlicky smell of her soup, which she pushed away; at another restaurant she got up and left the table midway through her fish dinner because she was too nauseated to finish it; she had to stand far away from the campfire because the odor of smoke had become abhorrent to her; and she couldn't tolerate the aroma of my faintly scented hand lotion, exclaiming, "Get that away from me. I can't stand that smell when I'm pregnant."

My mother is another example of pregnancy sickness amnesia, having claimed for years to have sailed through each of her pregnancies without pregnancy sickness. Yet at a celebration of my grandfather's eightieth birthday, she related a story in which my grandfather had dropped by her apartment late one night when she was two months into her first pregnancy; she had fixed some mushroom soup for them both and then promptly threw hers up.

Misconceptions about pregnancy sickness abound. "Sickness" implies disease, yet normal pregnancy sickness is a sign of health. As discussed in Chapter 3, women with negligible or only mild pregnancy sickness have about three times the risk of miscarriage as women with moderate or severe pregnancy sickness. Pregnant women without nausea often feel fortunate to have been spared, but they are actually at greater risk of harming their embryos.

PREGNANCY SICKNESS

Many people assume that all dietary changes during pregnancy are part of the same syndrome, confusing food aversions with food cravings. Movies and TV shows are sometimes the worst offenders in furthering this misconception, portraying women who have just found out that they're pregnant wolfing down every food in sight and then running to the bathroom to vomit. An insatiable appetite for all sorts of food accompanied by nausea and bouts of vomiting wouldn't make any physiological sense and doesn't occur. An insatiable appetite and idiosyncratic cravings for unusual foods, such as spicy pickles or hot curried lamb, may come in the second or third trimester. But during the first trimester, the pregnant woman should expect to be repulsed by many, if not most, foods, and to desire only nonpungent foods that are bland, sweet, or sour.

Why Understanding the Function of Pregnancy Sickness Is Necessary

One might reasonably ask why an explicit awareness of the function of pregnancy sickness should be necessary. After all, for pregnancy sickness to have evolved, it must have functioned well in ancestral women, who were presumably oblivious to its function. The ancestral hunter-gatherer environment that shaped our physiology, however, was radically different from ours. In a modern environment, failing to zero in on the function of a physiological mechanism, such as pregnancy sickness, can lead to terrible mistakes in managing it.

For one thing, modern medical technology enables women and their physicians to intervene when they shouldn't. In the case of pregnancy sickness, the most devastating example is the thalidomide disaster. In the late 1950s and early 1960s, many

Introduction

European women tried to alleviate pregnancy sickness with the drug thalidomide, which turned out to be a drug that causes severe limb malformations in human embryos. It is sadly ironic that women tried to inhibit a mechanism that protects against birth defects by taking a drug that causes them. Had the women and their physicians understood the function of pregnancy sickness, they might have elected dietary rather than medicinal intervention and thus averted disaster.

The field of medicine has a long history of mistakes in dealing with pregnancy sickness. In previous centuries in the United States and Europe pregnancy sickness was generally regarded as a "reflex" of pregnancy. Physicians who viewed this reflex as a nuisance used various questionable "treatments" to alleviate it, including leeches, vocal exercises, and dilation of the cervix. Although it's hard to imagine that vocal exercises did much harm (or good), many of the "treatments" were clearly dangerous, both to the mother and to the embryo. Dilating the cervix, for example, can lead to miscarriage or infection of the uterus.

Perhaps the most harmful attitudes about pregnancy sickness developed during the twentieth century. After the advent of psychoanalysis, some physicians and psychologists began to blame women for their pregnancy sickness, attributing it to female neuroses. Many pregnant women were told that their severe nausea and vomiting represented a subconscious rejection of pregnancy, an ambivalence about motherhood, a loathing of coitus, an unrelieved frustration at failing to find gratification in pregnancy, a rejection of femininity, or an oral attempt at abortion. The root of their pregnancy sickness was variously viewed as hysteria, an immature personality, or an undue attachment to their own mothers. Hurtful, punitive "treatments" were inflicted on women who were vomiting so severely that they required hospitalization. Such patients were first isolated in the hospital from their families and friends, and then their vomiting tubs were taken away, so that they had to vomit in their beds and wallow in whatever they expelled. Milder psychoanalytical "treatments" consisted of investigating the life situation of the pregnant patient and trying to reduce her guilt complexes. The misconception that pregnancy sickness was psychosomatic undoubtedly increased pregnant women's emotional distress because it made them feel guilty about feeling sick.

Understanding the function of pregnancy sickness can guide women in managing its unpleasant symptoms. Since pregnancy sickness protects the embryo, women should not normally seek to suppress it medicinally. On the other hand, as discussed in Chapters 6 and 7, nausea and vomiting can be minimized naturally by avoiding the odors and foods that trigger them. In agricultural societies, it is not uncommon to mask the bitterness (that is, the taste that signifies natural toxicity) of some foods with sugar, as in preparing chocolate; but during the first trimester of pregnancy it is important to recognize bitterness as aversive and not to fool the toxin-detecting mechanisms.

Modern diets differ nutritionally from ancestral hunter-gatherer diets, and these differences have consequences for the embryo's health, as discussed in Chapter 8. In order to ovulate and become pregnant, a woman normally must consume a certain level of fat and calories. It is unlikely that many ancestral hunter-gatherer women were vitamin deficient at conception, because much of their diet came from fresh fruits and vegetables, which are major sources of vitamins. In a modern environment, by contrast, much of the average diet comes from processed or fatty foods, which are usually relatively low in vitamins, and women can conceive even if deficient in certain vitamins crucial to the embryo's health. The food aversions, nausea, and vomiting of early pregnancy generally decrease nutrient intake, and certain vitamin deficiencies increase the risk of birth defects, so it is important that pregnant women understand the nutritional costs of pregnancy sickness and monitor their nutritional status accordingly.

Finally, in a modern environment, a pregnant woman can be exposed to a variety of toxins that do not emit the natural cues of toxicity. As discussed in Chapter 10, pregnancy sickness does not necessarily protect against such substances. The toxic substances in pills and injections, for example, bypass the taste and smell receptors that normally trigger aversions. Pregnancy sickness also does not generally deter the consumption of alcohol, which is not toxic to the embryo in the small quantities that exist naturally in plants consumed as food, but which *is* toxic in the large quantities available as beverages to modern women. It is important, therefore, for a pregnant woman to know what kinds of substances must be avoided consciously. In sum, by understanding the function of pregnancy sickness, a pregnant woman can make wiser decisions about managing her diet, obtaining adequate nutrition, quelling nausea, and avoiding high levels of toxins, including those that are unique to the modern environment. And a nonpregnant woman planning to conceive can also take specific steps to ensure that her embryo gets a good start in life.

How Can We Be Sure
We've Identified the Function?

In trying to understand any physiological mechanism, the fundamental question is that of function: what's the mechanism for? The question of function is not merely interesting or aesthetically pleasing; it's crucial for making good medical decisions. Blind intervention is not good medical practice. Imagine consulting a cardiologist who didn't understand that the function of the heart was to pump blood. How could this cardiologist define cardiac health, recognize heart disease, or know when and how to intervene surgically or medicinally? The function of pregnancy sickness is to protect against birth defects and miscarriage, and it is imperative that this knowledge underlie the practical advice given to first-trimester pregnant women.

Some people may wonder how we can be sure that we've pinpointed the correct function for pregnancy sickness. The process for determining the function of any physiological mechanism, whether it be pregnancy sickness or the heart, is basically the same. It entails, first, identifying the problem that the mechanism in question was designed to solve; and, second, demonstrating design, that is, showing that there is an adaptive fit between the characteristics of the mechanism and the problem that is too close to be merely the product of chance or the byproduct of other mechanisms. All the salient characteristics of the mechanism should be explained by the proposed function.

No Other Book Is an
Appropriate Guide to the First Trimester

At the time of this writing, no other book on pregnancy shows even a rudimentary understanding of the role pregnancy sickness plays in protecting the embryo. The focus of advice for the first trimester should be the prevention of birth defects, yet often women are given general advice about pregnancy, as though there is no need to distinguish the first trimester from the others. At present, much of the dietary advice offered to pregnant

Introduction

women by popular books and health educators is inappropriate for the first trimester, when the embryo is susceptible to major malformations. The needs of the first-trimester embryo differ dramatically from those of the second- and third-trimester fetus, and a woman's diet during pregnancy should reflect this difference. Furthermore, many of the physiological changes a woman undergoes in the first trimester are different from, or even opposite to, those that occur in the second and third trimesters. The sense of smell, for example, becomes much *more* acute during the first trimester but *less* acute during the third trimester.

Most popular books on pregnancy are not only incorrect on the topic of pregnancy sickness; they're also usually unsympathetic and often blameful. Some books treat pregnancy sickness as an attitude problem, as something that women should be able to control by an act of will. Many of them imply that severe pregnancy sickness stems from ambivalence about pregnancy or marriage. Some say that severe vomiting reflects an inability to cope emotionally, advising women with severe pregnancy sickness to try to think about what aspect of pregnancy they can't stomach. One popular book views pregnancy sickness as a cultural invention and even claims that it is going out of fashion. But pregnancy sickness is not subject to the whims of fashion. Human physiology was designed by nature, not culture.

Some of the advice popular pregnancy books offer is potentially dangerous. For example, one book advises pregnant women with nausea to try to quell it by drinking a tea made from fennel seed. Fennel seeds contain very high concentrations of estragole, a toxin that can damage the genetic material of cells. It is precisely this type of toxin that pregnancy sickness was designed to protect against. Other books advise pregnant women to eat ginger root. Although ginger root does contain a natural toxin that appears to have an antinausea effect on adults, it also contains many other toxins with as yet unknown effects, which may well endanger the embryo. A woman doesn't know what she's risking if she eats ginger every time she feels nauseated during pregnancy. Furthermore, if pregnancy sickness protects the embryo, a woman shouldn't be advised to interfere with this mechanism unless the nausea or vomiting become excessive.

What This Book Has to Offer

There are ways by which a first-trimester woman can minimize the risk that her baby will have birth defects. The main way, as this book will show, is by taking full advantage of nature's own protective mechanism—pregnancy sickness. Although it cannot protect against genetic defects in the egg or sperm—which cause such disorders as Down syndrome—pregnancy sickness can help to protect against nongenetic defects in the formation of the limbs, eyes, ears, brain, spinal cord, genitalia, heart, liver, and other organs. It is crucial to understand that the needs of the embryo differ from those of the fetus. The tiny embryo does not need many calories to thrive, but it does need vigorous protection against toxins. The fetus, by contrast, needs many calories, but not nearly as much protection against toxins.

Pregnancy sickness should be viewed as something a woman does for her baby-to-be. This book offers extensive advice on ways to manage pregnancy sickness without subverting its purpose. It shows the parenting partner that it's in his interest to help protect the embryo by helping the woman minimize her exposure to substances that nauseate her. Food aversions are the purpose of pregnancy sickness, and it is important to recognize them for what they are.

Introduction

This book also offers advice to women who experience either of the extremes of pregnancy sickness—a near absence of it or unrelenting nausea and vomiting. If a woman does not experience much pregnancy sickness, for example, she should consciously act to protect her embryo by modifying her diet to mimic that of a woman with pregnancy sickness (Chapter 9). This book also discusses nondietary hazards to the embryo (Chapter 11) as well as ways to help detect malformations that may have occurred (Chapter 12).

This book is divided into two parts: the theory—"How Pregnancy Sickness Protects the Baby-to-Be"—and the applications—"Managing the First Trimester." The first half of the book puts together and explains all the major pieces of the puzzle of pregnancy sickness. The second half applies this knowledge, providing the reader with a practical guide to the first trimester.

Although a wide range of things in the environment can cause birth defects—including various plant toxins, medicines, viruses, and metals—this book focuses mainly on things lurking in a woman's diet. Dietary toxins are constant, pervasive threats to the embryo but are grossly under-recognized as such. The other things in the environment that cause birth defects are not discussed in detail until later in the book, not because they are unimportant, but because the goal of this book is to alert first-trimester women to the dangers they will encounter most frequently and to give them information they can't obtain elsewhere. The information offered in this book is applicable to every pregnant woman every single day of the first trimester. In sum, it teaches women how to think about embryonic development, diet, and the first trimester in ways that will enable them to promote the health of their embryos.

PART I

How
Pregnancy Sickness
Protects the
Baby-to-Be

Chapter Two

Natural Toxins and Our Natural Defenses Against Them

SCANNING THE NATURAL LANDSCAPE, it becomes clear that people can eat only a tiny fraction of the vast spectrum of plants. We tolerate ripe fruits well, but we would get sick (and possibly die) if we ate the leaves, roots, stems, or flowers of most plants. Even among the plants we do eat, many are only "sort of" edible. Spices and herbs are edible only in tiny doses. And most people have ambivalent feelings about vegetables. What child hasn't lamented, "If vegetables are so good for us, how come they don't taste good?" Some common vegetables are so bitter that often it's hard to get young children to eat them without using bribes or threats or masking the bitterness with sugar. Even adults attempt to make vegetables more palatable—by coating them with salt and fat in the form of butter, salad dressing, cheese sauce, or cream sauce.

To the frustration of the typical woman who's just discovered she's pregnant, this already small set of edible foods abruptly shrinks. Suddenly, most foods smell bad and taste bad, to the point of being nauseating. The "sort-of-edible" foods become downright impossible to eat. It may seem paradoxical to a woman that just when she gets pregnant and is determined to "eat right" for her developing baby, she becomes repulsed by most sources of nutrients.

All Plants Manufacture Toxins

Many of us have taken nature tours with guides who alerted us to patches of poison oak. Plants often give the impression of being benign, passively allowing us to pick, cook, and devour them, so poison oak may appear to be an aberration. But it isn't. All plants manufacture poisons (toxins) to defend themselves against the animals that attempt to eat them and the microorganisms that attempt to invade them. Unlike animals, plants can't fight, hide from, or flee from their "predators." Their only means of defense is chemical warfare. A typical plant's chemical arsenal includes a few dozen different toxins to protect itself against a wide range of plant-eating animals and microorganisms. Although a given toxin may be produced by several plant species, each species produces a unique set of toxins. With about half a million plant species in the world, there are probably at least that many different plant toxins.

Producing toxins takes a lot of energy, and the resources of any plant are limited. So a plant faces a trade-off between surviving and reproducing: the more energy it expends making chemical defenses, the less is available to make offspring. A plant's usual "strategy" is to maintain only low or moderate levels of toxins, but to raise these levels immediately when it detects a threat, such as an insect nibbling on it. In other words, the plant normally operates on a tight defense budget, but in an emergency it mobilizes all its available resources for defense. For this reason, two plants of the same species can contain markedly different levels of toxins, depending on the particular stresses each has encountered.

Natural Toxins and Our Natural Defenses Against Them

A toxin, by definition, is any chemical made by a living organism (such as a plant) for the purpose of harming another organism (such as a plant-eating animal). Toxins disrupt the normal functioning of the "enemy's" organs. Some toxins cause blood vessels to constrict, for example, producing a sudden rise in

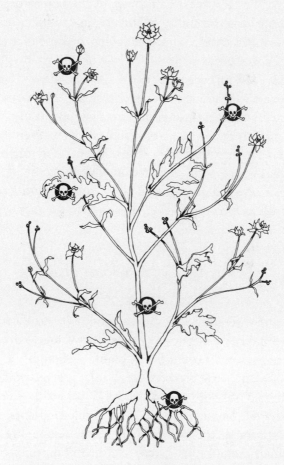

All plants and plant parts contain natural toxins.

blood pressure; others cause blood vessels to dilate, lowering the blood pressure dangerously. Some toxins coagulate the blood, rendering the victim susceptible to blood clots; others inhibit coagulation, preventing blood from clotting at wounds. Some toxins interfere with the transmission of nerve impulses, causing discoordination, paralysis, or hallucinations. Some toxins kill cells of specific "target" organs, such as the kidney or inner ear, thereby impairing the ability of such organs to function.

There is much truth in the saying "It's the dose that makes the poison." A single molecule of toxin—no matter how "poisonous"—can't kill or even noticeably harm a person. Depending on the type and amount of toxin consumed, the harm it causes can range from inconsequential to lethal, and from temporary to permanent. Types of permanent harm caused by toxins include organ malfunction, cancer, death, and birth defects. Toxins that cause birth defects are called "teratogens" (pronounced "te-RAT-o-gens"), and, as Chapters 3 and 4 will show, they are almost certainly the reason that pregnancy sickness evolved.

Why We Can Eat Some Plants Without Being Poisoned

The dilemma we and other plant-eating animals face is that in order to obtain a plant's nutrients we must eat its toxins, because toxins are present throughout a plant. Although the different parts of a plant—the roots, stems, fruits, petals, pollen, seeds, leaves, and so on—differ in the level of toxins they contain, all parts contain some toxins. Even if we didn't eat plants, we would still be exposed to their toxins: when we breathe "fresh" forest air we inhale plant toxins, because air is full of toxin-containing pollens; and when we walk outdoors and brush against grass or shrubs we touch plant toxins, because these plants secrete toxins that can penetrate our skin.

The solution to the problem of how to eat, inhale, and touch plant toxins without being poisoned by them is to have counter-defenses—that is, defenses designed to target and destroy toxins. Animal tissues have extensive arrays of specialized proteins known as "detoxification enzymes," whose function is to break toxins apart and convert them into harmless compounds that can be safely excreted. Detoxification enzymes are produced by almost all of our tissues, and they are produced in particularly large numbers by the liver and by surface tissues of organs that are directly exposed to the external environment, such as the skin, lungs, eyes, gastrointestinal tract, and vagina.

Because nature has produced a huge number of different toxins, and new ones can evolve at any time, we can't possibly have a different, specialized detoxification enzyme for each toxin. (For one thing, we don't have nearly enough genes to code for half a million different enzymes.) Instead, we produce a relatively small set of different types of detoxification enzymes, each capable of targeting the specific molecular characteristics shared by a broad class of different toxins. Since our bodies cannot know in advance which specific toxins we will encounter during our lifetimes, and in what quantities, our bodies cannot know in advance which detoxification enzymes need to be mass-produced. To get around this difficulty, our bodies regulate the production of detoxification enzymes in part by monitoring which enzymes are used the most. When tissues are first exposed to a certain type of toxin, they prepare for future encounters by boosting the production of the particular enzymes that can target that type of toxin. Still, the body's capacity to produce any enzyme is limited, so it can safely handle toxins only in certain doses.

PREGNANCY SICKNESS

Animals, like plants, have limited resources, and each species of plant-eating animal can successfully detoxify only a small number of plants and only certain plant parts. That's partly why different animal species have different ecological niches. People have sufficient defenses against the toxins in spinach, carrots, cabbage, apples, tomatoes, and peaches (at least in the quantities normally eaten), but we would become terribly ill if we ate a meal of eucalyptus leaves. Koalas, however, eat nothing else. They aren't poisoned by eucalyptus leaves because they produce very large quantities of the type of enzymes that rapidly detoxify eucalyptus toxins. But koalas won't and probably can't eat spinach, carrots, cabbage, and other plants people eat.

Why So Many Different Toxins Evolved

Plants and plant-eating animals are locked in an evolutionary "arms race." This is because throughout the course of evolutionary history plants kept evolving new adaptations to defend themselves against plant-eating animals, and animals kept evolving new adaptations to counter these defenses. Such adaptations arise gradually, through the process of natural selection. For example, say a chance mutation occurs in the hereditary material (DNA) of a seed that happens to cause the plant that grows from the seed to produce a new chemical. If this chemical happens to be especially harmful to the local animals that eat that species of plant, this plant will then have a better chance of surviving (and eventually reproducing) than other members of its species which lack the new chemical. The plant's offspring will inherit the ability to produce this chemical, and over the course of successive generations, plants producing this chemical will come to constitute an increasing proportion of the species. Natural selection eventually will "fix" the trait, which means that all members of the species will have it.

Similarly, a mutation that causes a plant-eating animal to cost-effectively produce a new enzyme that happens to destroy a toxin produced by a certain nutritious species of plant will increase the animal's chance of surviving, reproducing, and passing on this trait to subsequent generations. These "arms races" continue indefinitely: plants evolve new defenses; animals evolve new counter-defenses. The result of this ancient struggle is a huge spectrum of different plant toxins and detoxification enzymes.

How We Tell If a Plant Is Edible

To determine whether something is edible, we look at it, smell it, and taste it. If our senses say it's good, we assume it's edible. Our senses are designed to be on the lookout for dangerous levels of natural toxins and to perceive them as unpalatable. That's why we intuitively trust our senses with the job of telling us what we can and cannot eat.

Both the plant and the plant-eating animal benefit when the animal can immediately detect dangerous levels of toxins: the plant doesn't get eaten, and the animal doesn't get poisoned. Many plants even advertise their toxicity by emitting pungent toxins into the air, forewarning nearby animals. When plants are threatened directly—by being bitten into, for example—they often emit their strongest warnings. The distinctive pungent spray of an onion that's being sliced is such a warning. Since a given toxin won't harm all animals to the same extent, some plants' warnings will be ignored by some animals—onions, for example, can be eaten with impunity by most people. (In the 1980s I lived in a funky little apartment overlooking San Francisco Bay in an

PREGNANCY SICKNESS

area of the city known as Telegraph Hill, where I befriended a family of wild urban foxes—Red Snapper, Mrs. Snapper, and their little Whipper-Snappers. Since they were scrawny, I often left food for them out on my deck at night. One evening my friend ordered a pizza that came loaded with onions, and since I am terribly allergic to onions and cannot even tolerate smelling them, I immediately transferred the pizza to the deck, exclaiming that it smelled so bad even the foxes wouldn't want it. By morning, the foxes had carted off the entire pizza, but only after they had plucked off all the onions and deposited them on the deck.)

Many toxins that are perceived as edible at low doses are perceived as inedible at high doses. The pungent aroma rising from a pot of boiling cabbage—which comes from the natural toxin allyl isothiocyanate—may smell appetizing at low concentrations, but at high ones it would be nauseating.

Babies and small children usually have strong aversions to bitter and pungent substances and tend to be wary of new foods. This gives their toxin-detecting mechanisms time to determine which foods can be tolerated. The toxins of some bitter foods, but not others, can be readily detoxified in the human gut and liver. By adulthood, most people have acquired a dietary repertoire that includes many bitter foods, such as our common vegetables and spices (as discussed in more detail in Chapter 7). Most people, for example, don't become ill after eating a standard portion of cabbage or green beans, even though these foods contain toxins.

Why Fruits Are So Edible

Ripe fruits generally are the most palatable, least bitter parts of plants. That's because the tree produces fruit in order to attract birds and mammals to disperse its seeds. When a monkey climbs a tree and eats a piece of fruit, it usually swallows the seeds along with the fruit. Later, it deposits the seeds, via its feces, some distance from the tree. The seedling wouldn't have much chance of growing tall and strong if it rooted in the shade of its parent tree. When a tree's seeds mature and become ready for dispersal, the tree ripens the fruits enveloping them, which means it dramatically lowers their toxin content and raises their sugar content. Ripe fruits nevertheless retain some toxins in order to deter insects that would otherwise eat the fruit without dispersing the seeds. The seeds in ripe fruit remain bitter and often very toxic in order to discourage animals from chewing them up rather than swallowing them whole (if not bitten into, a seed's tough outer coat usually enables it to pass intact through an animal's gastrointestinal tract). Unripe fruits—that is, fruits enveloping immature seeds—are much more toxic and bitter, and much less sweet, than ripe fruits, which discourages animals from eating them. Although some unripe fruits are also much more sour than ripe fruits, it is their bitterness that generally makes them so aversive—as is probably apparent to anyone who remembers biting into an unripe banana, papaya, or cherimoya.

The parts of plants we find inedible usually are especially high in toxins. Although the succulent fruits of the fig make a tasty dessert, the leaves of the fig are not edible. For one thing, they contain high concentrations of a type of toxin that harms tissues when light strikes it. If a woman eats a fig leaf, gets fig leaf oil on her lips, and then goes into the sunlight, the toxins in the oil will be activated by the light and will damage the skin cells on her lips. Her body will react with intense itching, and she will try to scratch off the toxins. In many classical paintings nude people are depicted concealing their genitals with fig leaves. Such a practice would have assured not only daytime modesty but chastity as well: the itching that these people would have suffered had they removed their fig leaves and exposed their genitals to light would have ensured that the fig leaves were kept in place!

Plants as Drugs

One often hears of the healing powers of plants. But plants do not produce their medicinal chemicals for our benefit. Many plants do indeed have special healing properties, precisely because they produce toxins that we can exploit as drugs. A plant toxin that will harm a healthy person may benefit a person suffering from a disease. For example, a plant toxin that will lower the blood pressure of a healthy person to dangerous levels may bring down to normal the elevated blood pressure of a hypertensive person.

An example of a plant whose dangerous toxin is also an important drug is belladonna (*Atropa belladonna*). Belladonna, otherwise known as deadly nightshade, was a popular poison in medieval Europe, because it contains the toxin atropine, which can cause respiratory paralysis and coma. The name "atropine" is derived from the Greek mythological figure Atropos, who was one of the three fates to cut the thread of life. Although potentially lethal, atropine is commonly administered by physicians to prevent spasms during acute heart attacks. Ophthalmologists of recent decades applied atropine to their patients' eyes to dilate the pupils so that the retinas could be examined (synthetic drugs are now used for this purpose). For centuries European women took advantage of this ophthalmic property of belladonna in order to make themselves more alluring: a drop of belladonna extract in each eye simulates sexual arousal by dilating the pupils. Hence the name "belladonna"—Italian for "beautiful lady."

Natural Toxins and Our Natural Defenses Against Them

Even many of the common vegetables, spices, and herbs in our diets contain enough toxins to cause effects on the body that are believed by many people to be of medicinal value. And many were used in past centuries, by physicians and common folk alike, as remedies for various ailments. Herbal treatments prescribed by the renowned Greek herbalist Dioscorides of the first century A.D. included radishes to induce vomiting; cinnamon to cleanse the skin of venom; the juice of sweet bay, dropped into the ears, to lessen ear pain; walnuts, eaten in great quantities, to expel worms; cabbage leaves, beaten and applied to the skin, to decrease swellings; basil to neutralize scorpion bites; onion, in the form of a suppository, to treat hemorrhoids; garlic, eaten raw, to clear old coughs or to drive out worms; rhubarb, mixed in a drink, to stop convulsions, asthma, or dysentery.

In many parts of the developing world today people use common vegetables, unripe fruits, herbs, and spices as medicines. Onion juice dropped into the ear is supposedly a remedy for hearing difficulty. Garlic juice is said to act as an insect repellent, to neutralize the poison of insect bites and stings, and to lessen the pain of a decaying tooth. The juice from unripe pineapple is used to induce vomiting and to kill intestinal worms. Tarragon is applied to venomous bites and stings. Chili pepper is a folk remedy for rheumatism, asthma, and tumors, among many other ailments. The juice of papaya is applied to warts, tumors, and corns. Cinnamon is a folk remedy for arthritis. The cola nut is chewed as a remedy for dysentery, malaria, and toothache. Fennel is a folk remedy for cholera, spasm, stomachache, snakebite, and toothache, and it is also used to drive away fleas. Licorice is used as a laxative, and it is also used for ulcers and cough.

Although most folk remedies have not been tested scientifically—and some are probably ineffective and perhaps even dangerous—these examples clearly indicate how for centuries people have recognized that many common herbs and other plants included in human diets can have the properties of drugs. Even in industrialized countries today, herbalists use plants to try to induce therapeutic effects. The important point is that natural drugs are simply toxins that people have learned how to exploit for their own benefit.

How Toxic Are Modern Diets Compared to the Diets of Our Ancient Ancestors?

Sometimes pregnant women ask me questions of the sort, "Since nowadays we 'forage' in the supermarket instead of the savannah, do we still eat a lot of natural toxins?" The answer is yes, although our diets probably are considerably less toxic, on average, than ancestral hunter-gatherer diets were. That's because the picture-pretty fruits and vegetables lining the produce shelves of a modern supermarket generally have much lower levels of toxins than did the wild plants from which they are descended. By selectively breeding crops to taste better (which means breeding less bitter strains), farmers have progressively reduced the levels of natural toxins in domesticated plant foods. Wild cabbage and lettuce, for example, are much more toxic and bitter than are their domesticated descendants. The original strain of potato, a native of the Andes, was so toxic that it was edible only if baked in or eaten with clay; the main potato toxins adhere to the clay, which, when eaten, passes through the intestines without being absorbed.

In modern industrialized societies, however, we significantly increase the amount of toxins that we "have to" consume through diet by spicing foods and by drinking coffee and tea—things that our hunter-gatherer ancestors are very unlikely to have done. Spices, herbs, coffee, and tea have extremely high levels of toxins (roasted coffee contains more than 1,000 different kinds of toxins, caffeine being only one of them), almost no nutritive value, and, in fact, are consumed precisely for their toxins.

It may seem paradoxical that we deliberately consume these extra toxins after having taken so much trouble to breed vegetables that are low in toxins. In the case of coffee, there's an obvious reason for consuming it: many people enjoy its effect on the nervous system. Legend has it that the stimulating properties of coffee were first discovered centuries ago by a young Arabian goatherd named Kaldi, who noticed that his goats pranced about joyfully after eating the berries of the coffee plant. The goatherd ate some too and soon joined in the merriment. A passing monk, after inquiring into the cause of this frivolity and wakefulness, dried some of the berries and later boiled them, creating a beverage that helped him and his fellow monks stay awake during prayers. Ever since, coffee's stimulating properties have been enjoyed by people throughout the world. Although some Christian leaders once condemned coffee as Satanic, because it was discovered by "infidels," in the late 1500s Pope Clement VIII rendered coffee safe for Christians by baptizing it.

But spices and herbs, in the doses normally used to season foods, don't have stimulating effects. They are eaten for their distinctive flavors, which come primarily from their diverse arrays of toxins. It seems puzzling that people would develop a "taste" for the flavor of any toxin, when so many of the body's resources are devoted to protecting us from toxins. One explanation that has been proposed for why people spice their foods is that eating a variety of distinctive flavors mimics the sensation of eating a nutritionally adequate diet. In ancestral environments, a diversity of flavors would have reliably indicated a diversity of foods. Humans need to eat a diversity of foods because we require many kinds of nutrients that our bodies cannot manufacture on their own, and different foods contain different kinds of nutrients. For example, although most mammals can make their own vitamin C, humans can't, which means that we have to get this essential nutrient from foods that are rich in it, such as citrus fruits, tomatoes, and broccoli. Nutrients per se usually can't be smelled or tasted, so the only way that our ancestors could have ensured adequate nutritional diversity was to eat a varied diet. Humans therefore evolved a taste for flavor diversity. No one, however, has yet explained why the seeds and leaves of only a tiny fraction of plant species are palatable enough to be used as spices and herbs. Most strongly flavored, toxin-laden seeds and leaves simply taste bad to us.

Toxins in Nonplant Foods

Bacterial Toxins

Plants are not the only sources of natural toxins in our diets. Toxins are also produced by the bacteria that infest meats and dairy products. Unless such foods are stored in an environment that inhibits bacterial growth, such as a freezer, bacteria immediately begin to colonize and devour them. (Bacteria are everywhere—in the air, on our skin, even on "clean" kitchen counters.) Meats and dairy products that are "spoiled" (infested by large numbers of bacteria) typically have a putrid odor that deters people from eating them. But some bacterial toxins are so potent that they can cause food poisoning even in tiny, less easily detected amounts.

Mold Toxins

Many molds that infest plants, dairy products, and meats also produce toxins. Aflatoxins, for example, which are potent toxins produced by a kind of mold, are notorious contaminants of nuts and grains. At low levels they cannot be tasted, but at higher ones they simply taste "moldy." The bright colors of molds on fruits, vegetables, breads, nuts, and milk that are past their prime are warning signals of toxicity. In recent decades, however, we have learned how to exploit certain mold toxins: penicillin and many other life-saving antibiotics are derived from molds.

Toxins Created Through Cooking

Finally, many toxic chemicals are created through the process of cooking. Although intense heat destroys many toxins, it creates others by converting harmless compounds into toxic ones capable of mutating DNA. Frying or burning foods is particularly hazardous: the crusts on the surfaces of fried and barbequed foods are full of such toxic compounds. Thus, our normal, everyday diets are naturally full of toxins.

Ways We Avoid High Levels of Toxins

Detecting Toxins

The first line of defense against toxins is detecting and avoiding them. As discussed, smell and taste are two important ways of detecting toxins. Although toxicity itself cannot be smelled or tasted, chemical properties commonly associated with natural toxins are experienced by us as bitterness or pungency. By having natural aversions to bitter tastes and pungent odors, we can avoid many different toxins.

Processing Foods

Many plants contain both edible and inedible parts, so to access the edible parts, we "process" the plants before eating them. For example, we peel tough-skinned fruits, such as oranges, bananas,

PREGNANCY SICKNESS

and cantaloupe because the skins are full of bitter, unpalatable toxins. In addition, many foods contain inedible parts that can be transformed into edible ones. For example, soaking certain toxic foods in water often leaches out enough of their toxins to render them safe for cooking. Boiling them destroys many toxins as well. In many regions of Africa, one of the staple foods is cassava (tapioca), which naturally contains cyanide at such high levels that only a laborious process of soaking, grinding, fermenting, and heating prevents cyanide poisoning.

Diversifying the Diet

Humans, like many other animals, diversify their diets, which helps them to avoid overloading their systems with any one particular toxin. Almost all plant-eating mammals diversify their diets to some extent. Even koalas, which dine exclusively on eucalyptus leaves, seek out different eucalyptus species to vary the toxins they ingest. We appear to have an internal monitor to keep track of how diverse our intake of toxins is. For example, when people at a party are offered unlimited amounts of a variety of appetizers, they generally will consume much more total food if they eat a diversity of appetizers than if they only eat their favorite.

Fear of New Foods

One way that humans and many other mammals avoid eating high levels of potentially dangerous toxins is by being wary of foods they've never eaten before (this natural wariness is called neophobia). New foods usually are initially sampled in small amounts; if tolerated well, larger amounts can be eaten on the next occasion.

Natural Toxins and Our Natural Defenses Against Them

Shedding Cells

The shedding of cells is an important way that animals avoid building up harmful levels of toxins they've eaten, touched, or inhaled. In humans, the surface layers of the stomach, intestines, lungs, genital tract, eyes, and skin slough off every few days. In this way, cells that have become dysfunctional from having been contaminated by toxins or infected by bacteria or viruses are replaced by new cells (underlying "stem" cells divide to replenish the discarded cells).

Nausea, Vomiting, and Aversions

The defenses that are especially applicable to first-trimester women are nausea, vomiting, and food/odor aversions. These defenses are ancient parts of the nervous system. All mammals have the capacity to experience nausea and food/odor aversions, and almost all of them can also vomit. The basic function of nausea is to immediately deter us from continuing to eat or inhale a toxin. Nausea also provides the stimulus for food/odor aversions, which deter us from repeating bad experiences with the toxic substance that precipitated the nausea. Nausea is linked to vomiting in that when a person is nauseated, the contents of the upper intestines are pushed up into the stomach so that they can be expelled through vomiting.

Severe nausea is so actively unpleasant that it has inspired the saying "For the first hour you fear that you'll die, by the second hour you fear that you won't." Nausea is like pain, in that its purpose is to motivate the avoidance of whatever caused it. If we smell or taste a food that nauseated us on a previous occasion, we have an immediate aversion to it and refrain from eating it. Nausea and aversions are not "willed" or otherwise voluntarily controlled. The link between the experience of nausea and a particular smell or taste of food is etched in the nervous system, even if it is not consciously remembered. This point is dramatically illustrated by the following experiment that was performed on rats. Rats were anesthetized immediately after drinking sweetened water, which is a taste that appeals to them. While under deep anesthesia, they were injected with a drug that rapidly induces nausea. Weeks later, they were again offered sweetened water, and when they ran up to taste it they recoiled in revulsion. Even though they were unconscious when their brains made the association between sweetness and nausea, the aversion mechanism operated just as effectively as if they had been awake. (The reason food that is nauseating to a first-trimester woman becomes appealing again after the first trimester is dealt with in Chapter 4.)

A person cannot simply ignore or overcome nausea and aversions, just as a person cannot simply ignore or overcome pain. Cancer patients undergoing chemotherapy or radiation treatments, for example, are often plagued by nausea and vomiting, and if they eat anything around the time of their treatments they often develop subsequent aversions to those foods. The nausea, vomiting, and food aversions can be so debilitating that some patients stop life-prolonging cancer treatments. Certainly if these patients were able to "will away" nausea, they would do so.

Nausea, vomiting, and food/odor aversions are triggered primarily by the brain stem, which lies at the base of the brain just above the spinal cord. A part of the brain stem known as the chemoreceptor trigger zone (CTZ), which is part of the small organ known as the area postrema, continuously monitors the blood and the cerebrospinal fluid for toxic compounds. When the CTZ detects levels of toxins above a certain threshold, it activates nausea and a cascade of related defenses, including vomiting if the toxin level is high enough. Nausea and vomiting can also be triggered by special toxin-detectors in the gastrointestinal tract and lungs.

Women are more readily plagued by nausea than men. This sex difference begins at puberty—when girls start producing estrogen in much greater quantities than boys do—because estrogen stimulates the brain stem mechanisms that induce nausea. This difference between men's and women's susceptibility to nausea makes adaptive sense. The women who were our hunter-gatherer ancestors spent most of their reproductive years pregnant or nursing, and therefore they needed to be more sensitive than men to toxins that could be transferred to embryos and fetuses via the placenta, and to nursing children via milk.

The nausea-aversion system doesn't work perfectly in every case. Sometimes it can't precisely pinpoint the toxic culprit. For example, if a woman gets food poisoning (whose symptoms are nausea and vomiting) from eating bacteria-laden meat at the same time she eats artichoke salad, she may henceforth have an aversion to artichokes as well as to that particular meat, even though the artichoke was an innocent bystander. The human body can detect that a meal contained unacceptable levels of toxins, but it can't in every possible circumstance identify the specific ingredient responsible.

Pregnancy Sickness

One defense—pregnancy sickness—is specialized for protecting embryos. As described in detail in Chapter 4, it is essentially an exaggerated form of the standard defenses of nausea, vomiting, and aversions. The embryo has few defenses of its own against the toxins that the mother eats. It can't escape. It can't avoid or

PREGNANCY SICKNESS

expel toxins that get through the placenta. It can't shed many of its cells, because there are too few to spare. And the placenta's detoxification enzymes can handle toxins only in relatively low doses. The embryo's best defense against toxins is the mother's avoidance of them.

Chapter Three

❧

The Vulnerable Embryo

Early Formation of the Baby-to-Be

LIFE AS AN EMBRYO is tenuous. In an incredibly short span of time the embryo has to form all of its organs—without making mistakes, because there's no way for it to backtrack and correct them. Its development entails the transformation of a single fertilized egg cell into billions of specialized cells organized into different organs and other tissues, including the limbs, heart, spinal cord, brain, eyes, ears, genitalia, skin, and other parts of the body. For each organ to be formed properly a cascade of precisely timed events must take place, coordinated by the constant communication between the embryo's cells, which send each other information about who they are, what they are doing, and what they expect their neighboring cells to be doing. The sequence and timing of these events are key factors in the embryo's organ formation, because the formation of one part of an organ often triggers the formation of interacting parts, ensuring that all the components fit together.

Every day during the period of organ formation (called organogenesis), critical events take place. The illustrations that follow depict the normal week-by-week changes in the embryo's

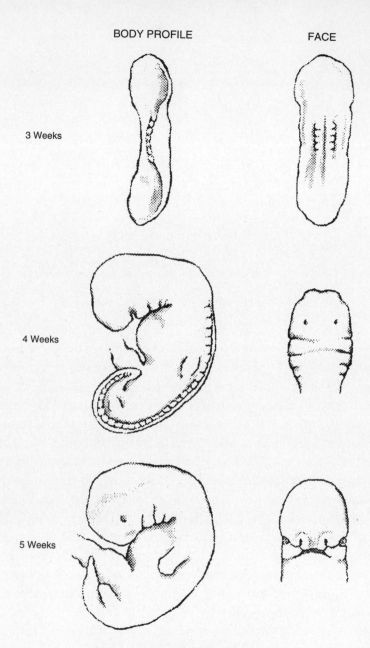

BODY PROFILE   FACE

3 Weeks

4 Weeks

5 Weeks

*The week-by-week changes in the
embryo's development are dramatic.*

BODY PROFILE   FACE

6 Weeks

7 Weeks

8 Weeks

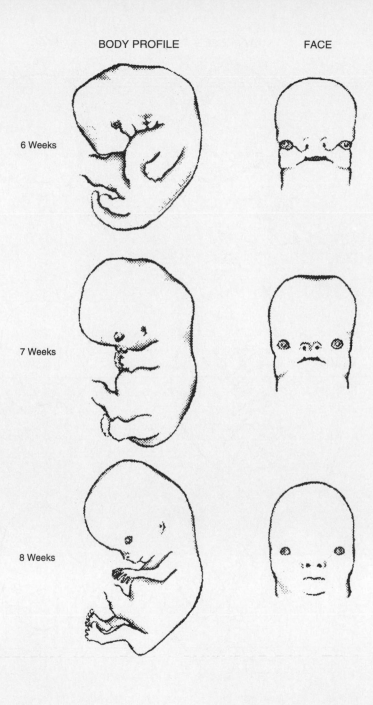

BODY PROFILE   FACE

10 Weeks

12 Weeks

14 Weeks

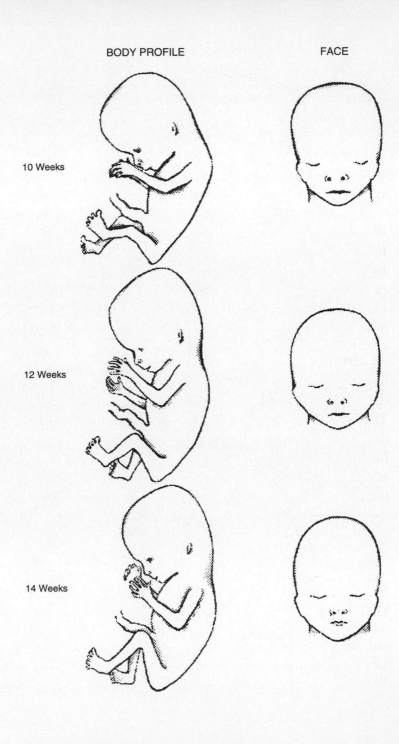

appearance, illustrating how rapidly its metamorphosis occurs. In order to emphasize how crucial it is that organ formation not be disrupted, even for a day, I'll briefly describe the embryo's development during a single week, the fourth week after conception.

On about day 22 after conception the neural tube—which will develop into the brain and spinal cord—begins to form from a flattened group of primitive nerve cells. A rudimentary heart begins to beat. On day 24 the eyes start to form, beginning with rudimentary pits and lenses. The opening at the top end of the neural tube closes. If the neural tube fails to close at both ends, serious defects result, such as spina bifida (when part of the spinal cord protrudes from the back, encased only in a thin sac) or anencephaly (when most of the brain is missing). On day 26 upper limb buds appear, which will become arms and hands. On about day 27 the opening at the bottom end of the neural tube closes. The otic pits, which will become the inner ears, appear. On about day 28 lower limb buds appear, which will become legs and feet. By this time, the rudiments of many of the internal organs, such as the gut and lungs, have also started to develop. As the illustration shows, the difference in appearance between the twenty-one-day-old and the twenty-eight-day-old embryo is striking.

When Organ Formation Goes Awry

At any point in the development of any organ things can go wrong. Even a small disturbance in a single developmental event can doom the embryo to birth defects or death. Many embryos with defects are spontaneously aborted, and it even appears that the uterus tries to detect defective embryos and selectively abort them. But if the uterus cannot detect the defects, the pregnant

woman remains oblivious to them (unless, of course, she has prenatal testing—an option that has been available to women only
for the last couple of decades). A woman can take specific actions
to reduce the chance that defects will occur, but once a defect
does occur, there is nothing she can do to transform an abnormal
embryo into a normal one.

Many embryos with defects do survive the entire pregnancy.
Of all infants born in North America, about 2–3 percent have
major birth defects and another 4–10 percent have minor
defects. These so-called minor defects, however, usually do not
seem so minor to the persons affected by them. They can seriously diminish the quality of a person's life by causing problems
such as partial deafness, incomplete bladder and bowel control,
strabismus (crossed eyes), and various learning disabilities. Some
defects are apparent at birth, but many birth defects of the brain
and other internal organs don't become apparent until later in
infancy, in early childhood, or at puberty. In the United States,
birth defects are responsible for about 14 percent of infant
deaths.

When a baby is born with defects, the parents almost always
want to know what caused them. Sometimes they want to be
able to blame something or someone; sometimes they simply
want an explanation of their fate. As with other life traumas, it is
probably easier to accept the birth of a baby with defects if
the event is seen as fitting into a web of causality. But often the
cause of an infant's birth defects is not identifiable. In many
cases, it's not even clear whether the cause is genetic or environmental. If the cause is genetic, it means that the genetic material
of the mother's egg, the father's sperm, or the fertilized egg was
abnormal and, consequently, that the embryo's development was

The Vulnerable Embryo

directed by flawed genetic instructions. If the cause is environmental, it means that something external to the embryo, such as a drug, plant toxin, or virus, disrupted organ formation, even though the embryo started out with normal genetic material.

Although many specific birth defects and birth defect syndromes can be linked to known genetic or environmental culprits, in about two-thirds of the actual cases of birth defects the cause remains elusive. That is, the investigator rounds up the usual suspects but has to rule them all out: genetic testing of the baby does not reveal an obvious abnormality, nor does probing into the mother's recent history of exposure to drugs and viruses reveal a culprit. Many unexplained birth defects are probably caused by genetic abnormalities too subtle to be detected by current technologies. Many other unexplained defects, however, are probably caused by natural dangers lurking in the environment—in particular, by natural toxins in the mother's diet. As explained in the following sections, natural toxins are significant threats to embryos, yet they have been overlooked in almost all investigations of the causes of human birth defects.

Environmental Causes of Birth Defects

A pregnant woman is surrounded by teratogens—agents that can cause birth defects. Strictly defined, teratogens are things that increase an embryo's risk of birth defects without significantly harming the mother (this book uses this strict definition of "teratogen"). More loosely defined, teratogens also include things that increase the risk of miscarriage. The spectrum of natural teratogens in the environment includes various plant toxins, metals, vitamins (in megadoses), and infectious microorganisms. The natural teratogens that are highlighted in this book are the chemical ones that come from plants.

Different teratogens cause malformations in different ways—some direct, others indirect. For example, some teratogens can enter an embryo's cells, where they can break the cell's chromosomes or alter key genes, thus preventing the genes from properly directing the development of a particular organ. Other teratogens are thought to interfere with the chemical signals that the embryo's cells send one another, thus disrupting the flow of developmental information. Still other teratogens are thought to interfere with the functions of the placenta, preventing it from properly nourishing and protecting the embryo. For most teratogens, however, it is not yet known exactly how they wreak their havoc.

With teratogens, as with all toxins, "it's the dose that makes the poison." Below a certain dose, a teratogen will not harm the embryo; above this dose, it can cause birth defects or kill the embryo without significantly harming the mother; at still higher doses, it can harm or even kill the mother. Although a single, nonlethal dose of toxin rarely causes permanent harm to an adult, it may injure an embryo irrevocably. Whereas the mother is fairly resilient to the nonlethal effects of toxins, the embryo is extremely vulnerable.

Natural Toxins That Cause Birth Defects

The placenta is a protective barrier, but not an absolute one. In order to perform the function of nourishing the embryo the placenta has to be sufficiently permeable to enable vitamins and other nutrients to pass from the mother's bloodstream to the embryo's. But this renders the placenta permeable to the small *non-nutritional* molecules—such as plant toxins—that happen to be circulating in the mother's bloodstream. In fact, most plant toxins are very small molecules that can readily cross the placenta.

A first-trimester woman needs to be aware that whatever she allows into her bloodstream may end up in her embryo's, and that, for the most part, she can control what enters her bloodstream. The naturally occurring teratogens in plants— although intended to inflict harm on the plants' predators—are not like snares or bullets; evading a plant toxin means simply not eating or touching the plant that contains it. To help convince a reader who is in the first trimester of pregnancy that plant toxins can seriously endanger her embryo, the following section describes the widespread occurrence of birth defects and other reproductive problems in animals that have grazed on teratogenic plants. The section after that explains why a first-trimester woman should be concerned about common plant foods that humans eat.

Birth Defects in Farm Animals

People who grew up on a farm may be more aware than most people that plants endanger embryos, because plant toxins are notorious causes of birth defects in livestock. Farm animals that are allowed to range freely within the farm boundaries often graze on a variety of plants, and if teratogenic plants happen to grow there, then the animals may eat them. Lambs, piglets, calves, colts, and goat kids are common victims of plant teratogens. Plant toxins have caused many different types of birth defects among these farm animals, including cleft palate, eye malformations, limb deformities, and scoliosis (curvature of the spine).

In many such cases, the birth defects were initially attributed to "bad genes." This explanation seemed to account for the fact that successive generations of animals on the same farm were giving birth to offspring with the same defects. But, in reality, in some of these cases each generation of animals was grazing on the same species of teratogenic plant, causing the same birth defects to occur. In one case in rural California, the source of the birth defects was discovered after the same defect showed up in different kinds of animals on the same farm. It turned out that the family goat had been grazing on lupine, a plant known primarily for its beautiful purple flowers, but one that is so teratogenic that severe bone deformities can occur in an embryo if a pregnant woman even drinks the milk from an animal that has recently grazed on it. After the family's pregnant goat foraged on lupine and her milk was drunk by the pregnant dog and the pregnant woman, a litter of goat kids, a litter of puppies, and a baby boy were all born with "crooked calf syndrome."

Do Plants Do This on Purpose?

Although many plant toxins that cause birth defects probably do so incidentally—that is, embryos are not their main targets— many other plant toxins probably cause birth defects "deliberately"—that is, they were designed to do precisely that. The reproductive systems of plant-eating animals are common targets of plant weaponry. By distorting an animal's uterus, disrupting its reproductive cycles, inducing it to abort, or deforming its offspring, a plant can prevent the creation of a new generation of local plant-eaters. Free-ranging, grass-grazing animals are frequent victims of reproductive toxins. Many grasses produce reproductive toxins because they are surrounded by their own seedlings, with whom they share many or all genes; when they depress the local plant-eating animal population, they spare their seedlings and promote their own genetic stock. Although many reproductive toxins appear to be designed to harm insects, they often also harm mammals. In New Zealand, grasses have thwarted the fertility of millions of sheep.

One of the most common ways that plants disrupt animal fertility is by producing chemicals that mimic the animals' reproductive hormone estrogen. These chemicals are called phytoestrogens, and although they do not necessarily resemble estrogen in their chemical structures, they are nevertheless able to bind to the special receptors in animal tissues that are supposed to bind estrogen, leaving fewer receptors free to bind estrogen itself. Soy beans, many species of clover, and alfalfa are among the plants that produce estrogen mimics. In livestock, these mimics have caused such problems as permanent sterility, ovarian cysts, premature delivery, and miscarriage. The fact that so many diverse estrogen mimics are produced throughout the plant kingdom means that many different plants independently evolved this strategy for harming the animals that prey on them (which means that the strategy is pretty effective).

Some plant toxins disrupt fertility by causing the embryo to abort—either by killing the embryo directly or by causing the uterus to have sudden, strong contractions. Some plants that cause abortion do so deliberately, others incidentally. Throughout the nonindustrialized world, women who want to abort their embryos have taken advantage of such abortifacient plants, consuming them despite their terrible taste. (Of course, they are foiling the goal of pregnancy sickness by doing so.) For example, in Guam, the Chamorro women who want to abort their embryos drink a beverage made from the bark of the shrub *Ephedra vulgaris*. In the Murray Islands, the Miriam women chew certain poisonous leaves called *tim, sobe, bok, or sem,* which they say causes great pain to the pregnant woman but kills the embryo. And in Mexico, the Cahita Indian women drink a tea made from the corklike pine *corcho.*

The practice of using plants to induce abortions probably is many thousands of years old, since it is not uncommon among contemporary hunter-gatherers, whose ways of life are ancient. For example, !Kung women of the Kalahari Desert in Africa try to terminate unwanted pregnancies by drinking beverages made from certain poisonous plants. Mbuti Pygmy women of Central Africa try to induce abortion by drinking beverages made from *gorogoro* bark, or by burning and inhaling the smoke from the highly toxic *ikanya* bark. That people of many cultures have independently discovered the connection between toxic plants and abortion underscores the fact that a large number of plants in the world can greatly endanger embryos.

Toxins from Bacteria Can Also Harm Embryos

Human diets typically contain some bacterial toxins. Since most women eat meat, poultry, fish, and dairy products—which bacteria will contaminate at their earliest opportunity—pregnancy sickness discourages women from eating foods that smell like they have been contaminated by bacteria. Because bacterial toxins are large molecules, most of them cannot cross the placenta to harm the embryo directly (although some appear to be able to do so despite their large size). Many bacteria, however, can harm the embryo indirectly, or even kill it, by damaging the placenta or altering certain aspects of the mother's body. For example, when a woman is infected by bacteria, her body combats the infection by raising the temperature—inducing a fever—because this usually helps to inhibit bacterial growth. But an elevated body temperature can impair the development of an embryo's nervous system (as discussed in Chapter 11). Thus, bacteria can indirectly harm an embryo when they invade a first-trimester woman's body.

How Risky to Human Embryos Are the Toxins in Our Diets?

The compelling question to the first-trimester woman is "Can normal, everyday foods endanger my embryo?" The answer is that we don't know for certain, but we should assume that some of the natural toxins in our diets can cause birth defects in doses that are within the range of what humans consume. First I'll discuss the reasons why we don't yet know exactly how dangerous food toxins are for human embryos, and then I'll discuss the reasons why we should act on the assumption that the normal diets of nonpregnant people are dangerous for embryos.

We Don't Yet Know Which Dietary Toxins Are Dangerous for Embryos

When a baby is born with birth defects, plant toxins are almost never suspected by the obstetrician, pediatrician, or parents of having caused them because the harm that plants can inflict on people has been grossly under-recognized. Most people are not even aware that plants—and foods derived from plants—are full of natural toxins. Although biologists have discovered thousands of plant toxins so far—including many in our foods—relatively few resources have been spent to investigate the natural toxins in foods, so most of them have not even been identified. It is simply not known how many and precisely what kinds of natural toxins most foods contain. And for most of the natural toxins in foods that have been identified, it is not known what effects they have on human embryos.

PREGNANCY SICKNESS

People's diets vary dramatically from region to region around the globe, and so do the rates at which different types of birth defects occur. But differences in the natural toxins that people eat are almost never suspected of being responsible for the differences in the types and rates of birth defects. One recent study in Norway found that although women who had given birth to one baby with defects were at greatly increased risk (compared to other women) for giving birth to a second baby with defects, women who moved to a new municipality before conceiving the second baby cut this increased risk roughly in half. These results suggest that certain factors in the initial environment of these women—such as the particular foods they ate—were interfering with embryonic development.

Very few natural food toxins have been investigated for their ability to cause birth defects, and so the information that is currently available linking particular dietary toxins with particular birth defects is extremely sparse. People in Central and South America, for example, eat a lot of hot peppers—which are loaded with natural toxins. But no one has yet investigated the potential of pepper toxins to cause birth defects. When a physician or researcher does suggest that a certain baby's birth defects might be connected to a mother's diet during pregnancy, it is usually because the mother's diet was deficient in vitamins that we know are essential for embryonic development, or because her diet was "weird." For example, one obscure medical article reported on a woman who gave birth to a baby with multiple defects after eating almost nothing for the first four months of pregnancy except boiled vegetables (this woman also experienced no pregnancy sickness, according to the article, which is probably why she was able to eat a first-trimester diet of vegetables).

The Vulnerable Embryo

In the future, a first-trimester woman ideally would be able to look up any food in a compendium that rates thousands of different foods for their safety to embryos and that even rates them at different quantities, methods of cooking, and degrees of freshness or ripeness. Perhaps an abbreviated form of such a compendium will be compiled for the first-trimester woman of the future, but only if many more studies are done to investigate the link between dietary toxins and birth defects.

Ways We Might Be Able to Figure Out This Information in the Future

We're a long way from being able to construct even a rudimentary chart mapping specific birth defects to specific dietary toxins. It might seem relatively easy and straightforward to do this, but it isn't. For one thing, we can't tell from simply looking at the chemical structure of a plant toxin whether or not it is capable of causing birth defects. In fact, two different chemicals with very similar structures often differ markedly in their effects on embryos. For another thing, although a given toxin that causes human birth defects causes the same kind of defects in all the babies it affects, the reverse is not necessarily true: some birth defects, such as spina bifida, can have multiple causes—natural toxins, medicinal drugs, or genetic aberrations. There's not a simple one-to-one correlation between teratogens and birth defects. Furthermore, trying to figure out which toxins are teratogens, out of the huge array of food toxins people eat, is tricky. If a genetically normal baby is born with birth defects to a mother who did not experience much pregnancy sickness, and who therefore ate a wide array of spices, herbs, condiments, vegetables, fungi, fruits, and grains during the first trimester, it's not at all obvious which food, if any, caused the defects.

PREGNANCY SICKNESS

In the hope of finding links between certain birth defects and certain foods, we could survey women who have delivered babies with birth defects to find out what foods they ate during the first trimester, but we would need to survey a lot of women who could recall with reasonable accuracy the foods and beverages they consumed. Such a study might not be terribly reliable, since memories fade quickly, but it might, nevertheless, yield some important clues. Many studies of this type have been done successfully when the substances being investigated were medicinal drugs, rather than foods, because memory isn't such a problem with drugs: a woman is likely to remember most of the drugs, if any, that she took during pregnancy, and her physician and pharmacist keep records of the drugs prescribed to her. Furthermore, drugs have been prime suspects in cases of birth defects ever since the thalidomide disaster; whereas natural food toxins have yet to be widely recognized as potential culprits.

One way we could sleuth out the foods most likely to cause birth defects would be to test different human foods on pregnant laboratory animals.* So far, only a smattering of human foods have been tested for their ability to cause birth defects in animals (whereas more than 3,000 drugs, occupational chemicals, food additives, pesticides, and other substances have been tested).

---

*Readers who are especially sensitive to animals' feelings may feel uneasy about discussions of animal experimentation for human benefit. Having cared for and loved many wild and domestic animals, I sympathize with the plight of animals who are caged and made to suffer emotionally or physically. Nevertheless, I think it's a lot sadder when a human baby is born with defects than when a mouse, rabbit, or monkey baby is. The apparently transient emotional anguish experienced by animal mothers who deliver babies with birth defects does not parallel the deep, long-term anguish experienced by human mothers and by their children. All in all, I think that some experiments using animals are justified for discovering the causes of human birth defects.

The Vulnerable Embryo

Chick peas, sweet peas, cassava, and potatoes, for example, have been found to cause birth defects in rats, mice, or hamsters when the pregnant females were fed large amounts of these foods. But what this means for humans isn't clear, because tests on animal embryos don't necessarily mimic events that happen in human embryos. A substance that causes a certain type of birth defect in one species may cause a different type of defect in another species, or no defect at all. In fact, many substances that are tested on animals and found to cause birth defects in at least one species do not appear to cause birth defects in people, at least in the amounts that people are normally exposed to them. Substances that cause birth defects in many different animal species, however, are likely to cause them in humans as well. Megadoses of vitamin A, for example, are teratogenic in humans and in all species of mammals tested.

Since people around the world eat thousands of different foods, and it's too expensive to perform animal tests on all of them, we should select foods to test that would yield the most useful information. Of highest priority are foods that are eaten by large numbers of people and that are either eaten in large quantities (such as staple foods) or contain high levels of toxins (such as pungent foods used primarily to impart flavor). Staple foods of large regions include, for example, cassava (eaten in many parts of Africa), lentils (eaten in India and Pakistan), and potatoes (eaten in Ireland and in many other countries around the world); foods used extensively as flavoring agents include, for example, hot peppers, mustard, oregano, garlic, and onions.

Why We Should Assume That Human Foods Can Cause Birth Defects

We should not assume that our diets are free of toxins that cause birth defects just because no one has yet done studies linking specific dietary toxins to specific defects. In other words, the fact that plant toxins in the normal human diet have not been proven to be unsafe for human embryos does not mean that they are safe. Claims are often made in the medical sciences that there is no evidence for a causal association between two things when, in fact, "no evidence" may simply mean that no one has done the studies necessary to determine whether such an association exists.

One researcher, for example, after listing dozens of plant toxins that are known to cause birth defects in livestock, stated that there is no evidence that plant toxins are associated with birth defects in humans. There are at least two things wrong with this kind of statement. First, nature has not singled out humans for special protection. Humans are not immune to other natural dangers, such as viruses and venoms, and they should not be expected to be immune to natural teratogens either. Second, the statement gives the reader the false impression that the studies that would be needed to detect an association between plant toxins and human birth defects have actually been done. A hundred and fifty years ago the statement could have been made that "there is no evidence that germs cause disease," because science had not yet advanced enough to demonstrate the causal link between germs and disease.

In making good health decisions, such as how to care for one's embryo, it is important to consider all pertinent scientific information. There is overwhelming circumstantial evidence that many plants—including some of those we eat—contain toxins that can harm human embryos. The following set of well-established facts summarizes this evidence.

- All plants produce toxins in order to harm the animals that eat them.

The Vulnerable Embryo

- Embryos can be harmed by plant toxins in amounts too tiny to harm the mother.

- Many plant toxins are known to cause birth defects in animals.

- Nature has not exempted humans from the effects of toxins (or other natural dangers).

- A number of drugs are potent teratogens in humans, and drugs are not fundamentally different from plant toxins. In fact, many drugs are derived from plant toxins or are synthetic analogs of them.

- Several human foods (examples of which are mentioned in this chapter) have already been shown to cause birth defects in animals when fed at high doses to pregnant females.

When a nonpregnant adult makes the mistake of eating too many food toxins, the consequences tend to be merely unpleasant, such as stomachaches or throwing up; only on rare occasions are the consequences lethal or otherwise irreversible. But during the first trimester the consequences of making the mistake of eating too many food toxins can be devastating and irreversible. Each year in North America hundreds of thousands of babies are born with birth defects. We can't afford to wait until the definitive scientific investigations of dietary toxins and human birth defects have been completed before we actively protect our embryos from dietary toxins. Every time a pregnant woman chooses to eat or not to eat something she makes a decision that affects her embryo, and a teratogen is a teratogen whether or not scientists have gotten around to documenting it as such. Dietary decisions should be based on the best information available, however incomplete, and on the best reasoning we can do.

Why It Helps to Know
the Purpose of Pregnancy Sickness

Since pregnancy sickness causes the mother to dramatically reduce the amount of natural dietary toxins she consumes, most first-trimester women are unlikely to eat plants in quantities large enough to cause birth defects. So, one might ask, if pregnancy sickness is already protecting the embryo from dietary teratogens, why does a first-trimester woman need to be consciously aware of them? There are several reasons.

First, the degree of pregnancy sickness varies greatly among women, as explained in detail in Chapter 5. Although pregnancy sickness causes women of all regions to decrease their consumption of foods that have high levels of natural toxins, some women do not experience a sufficient degree of pregnancy sickness to adequately protect their embryos. Consequently, they end up eating the flavorful foods of their regional cuisines and thus inflict high levels of toxins on their embryos. These women, in particular, would benefit from knowing which types of foods are most likely to contain toxins that cause birth defects. Chapter 7 ranks different kinds of foods according to their levels of natural toxins and their probable danger to the embryo. This ranking should alert a first-trimester woman who does not have much pregnancy sickness to the types of foods she should avoid, enabling her to screen out those dietary items most likely to harm her embryo.

Second, a physiological mechanism designed to protect embryos in the ancestral environment of the hunter-gatherer is not necessarily as effective in the modern environment, because the invention of agriculture has changed the human diet dramatically in a relatively short span of time. For example, although pregnancy sickness is designed to discourage women from eating foods that taste bitter, the mass production of sugar has enabled people to mask the bitterness of some plants with sweetness, and thus to fool the taste mechanisms that are supposed to detect bitterness. Chocolate and cola without the added sugar would be exceedingly unpalatable and probably would not be tolerated by first-trimester women. (As discussed in Chapter 7, it is not yet known whether eating large quantities of chocolate and cola can cause birth defects in human embryos.) Plants containing toxins that give food the sensation of "hotness" also can mask the bitterness of other toxins, because the burning can overwhelm other sensations. Hot peppers, which are used extensively as flavorings in the cuisines of many cultures, probably render other dietary toxins in foods flavored by peppers hard to detect. Our hunter-gatherer ancestors, whose diets were already high in natural toxins, are unlikely to have flavored their meals with high-toxin foods, such as hot peppers. Knowing which toxic foods of modern cuisines are fooling our toxin-detection mechanisms and hindering the operation of pregnancy sickness enables a first-trimester woman to consciously avoid these foods.

Third, many women are given dietary advice for the first trimester that is not only incorrect but potentially dangerous. Telling people to eat lots of cabbage and other vegetables is generally good advice, but it is bad advice for first-trimester women, who need to protect their embryos from the high levels of natural toxins contained in vegetables. Alerting first-trimester women to the types of foods that are most likely to endanger embryos (see Chapter 7) counters the bad advice they've heard elsewhere and reinforces the good advice that pregnancy sickness is trying to convey.

Fourth, the more food toxins that are correctly identified as teratogens, the better chance a first-trimester woman has to protect her embryo. There is no way for the body to know inherently which toxins can cause birth defects: the natural environment contains a vast spectrum of toxins, new ones can evolve at any time, and toxins that happen to cause birth defects do not share a common chemical structure. Pregnancy sickness therefore cannot selectively zero in on teratogens. Instead, pregnancy sickness gives a woman aversions to toxins *in general*, a strategy that ensures that she has aversions to teratogens. Although the function of pregnancy sickness is to recognize the cues of toxins—bitter tastes and pungent odors—and produce aversions to them, a toxin's degree of bitterness or pungency does not always correlate perfectly with its potential to cause birth defects. In other words, the most bitter and pungent toxins will not necessarily turn out to be the most dangerous for embryos, and the most dangerous toxins for embryos are not necessarily extremely bitter or pungent. So the strength of the warning that a woman gets from pregnancy sickness about a particular food doesn't always accurately represent the degree of danger that the food poses for her embryo. If a first-trimester woman's diet includes large quantities of any particular food that is derived from plants, then knowing whether that food contains toxins that can endanger her embryo is important, especially if that food lacks a strong taste.

Example: Potatoes and Spina Bifida

The potato is an example of a food that many people eat in large quantities, that most people do not perceive as particularly bitter, but that some researchers suspect of causing birth defects in humans. Potatoes produce the toxins solanine and chaconine, which are present at especially high levels in the potato skins. When potatoes become infected with the fungus that causes

The Vulnerable Embryo

"potato blight" they dramatically increase their levels of toxins to combat the fungus. In experiments on some mammals (but not others), these potato toxins have increased the incidence of neural tube defects in embryos, even at doses that were not toxic to the mother. It is not yet known for certain whether potato toxins can cause birth defects in humans. Ireland, a country with heavy potato consumption, has the highest rate of neural tube defects in the world, and this rate increases during years of severe potato blight, when potatoes boost their levels of toxins (but this correlation does not necessarily imply a cause-and-effect relationship).

These potato toxins persist in the body for long periods of time, penetrating tissues and fat, then slowly reentering the bloodstream. Whereas the half-life of most toxins (that is, the time it takes the body to excrete half the amount of toxin that has been absorbed) is only several hours or days, the half-life of potato toxins is several weeks. Since the human body eliminates potato toxins very slowly, a person whose dietary staple is potatoes maintains a large store of these toxins, primarily in the liver (autopsies have verified this). A woman who abstains from potatoes during early pregnancy but eats them regularly during the months preceding conception could, therefore, still have high levels of potato toxins in her bloodstream during early pregnancy. One researcher has suggested that this may explain why, in one study, women who had previously given birth to an infant with neural tube defects but who avoided potatoes during the next pregnancy and shortly prior to conceiving did not decrease their risk of having another infant with neural tube defects. In any case, neural tube defects appear to have many different causes—including certain genetic abnormalities, nutritional factors, and environmental insults—so even complete avoidance of potatoes would not eliminate the risk of these defects. Since the verdict isn't in yet on the risk of potatoes to human embryos, women in their first few weeks of pregnancy and women trying to conceive should be wary of this otherwise valuable source of nutrients.

In Practical Terms, What Does All This Mean to the First-Trimester Woman?

The best dietary strategy during the first trimester is to play it very safe, which means to regard plant toxins as "guilty" of being able to harm the embryo until proven "innocent." We don't yet know which specific toxins in our diets are able to cause developmental defects in human embryos, but we do know which kinds of foods contain high levels of toxins and are, therefore, most likely to endanger embryos. These are listed in Chapter 7.

In order not to alarm the first-trimester woman into starving herself, it's important to emphasize that what matters most is the amount of a given toxin. Most foods, if eaten by a first-trimester woman in *huge* amounts, probably could harm an embryo. Every food and beverage that a woman consumes is a combination of chemicals. And when chemicals are tested in pregnant laboratory animals at very high doses, more than a third of them turn out to increase the rate of birth defects. (This is true whether the chemicals are natural ones, from plants or molds, or synthetic ones, from various industries.) But because the doses in these animal tests are so high, the tests don't usually reflect human exposures to these chemicals. In reality, only a small—but critical—percentage of the thousands of natural and synthetic chemicals that first-trimester women encounter in their daily life is likely to significantly increase the risk of birth defects.

The Vulnerable Embryo

Before women even conceive, they can help protect their future embryos by being aware of the rare dietary teratogens that persist in tissues for unusually long periods of time. Thus far, potato toxins are the only common dietary toxins that have been flagged as possible human teratogens and that persist long enough in the body to be there in large doses weeks later. Women trying to conceive should probably eat a diversified diet in order to avoid accumulating high levels of any one toxin in their tissues.

Pregnancy Sickness Is Timed to Protect the Vulnerable Embryo

The mother's pregnancy sickness coincides with—and is therefore able to protect—the embryo's organ formation. Organ formation begins toward the end of the third week after conception, the most critical period being from 20 to 56 days after conception. After day 56, the end of the eighth week of pregnancy (dated from conception, *not* from the last menstrual period), the most precarious period of prenatal development is over, and the baby-to-be is henceforth referred to as a fetus. But sensitive developmental periods of some organs extend several weeks into the fetal period. For example, although the embryo's internal reproductive organs are fairly well formed at eight weeks after conception, its external genitalia are still ambiguous—that is, they have not yet differentiated into male or female. This basic sex differentiation is not completed until week 12 after conception.

By the end of the fourteenth week after conception all the organs are essentially formed, and the fetus even looks like a tiny human being, both in face and in body. Since organ formation is confined to the first trimester, major malformations can occur

PREGNANCY SICKNESS

only during that period. During the second and third trimesters the fetus grows rapidly, as its organs mature, but only relatively minor development takes place, such as the formation of fat deposits. If one were to take a snapshot of the fetus every month from four months after conception until birth, the series would resemble a set of nested Russian dolls—graduated in size, yet otherwise almost identical.

Pregnancy sickness usually begins by the end of the third week after conception (although a pregnant woman may not be aware of her food and odor aversions immediately). It typically peaks at about eight weeks after conception and then gradually wanes, ending during the fourth month after conception, usually by about the end of week 14. In some women pregnancy sickness persists for a few more weeks; only in rare, dysfunctional cases does it persist throughout pregnancy. Thus, the woman's aversions to toxins are greatest precisely when her baby-to-be is most vulnerable to toxins.

Why Pregnancy Sickness Doesn't Begin at Conception

Pregnancy sickness does not occur during the first two weeks after conception, nor should it: at this very early stage the embryo is not particularly susceptible to harm from toxins, even if it comes into contact with them, and, in any case, it is unlikely to come into contact with toxins. The reason the embryo is not very vulnerable to toxins immediately after conception is that organ formation does not begin until the third week. During the first two weeks the embryo is really just a fertilized egg cell that divides many times, forming a mass of identical cells inside an outer shell of identical cells; none of these cells has begun to differentiate into specific types of tissues. Since organ formation is not occurring, organ malformation is not occurring either.

The Vulnerable Embryo

Experiments on many different animal species have shown that before the start of organ formation, toxins rarely cause malformations in embryos. Instead, when toxins do reach an embryo at this early stage, they kill some of its cells, in which case the other cells simply divide to replace them (since at this stage all the cells are identical); or, on occasion, they may kill all the cells, in which case the woman simply has a very early miscarriage and starts her next menstrual cycle.

Toxins from the mother's bloodstream are less likely to reach the embryo during the first two weeks after conception than during the rest of pregnancy. For the first six or seven days after conception the embryo (which is actually called a blastocyst at this early stage) travels down the Fallopian tubes to the uterus, where it will implant and grow. Although it begins implanting in the uterus at the end of the first week after conception, not until day 15 after conception does it form a rudimentary placenta capable of absorbing blood from the arteries in the mother's uterus. Since the main route by which toxins reach an embryo is via the mother's bloodstream, which floods the placenta to deliver vital nutrients, the embryo is not usually exposed to large quantities of dietary toxins until it begins to depend on maternal blood for nourishment. A small amount of toxins may reach the embryo before it implants in the mother's uterus, since toxins in the bloodstream can circulate to most tissues and fluids of the body, and the uterus secretes fluids that undoubtedly reach the embryo. But until organ formation begins, the embryo is just not especially vulnerable.

Most of the toxins the woman eats before the start of organ formation do not linger in her body for a long time and so do not pose future threats to her embryo. Most toxins, in fact, are cleared from the body within hours or days, so that by the time

PREGNANCY SICKNESS

organ formation and pregnancy sickness begin, the toxins the woman ate during the first two weeks of pregnancy have been virtually eliminated from her body. Some toxins are cleared from the body exceptionally slowly and may be able to cause malformations even weeks after being eaten, but these appear to be rare. In general, pregnancy sickness is not needed until the third week after conception.

Why Pregnancy Sickness Lasts Only Three Months

Pregnancy sickness would cause more harm than good if it lasted past the stage when it's needed, because it inflicts a nutritional cost on both the woman and her baby-to-be. For example, pregnancy sickness discourages the woman from eating vegetables— a major source of vitamins. But as long as a woman is not deficient in nutrients at the time of conception, the nutritional deprivation she experiences as a result of pregnancy sickness is unlikely to harm her embryo. Because of the embryo's small size—at eight weeks after conception it only measures a little more than an inch from the top of the head to the rump—it needs only a small amount of calories and nutrients to fuel its development. (See Chapter 8 for information about nutrition during the first trimester.)

But the dietary needs of the fetus differ from those of the embryo. During the second and third trimesters the fetus grows rapidly and needs a substantial amount of calories and protein to thrive. If the fetus suffers nutritional deficiencies its growth can be retarded, and its health can be compromised in other ways as well. The woman therefore needs to regain her appetite for nutritious foods. Pregnancy sickness spans only the period during which the baby-to-be is most vulnerable to toxins in its mother's diet and least vulnerable to shortages in its mother's intake of food.

The Vulnerable Embryo

Pregnancy Sickness Protects Against Miscarriage

Pregnancy sickness is a sign of a healthy pregnancy. Although many women feel unlucky if they suffer a moderate to severe case of pregnancy sickness, they should actually count themselves lucky, because their embryos are much more likely to survive the entire pregnancy and be born healthy. Many studies over the last four decades, involving thousands of pregnant women, have shown that women who have only mild or nonapparent pregnancy sickness are about three times as likely to miscarry as are women with moderate to severe pregnancy sickness. One study also found that women with moderate to severe pregnancy sickness were less likely to deliver infants with birth defects.

What These Studies Do and Don't Mean

Women suffering from moderate to severe pregnancy sickness who hear about these statistical studies often feel consoled by them, pleased that their suffering is at least a healthy sign. But these studies don't tell them *why* pregnancy sickness is associated with a successful pregnancy. The studies don't even tell them that the unpleasant symptoms of nausea, vomiting, and food aversions have functions in and of themselves. Someone who understands that the function of pregnancy sickness is to protect the embryo from birth defects will not be surprised to learn that moderate to severe pregnancy sickness is associated with a lower risk for miscarriage. After all, defective embryos are much more likely than healthy embryos to be miscarried. But someone pondering the meaning of these studies should not read too much into them, because the relationship between abnormally low degrees of pregnancy sickness and miscarriage may not always be a causal one. The hormones of pregnancy are necessary both for causing pregnancy sickness, as explained in Chapter 4, and for maintaining the lining of the uterus (which would otherwise be shed via menstruation or miscarriage). In some pregnancies, the placenta and ovaries produce abnormally low levels of hormones, resulting both in attenuated pregnancy sickness and in an insufficient uterine lining.

Furthermore, the fact that pregnancy sickness serves an important function does not mean that severe pregnancy sickness is superior to mild pregnancy sickness. The "optimal" degree of pregnancy sickness, in fact, could not be the most severe, because extreme pregnancy sickness prevents the woman from eating almost anything, endangering her life and that of her embryo. By analogy, even though fever is known to serve the important function of combating bacteria and viruses, the highest fevers can actually be life-threatening.

The Best Evidence That Pregnancy Sickness Protects the Embryo

In sum, the embryo presents a special problem of defense because it is extremely susceptible to damage by toxins. Pregnancy sickness helps to solve this problem by causing the woman to become more vigilant toward toxins and less tolerant of them. When a first-trimester woman is suffering from intense nausea, however, it can be difficult for her to believe that nausea really is a good thing. Perhaps the best way for a first-trimester woman to feel good about feeling nauseated is to convince herself that pregnancy sickness is indeed protecting her embryo, which she can do by looking at its "design":

The Timing of Pregnancy Sickness. It coincides precisely with the baby-to-be's organ formation, the peak period of vulnerability to toxins.

The Vulnerable Embryo

The Symptoms of Pregnancy Sickness. Nausea, vomiting, and food aversions have known antitoxin functions in nonpregnant people and in other mammals. In fact, the area of the brain stem that triggers these symptoms is an ancient part of the mammalian nervous system.

The Cues That Trigger or Increase Pregnancy Sickness. Bitter tastes and pungent odors are cues of toxins in the natural world, and they are also the main external triggers of nausea, vomiting, and food/odor aversions during the first trimester.

The Physiological Changes in a Woman's Body that Accompany Pregnancy Sickness. During the first trimester, the woman's body mobilizes various other defenses against toxins, complementing pregnancy sickness, as described in the following chapter.

Chapter Four

How a Woman's Body Defends Her Embryo Against Toxins

THE GOAL of this chapter is to further demystify pregnancy sickness—to explain how it happens. This chapter also will make sense of other first-trimester changes in a woman's body—such as the acute sense of smell, frequent urination, and drooling—showing how they may help to protect the embryo from the naturally toxic environment. This chapter connects pregnancy sickness with other first-trimester physiological events, so that a reader experiencing her first trimester will be better able to visualize what's going on in her body.

Hormones and Pregnancy Sickness

The hormones of early pregnancy probably trigger, maintain, and, ultimately, terminate pregnancy sickness. A hormone is a substance that can be secreted in one part of the body, circulate in the bloodstream, and trigger events in other parts of the body. It is hormones that cause females to menstruate, ovulate, and maintain a pregnancy. Organs whose cells have hormone receptors (molecules with strong affinities for particular hormones) can "sense" what's happening in other parts of the body and respond appropriately.

PREGNANCY SICKNESS

Hormones and the Brain Stem

The brain stem's CTZ (chemoreceptor trigger zone), which was introduced in Chapter 2, is the body's central toxin sensor. Like most parts of the brain stem, the CTZ is evolutionarily ancient. Every mammal has one. Unlike most parts of the brain, however, the CTZ is bathed by circulating blood (so that it can analyze the blood's constituents). Lining the blood vessels of the CTZ are many different toxin sensors, whose function is to detect the kinds and amounts of toxins circulating in the bloodstream. When toxin levels are above a certain threshold, the CTZ triggers the cascade of signals that travel to various parts of the nervous system to induce nausea, vomiting, and food aversions.

The CTZ apparently "knows" whether or not a woman is pregnant. It acquires this information by sensing the types and amounts of hormones circulating in the bloodstream. It then responds appropriately, increasing its sensitivity to toxins in the first trimester, then decreasing its sensitivity subsequently.

Which Hormones Control Pregnancy Sickness?

There are three hormones that are likely candidates for influencing pregnancy sickness. They are estradiol (a form of estrogen), progesterone, and human chorionic gonadotropin (HCG). For readers who are interested in knowing more about these hormones, I'll briefly introduce each and describe how it may influence pregnancy sickness. Other readers may want to skip to the next section.

Estradiol. At the start of a woman's menstrual cycle (i.e., when menstrual bleeding starts), her ovaries begin to secrete estradiol, which causes her endometrium (the tissue that lines the uterine cavity, where an embyro implants) to thicken in

How a Woman's Body Defends Her Embryo Against Toxins

preparation for a possible pregnancy. Estradiol levels rise sharply at ovulation (about two weeks into the menstrual cycle) and then wane, dropping steeply toward the end of the cycle if the woman has not conceived. If the woman has conceived, however, estradiol levels rise as soon as the embryo implants in the uterus. By the sixth week of pregnancy the placenta, rather than the ovaries, produces most of the estradiol. Estradiol levels continue to rise steadily throughout pregnancy.

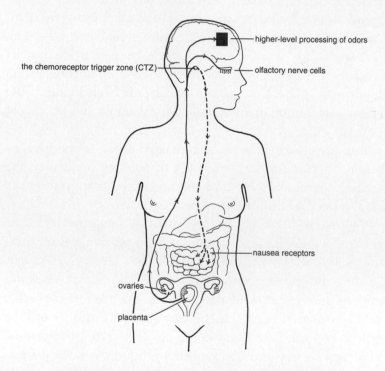

The hormone estradiol, which is secreted by the ovaries and the placenta, can stimulate certain parts of the brain to induce food/odor aversions, nausea, and vomiting.

PREGNANCY SICKNESS

Estradiol almost certainly plays an important role in pregnancy sickness because it and other forms of estrogen have such dramatic pregnancy sickness–like effects on the CTZs of nonpregnant women and other mammals. When girls go through puberty their ovaries begin producing estradiol and they suddenly become more susceptible than boys to nausea. Women who take high-estrogen birth control pills often suffer the side effect of nausea (although nowadays most birth control pills on the market have relatively low levels of estrogen). In experimental animals high doses of estradiol and other estrogens commonly cause nausea and the development of food aversions. The CTZ is able to "track" estradiol levels because it has special receptors that gauge how much estradiol is circulating in the bloodstream. (These receptors have already been found in the CTZ of rats, but no one has looked for them yet in the CTZ of humans.)

Since pregnancy sickness is normally limited to the first trimester, whereas estradiol levels rise throughout pregnancy, the puzzling question is what shuts off pregnancy sickness after the first trimester. The answer may be progesterone.

Progesterone. During the menstrual cycle, progesterone is secreted by the ovary that ovulates (each ovary ovulates on alternate cycles). After ovulation, progesterone levels rise sharply, signaling the endometrium to mature. If the woman does not conceive during that cycle, progesterone levels fall precipitously and menstruation occurs. If the woman does conceive and the embryo implants, the ovary continues to secrete progesterone for several weeks, until the placenta produces enough progesterone to maintain the pregnancy. Although levels of progesterone rise as soon as the embryo implants, they plateau from about weeks 3 through 8 of pregnancy—the rest of the embryonic period. After week 8 they begin to rise again, climbing steadily until birth.

The reason that progesterone appears to be the hormone that shuts off pregnancy sickness is that some of progesterone's effects oppose those of estrogen. For example, progesterone has a calming effect on smooth muscle tissue, such as the lining of blood vessels (presumably including blood vessels in the CTZ). During the peak period of pregnancy sickness, from three to eight weeks after conception, progesterone levels generally remain flat, whereas estradiol levels rise sharply, causing the ratio of estradiol to progesterone in the mother's bloodstream to increase up to tenfold. After week 8, as progesterone levels rise, the rate of this increase declines, and pregnancy sickness wanes.

Human Chorionic Gonadotropin. HCG has long been suspected of playing a role in pregnancy sickness because of its timing: HCG levels rise when pregnancy sickness begins, and they fall when it ends. As soon as an embryo implants, its placenta produces HCG and releases it into the mother's bloodstream. (HCG is the hormone measured in tests for detecting pregnancy.) HCG levels in the mother's bloodstream rise until about week 8, and then begin to decrease, falling steeply after week 10 and remaining low from week 14 until birth.

HCG plays at least an indirect role in pregnancy sickness, in that it stimulates the mother's ovaries to keep producing estradiol and progesterone through the first several weeks of pregnancy. It isn't yet known, however, whether HCG actually stimulates the CTZ to trigger nausea and aversions, as estradiol does. If both estradiol and HCG trigger pregnancy sickness directly—via effects on the CTZ—it seems likely that each has a slightly different effect on the CTZ. Otherwise, since estradiol alone is known to cause nausea and food aversions, and since

HCG is produced only when there are already high levels of estradiol in the mother's bloodstream, it would seem unnecessary for both to have the same function. Food aversions and odor aversions are complex behaviors that involve communication between the brain stem and higher levels of the brain. Perhaps the timing of HCG levels in the bloodstream and pregnancy sickness is just a coincidence, or perhaps HCG plays some kind of complementary role in triggering pregnancy sickness. In any case, the main hormone responsible for pregnancy sickness appears to be estradiol.

Who Controls Pregnancy Sickness, Mother or Embryo?

Assuming that hormone dynamics trigger, maintain, and terminate pregnancy sickness, then who controls pregnancy sickness, the mother or the embryo? The answer is that either can potentially control it, because both produce hormones that can affect the CTZ: the mother's ovaries produce estradiol and progesterone; the embryo's placenta (the placenta develops from the embryo's cells, not the mother's) produces estradiol, progesterone, and HCG. When the embryo implants, it suddenly acquires the capacity to tap the constituents of the mother's bloodstream and the capacity to release hormones into her bloodstream. The embryo thus simultaneously becomes vulnerable to toxins and able to trigger pregnancy sickness. By regulating the amounts of hormones the placenta produces, the embryo may be able to regulate the severity of its mother's pregnancy sickness. The mother's ovaries, however, may counter by adjusting their hormone production in response to the embryo's.

But would the mother's and embryo's "interests" in pregnancy sickness ever be likely to diverge, resulting in a hormonal "tug-of-war"? Usually it is in the interests of both mother and embryo for the mother to have at least a moderate degree of pregnancy sickness: the embryo doesn't "want" to be malformed, and the mother doesn't want her baby to be malformed. If the mother is still nursing a previous baby, however, moderate pregnancy sickness may prevent her from eating enough nutrients to nourish that baby. In this case, it may be in her interest to have no more than mild pregnancy sickness—that is, she may be better off nourishing her nursing baby and risking possible malformation of her embryo. It's even possible that the mother's ovaries can detect the hormones of breastfeeding and use them as a signal to lower their estradiol production if she is pregnant.

In the environment of our hunter-gatherer ancestors, where there were no baby bottles full of formula, the trade-off between nursing an older baby and protecting an embryo would have been especially stark. If the mother didn't have sufficient milk to nurse her baby, it died. But eating enough food to breastfeed usually entailed eating a lot of plants, which meant eating a lot of toxins. It would still have been in the embryo's interest for its mother to have pregnancy sickness so that she would refrain from eating foods high in toxins. Thus, at times there would have been a conflict of interest between the mother, who was capable of eating nutritious plant foods and inadvertently inflicting plant toxins on her embryo, and the embryo, who was capable of inflicting pregnancy sickness on its mother.

Sensitivity to Odor Increases Dramatically

A first-trimester woman becomes extremely sensitive to odors, almost all of which smell bad to her. She may now be able to smell laundry detergent two rooms away or mold in a closet

PREGNANCY SICKNESS

down the hall. Many aromas that were attractive before pregnancy all of a sudden become repulsive. For example, most non-pregnant women enjoy the aroma of fresh coffee brewing and the anticipation of drinking some. It is even said that among the Turks in the 1700s, a husband's refusal to give his wife coffee was legitimate grounds for divorce. One of the telltale signs that a woman is pregnant, however, is her sudden aversion to the aroma of coffee.

Odors, Fumes, and Toxicity

The sense of smell is a major way that humans and other mammals detect natural toxins, and women with pregnancy sickness become especially intolerant of odors that indicate toxins. We can't smell all plant toxins, but we can smell many of them. As discussed in Chapter 2, the pungent aromas of plant foods are usually caused by the toxins they contain because plants advertise their toxins to ward off plant-eating animals. Mustard and broccoli, for example, get their pungent aromas from the toxin allyl isothiocyanate. Meats, fish, and dairy products acquire pungent aromas as they become contaminated by bacteria. By having a greatly increased sensitivity to odors, a first-trimester woman detects toxins more readily without having to be consciously aware of them.

The odor of cooking fumes often triggers strong aversions—and sometimes nausea and vomiting—in a first-trimester woman because the fumes are potentially dangerous. Heating a plant converts many of its toxins to gasses, which can then be inhaled, absorbed into the bloodstream, and circulated to the placenta. Some cooking fumes are toxic even for adults, as illustrated by the following example of false morel mushrooms. Eaten raw, false morel mushrooms are poisonous (and often lethal), but when they are well-cooked they are considered edible. Cooking them, however, can be dangerous, because the steam they produce contains the toxin monomethylhydrazine. This same toxin, in fact, is synthesized by the chemical industry for use as rocket fuel. Needless to say, the embryo is better off without it.

Cooking poses other potential hazards to the embryo. As discussed in Chapter 2, cooking transforms some harmless food compounds into compounds capable of mutating the DNA of some cells. When a pregnant woman eats fried meat, for example, some of the compounds produced by frying are absorbed into the bloodstream, where they can circulate to the placenta.

Cooking over a barbeque or campfire can be especially nauseating to a first-trimester woman because vaporized food toxins are mingled with toxins from the charcoal or wood. Burnt material, such as charcoal and burnt wood, is toxic because it can mutate DNA. Wood also contains resins and other toxins that can be vaporized and then inhaled when heated. These types of fumes are potentially harmful to the developing embryo and should be expected to repulse first-trimester women. All in all, the nausea that a woman experiences when inhaling cooking fumes should discourage her from continuing to inhale these fumes, from eating the foods that emit these fumes, and from wanting to cook or eat these foods in the near future.

Odor Aversions to Nonfood Substances

Many of the most severe odor aversions during early pregnancy are to substances that aren't even potential sources of food, such as perfumes, scented products, cleaning fluids, ink, and so forth. Although aversions to such substances may seem puzzling or even dysfunctional, they are actually necessary components of pregnancy sickness.

PREGNANCY SICKNESS

The purpose of odor aversions during early pregnancy is almost certain to prevent the woman from eating toxic substances and inhaling toxic vapors. Many inedible substances are inedible precisely because they are toxic, and the vapors they emit are often toxic, too. Therefore, the odors of inedible substances can be expected to trigger strong aversions during the first trimester. Perfume, for example, has a high concentration of inedible, aromatic plant oils that contain a wide spectrum of plant toxins. Drinking a bottle of perfume would make even a nonpregnant person ill. The fumes from inedible substances may typically be harmless, or only transiently harmful, to adults, but they are not necessarily harmless to embryos.

The brain mechanisms that assess toxicity and produce aversions may allow an inedible substance, such as perfume, to smell pleasant (yet still not edible) to a nonpregnant woman. But during the first trimester these mechanisms probably are designed to err on the side of caution. The messages they convey to a first-trimester woman are "Don't inhale the fumes from this substance and don't even think about eating it."

A superacute sense of smell combined with aversions to most odors may seem like a handicap—and it would be at times other than the first trimester of pregnancy. But it is extremely important for protecting embryos.

Intensity of Odors

We tend to think of odors as good, bad, or somewhere in between. To most nonpregnant people, lemons and pine trees smell good, and skunk and feces smell bad. In nature, sweet odors and certain other kinds of odors are meant to attract animals; pungent odors are meant to repel animals; and many other odors are meant neither to attract nor to repel. But the attractiveness or repulsiveness of an odor also depends on its concentration. The intensity of an odor, in fact, greatly affects how we perceive it. For example, the natural chemical in bananas that creates the familiar banana odor is amyl acetate. In normal concentrations, this odor appeals to most people, but as its concentration increases it begins to smell like airplane glue. The odor not only turns from pleasant to repulsive, but its quality changes—it doesn't smell like the same substance.

This transformation in how the brain perceives odor when the intensity of the odor changes may protect us from inhaling high concentrations of substances that we can detect by smell. All vapors, even normally nontoxic ones, become toxic at some concentration. Although it's not dangerous to inhale small concentrations of impurities, such as a few perfume or diesel fuel molecules, it is dangerous to saturate the lungs with such impurities.

This connection between the intensity of an odor and its repulsiveness becomes greatly exaggerated during early pregnancy. Almost all intense odors repulse first-trimester women. In cases of severe pregnancy sickness, almost any detectable odor becomes repulsive. The lungs are supposed to carry oxygen, not perfume, to the embryo, and the odor-assessing mechanisms of the brain help to ensure that this is what happens.

Another reason why intense odors should trigger repulsion in a first-trimester woman is that her brain may use the intensity of an odor to estimate the amount of a particular food she's considering eating. Even substances that are fairly low in toxins are not necessarily safe to eat during early pregnancy in amounts large enough to produce an intense odor. Ripe fruits, for example, which are relatively low in toxins so that certain animals will be enticed to eat them and disperse their seeds, nevertheless contain some toxins to ward off insects that devour fruits without dispersing the seeds. Furthermore, much of the odor of many fruits comes from the peel, which may be high in toxins. (That's why we peel many kinds of fruit.) Aromatic but inedible peels help attract seed-dispersing animals while deterring animals that are unable to peel the fruits and carry away the seeds. Whereas a mild fruit odor would not be likely to bother most first-trimester women, an intense fruit odor probably would.

How a First-Trimester Woman's
Sense of Smell Is Heightened

When a person's sense of smell changes, it means that some change has taken place in the nose or in one of the areas of the brain that perceives smell. In order for a person to smell an odor in the first place, molecules of that odor must enter the nose and bind to olfactory nerve cells, which are embedded in the mucous membranes of the upper part of the nasal passages. The nerve cells extend up to the brain's olfactory bulb, where they transmit odor information to other nerve cells, which carry this information to odor-assessing parts of the brain. In order for a molecule to bind to an olfactory nerve cell and create the sensation of smell, there must be sensors (receptors) for it on the olfactory nerve cells. If a substance we inhale doesn't have an odor, that means that its molecules don't bind to our types of odor receptors.

One way that the body may heighten its sense of smell during early pregnancy is by increasing the number of olfactory nerve cells and their receptors. This would enable the woman to suddenly detect much fainter odors, because any given odor molecule entering her nose would have a greater chance of landing on a receptor that can bind it. It has already been shown that olfactory nerve cells in rats increase during pregnancy, in response to the high levels of estrogen, but the relevant studies have yet to be done in humans. One reason that an increase in olfactory nerve cells is a likely physiological explanation for the first-trimester woman's heightened sense of smell is that olfactory nerve cells do fluctuate in number throughout life, and it makes sense that pregnancy would be one of the events designed to stimulate them to proliferate. (Unlike non-nerve cells, such as skin, blood, and liver cells, most types of nerve cells in an adult's body cannot proliferate, and they don't even get replaced if they die—that is, no neighboring cell divides in two to make up the loss. Olfactory nerve cells are exceptions: they are renewed throughout much of life.)

Women in general have a more acute sense of smell than men do, presumably because of the huge sex difference in estrogen levels. This means that women, on average, are probably more alert than men are to natural toxins. During early pregnancy, the difference between a woman's and a man's sense of smell widens greatly. So if a first-trimester woman complains that she can smell a certain odor, and her male partner thinks that she must be imagining it, he needs to realize that her acuity to odors is a lot more like the pet dog's or cat's than his is.

Odor Aversions Wane After the First Trimester

After the first trimester, the change in a woman's sense of smell reverses direction, becoming much less acute. By the third trimester, her sense of smell may even be subnormal—that is, less acute than it was before she got pregnant—so foods and other things don't seem to have such strong smells anymore.

PREGNANCY SICKNESS

Hormones are probably responsible for this change: whereas the high levels of estrogen in early pregnancy may stimulate olfactory nerve cells to proliferate, the high levels of progesterone in the second and third trimesters may suppress such proliferation, causing a woman's sense of smell to wane.

This reversal may be necessary to counteract the food aversions developed during the first trimester. By the end of the first trimester, a woman has developed aversions to a huge assortment of foods because her brain stem's CTZ has been hyperstimulated and her sense of smell heightened. The problem is that, even though her CTZ returns to normal after the first trimester, her brain remembers which foods nauseated her. The brain mechanisms that induce food aversions are supposed to protect the body from repeated experiences with toxic foods. These mechanisms were designed to induce aversions on a long-term basis, since foods containing high levels of toxins on one occasion are very likely to contain them in the future.

But pregnancy sickness is supposed to be short-term. It would not be adaptive for pregnancy sickness to cause permanent food aversions or even aversions that lasted throughout pregnancy. In order to nourish her rapidly growing fetus, a woman needs to start eating normally again after the first trimester, and aversions would hinder this. So her brain needs to forget. It is harder to "erase" an aversion, however, than it is to develop one. So one way that the body apparently solves the problem of aversions to too many foods after the first trimester is to reduce the sense of smell to a subnormal level. Food odors therefore aren't as intense, which means that food aversions can't be triggered as easily.

But a diminished sense of smell means a diminished ability to detect toxins. Therefore, overcoming the food aversions acquired during the first trimester may entail some risk of eating higher-than-normal levels of toxins during the second and third trimesters. Some women even report that late in pregnancy they seek out spicy foods, which are high in natural toxins (see Chapter 7). Since a diminished sense of smell means a diminished sense of taste (because most of the taste of a food is really its smell), some third-trimester women may require spices or other pungent foods in order to experience taste sensations that are strong enough to be satisfying. Thus, instead of inflicting large quantities of plant toxins on the highly vulnerable embryo, pregnant women inflict them on the much less vulnerable fetus.

A Suite of Physiological Changes Helps Protect the Embryo from Toxins

Because an embryo's vulnerability to toxins is so great, various other changes take place in a woman's body during the first trimester to help shield her embryo from toxins. Some of these changes are regulated by the brain stem's CTZ and are designed to accompany nausea. Other changes also complement pregnancy sickness but are not regulated by the CTZ. Many of the unpleasant or annoying symptoms of early pregnancy are actually ways of protecting the embryo.

Information is still sparse regarding changes that occur in the mother's body specifically in the first trimester, because so few pregnancy researchers have been on the lookout for them. Most studies of the physiology of pregnancy simply compare women who are pregnant with those who are not, rather than comparing women in the first trimester with those in the second and third trimesters. Because many of the needs of the embryo differ greatly from those of the fetus, many aspects of the

PREGNANCY SICKNESS

woman's physiology should be expected to change when pregnancy shifts from the formation stage to the growth stage.

Common Symptoms Linked
to Pregnancy Sickness via the CTZ

Increase in Saliva Production. Some women find that they salivate so much during the first trimester that they outwardly drool. What may seem puzzling to people is that they usually associate salivating profusely with thinking about foods that are appetizing, whereas many first-trimester women salivate profusely even when they think almost nothing is appetizing.

When the CTZ is stimulated, it, in turn, stimulates the part of the brain stem that controls salivation. Salivation accompanies nausea because it facilitates vomiting, providing a slippery coating for expelling the contents of the stomach. It's also possible that overt drooling helps to expel toxins that are released from plant foods into the mouth during chewing. Many plant toxins, in fact, are not actually toxic until they are "activated" to their toxic forms, which happens when the plant tissues are torn or crushed (such as when a person chews on them). Drooling may prevent at least some of these toxins from entering a woman's tissues.

Drop in Blood Pressure. Blood pressure decreases during early pregnancy and remains below normal for the first trimester. (Blood pressure usually returns to normal during the second trimester and rises slightly above its pre-pregnancy value during the third trimester.) This first-trimester drop in blood pressure may be caused by the CTZ. In animal experiments, stimulating the CTZ directly (via electrical impulses) triggers an abrupt drop in blood pressure. This effect probably also occurs when animal or human CTZs are stimulated naturally. The benefit of lowering the blood pressure is probably to slow the rate at which toxins are circulated to organs they could damage. The body can detoxify only a certain amount of toxin during any given interval of time, and slowing the rate at which toxins are circulated buys extra time. This strategy is essentially the same one we use for snakebite. We try to prevent snake venom from circulating rapidly throughout the bloodstream by tying a tourniquet above the bite—which cuts off much of the blood flow from the venomous area—and by remaining as still as possible—which prevents the heart from pumping rapidly and transporting the venom quickly throughout the body.

Maladaptive side effects, such as dizziness and fainting, sometimes occur as a result of the first-trimester drop in blood pressure. There is a subtle compromise between lowering blood pressure enough to reduce the rate at which toxins are circulated and maintaining blood pressure high enough to enable the woman to engage in necessary activities.

Diarrhea. Some first-trimester women experience more diarrhea than usual. Diarrhea is the body's way of quickly expelling toxins, bacteria, and other harmful things from the intestines. When the CTZ detects high levels of toxins, it sends a signal to the large intestines to induce muscle contractions, which push digested foods toward the rectum where they can be expelled. That's why severe or persistent nausea—which is often the result of a stimulated CTZ—is commonly accompanied by diarrhea. (Severe diarrhea, however, may be a response to bacterial infection rather than a normal symptom of pregnancy sickness.)

Aversions to New Foods. A stimulated CTZ tends to discourage people from experimenting with new foods (this type of aversion is called neophobia). When mammals sample foods that are new to them, they usually do so gingerly, limiting their initial portion to a small amount. During the first trimester of pregnancy, women are likely to be especially wary of new foods. A woman doesn't know beforehand whether a food she has never tried harbors toxins that she cannot tolerate, and the first trimester of pregnancy is not the time to experiment. Rather, the body's best strategy during this critical time is simply to play it safe and avoid new foods ("new foods" means new ingredients, not necessarily new recipes).

The following incident illustrates the dangers of experimenting with unfamiliar plants. In the African country of Zambia, the people known as the Gwembe Tonga subsist by planting crops, but when agricultural yields are poor they gather wild plants to supplement their diets. When food is especially scarce, they resort to eating wild plants that are considerably more toxic than their usual foods, and they will even eat plants that give them stomachaches and headaches (still preferable to starving!). But such foraging can have tragic consequences. In 1958, when 600 Gwembe Tonga were forcibly relocated by the Zambian government to a new settlement, the economic hardships of resettlement drove them to forage unfamiliar wild plants. In one year, nearly 10 percent of the settlers died from apparent poisoning by wild plants.

When a woman in an industrialized society goes "foraging" in a supermarket and selects foods she has never eaten before, she generally doesn't have to worry that the foods might poison her. The foods will already have been "tested" on many consumers. But new foods (that is, foods she has not eaten before) probably are more risky for her embryo, on average, than are familiar foods, since she will not have built up an arsenal of detoxification enzymes against the toxins of unfamiliar foods. Even though the problem of experimenting with new foods is not as serious for women and embryos in an industrialized society as it was for our hunter-gatherer ancestors, the brain mechanisms that cause a first-trimester woman to be wary of new foods haven't disappeared just because the original environment has.

Intolerance of Bright Colors. Nausea sometimes makes the sufferer intolerant of bright colors, and some women with pregnancy sickness find that looking at bright colors worsens their nausea. The connection between bright colors and nausea may stem from the association between bright colors and toxins in the natural environment. A variety of organisms advertise their toxins with bright colors. Many molds, for example, which are notorious for producing potent toxins, come in a spectrum of bright reds, yellows, greens, and blues. We know instinctively that the blue mold infesting the bread and the green mold infesting the peach should not be eaten. Many toxic insects and reptiles, such as the monarch butterfly and the poison dart frog, also display bright colors to warn potential predators of their toxins.

Since bright colors are attention-grabbers, however, they are also used by many plants to attract animals to pollinate them or disperse their seeds. Flowers and ripe fruits, for example, typically have bright colors in order to stand out clearly from the rest of the plant. It is not known how the human brain distinguishes bright colors that are meant to repel from those that are meant to entice. During periods of intense or persistent nausea, as occurs with moderate to severe pregnancy sickness, the brain probably errs on the side of caution and assumes that all bright colors

PREGNANCY SICKNESS

signal potential toxic danger. A first-trimester woman thus may find that all bright colors exacerbate her nausea, and she may be averse to eating brightly colored foods.

Other Protective Changes in the First Trimester

Frequent Urination. Early in the first trimester women begin to urinate more frequently than usual. Frequent urination is easily understandable as a side effect during the third trimester, when the fetus is large enough to put substantial pressure on the bladder, but it seems perplexing during the first trimester, when the embryo is tiny and the uterus is correspondingly small.

The main reason for frequent urination so early in pregnancy is probably that the woman's kidneys start working overtime, apparently to flush out toxins at a faster-than-normal rate. The function of the kidneys is to filter out waste products from the blood. Some of these waste products are toxic molecules. During the first trimester the blood flow to the kidneys is about 75 percent greater than usual, and the kidneys start filtering the blood at a rate of about 50 percent greater than usual. If these changes were not adaptations of some sort, they would not be expected to occur until after the first trimester. During the second and third trimesters, the woman's body begins producing much more blood, in order to more efficiently convey oxygen and nutrients to the rapidly growing fetus. This increase in blood volume creates more work for the kidneys, which have to filter it. But during the first trimester, the total volume of blood in the woman's body does not increase, yet the kidneys are made to work as hard as they do during the second and third trimesters.

The fact that the kidneys begin working overtime so early in pregnancy seems to indicate that they do so in order to filter toxins from the blood more rapidly. Women whose kidneys do not work much overtime during the first trimester are more likely to miscarry (but it's not known whether these miscarriages are caused by the kidneys' failure to clear toxins quickly enough).

Fatigue. Fatigue is a common symptom of first-trimester women, and there may be an adaptive reason for it. In the environment of our hunter-gatherer ancestors, women had to expend a lot of energy to gather food. Although people living and traveling together almost certainly shared some of their food, most pregnant ancestral women would not have had abundant, easily obtainable supplies of food. Furthermore, hunter-gatherer women did not have a wide choice of foods that were low in toxins, since they lacked the low-toxin staples of modern agricultural diets, such as processed grains and dairy products—foods that tend to be favorites of first-trimester women living in modern industrialized societies. Fatigue would have caused ancestral first-trimester women to be less physically active, which, in turn, would have caused them to need less food. Since getting food required a lot of labor, needing less food meant eating less food, and, consequently, eating fewer toxins.

But fatigue in a first-trimester woman living in a modern industrialized society is not necessarily advantageous. For her, eating simply entails shuffling over to the refrigerator or driving to the supermarket. Obtaining large quantities of low-toxin foods—such as breads, cereals, pastas, rice, staple fruits, milk, and yogurt—is an easy task. Fatigue and lethargy in an industrialized society, unlike in a hunter-gatherer one, often even lead to an increase, rather than a decrease, in food intake, because the fatigued person sits around eating instead of engaging in more vigorous activity. Unless her pregnancy sickness is severe, a first-trimester woman in an industrialized society may end up eating more total calories per day than she did before pregnancy. This isn't necessarily bad, as long as the foods she eats are relatively low in toxins, but her fatigue has no benefits to compensate for its unpleasantness.

Some cases of fatigue in early pregnancy are probably incorrectly diagnosed as anemia. It is very important to distinguish between the two. As explained in Chapter 8, the standard treatment for anemia—supplementation with iron—can harm the embryo if the mother is not really anemic.

Drug Resistance

Several of the first-trimester antitoxin defenses described above reduce the harm that toxins do if they enter the woman's body. A consequence of this, however, is that the woman becomes more resistant to many medicinal drugs (which are, by definition, toxic substances). A dose of medicine that was effective before pregnancy suddenly may not be. (As emphasized in Chapters 9 and 10, a first-trimester woman should always consult her obstetrician before taking any medication.)

During pregnancy a woman's susceptibility to drugs can also change because of the effects of pregnancy hormones on levels of detoxification enzymes. But the effects of hormones on susceptibility to drugs are not consistent for all women or for all drugs. Pregnancy hormones enhance the rates at which some toxins are detoxified but depress the rates of others. Even though the body has a number of different first-trimester defenses to prevent toxins from reaching the embryo, it doesn't seem to have one that simply detoxifies all toxins at a faster rate. The reasons for this apparent "oversight" on the part of nature are explained in the following section.

How a Woman's Body Defends Her Embryo Against Toxins

Is Pregnancy Sickness the Best Strategy?

It may seem puzzling that nature didn't design the first-trimester defense system to consist of a huge increase in the production of detoxification enzymes in the mother's liver and gastrointestinal tract and in the embryo's organs and placenta. At first glance, such a defense system might seem to be a less costly way of protecting the embryo from toxins than for the mother to undergo many weeks of aversions, nausea, and vomiting. On closer inspection, however, this would not be a good solution, because it could backfire. Many plants avoid harming themselves with their own arsenal of toxins by exploiting the detoxification enzymes of the animals that devour plants: the plants manufacture toxins that remain inert (harmless) until the animals' enzymes try to destroy them. To be excreted safely, most toxins must be converted by enzymes into "intermediate" compounds, which are then attached to specialized molecules that prevent them from doing damage. But many of these temporary intermediate compounds are themselves toxic. If they are not immediately attached to molecules that render them harmless, they are free to do damage. Thus, accelerating the rate at which toxins are detoxified would accelerate the rate at which toxic intermediate compounds are produced, thereby jeopardizing the embryo. That is why the mother's pregnancy sickness—that is, avoidance of toxins—is the embryo's best defense.

Not All Symptoms of Early Pregnancy Have a Purpose

Some symptoms of early pregnancy have no function. They are merely side effects or by-products of first-trimester changes that do have functions. Fainting, as mentioned above, is an occasional dysfunctional by-product of the functional drop in blood

PREGNANCY SICKNESS

pressure that occurs during the first trimester. Headaches, which plague many first-trimester women, may also be side effects of the cardiovascular adaptations of early pregnancy. But headaches themselves are extremely unlikely to be adaptive. (First-trimester women suffering from them may be comforted to know that headaches that begin during pregnancy are usually limited to the first trimester.)

Many unpleasant symptoms of early pregnancy are normal and are not cause for alarm. But some common symptoms can also stem from genuine medical problems. Vomiting and headache during the first trimester, for example, are usually just "part of the package" of pregnancy, but they also can be caused by things that have nothing to do with pregnancy, such as certain viral infections, bacterial infections, and neurological disorders. Since the normal symptoms of pregnancy can mask serious underlying medical problems, a physician should be alerted if any symptom becomes extreme.

Chapter Five

$\sim\!\!\infty\!\!\sim$

Why Pregnancy Sickness
Varies So Much in Severity

A FEW YEARS AGO, while shuttling her six-year-old daughter Lisa and Lisa's girlfriend to soccer practice, my sister overheard the friend explaining the "facts of life." "Lisa," the friend began, "do you know what French kissing is?" "No," said Lisa. "It's when a man and woman put their tongues in each other's mouths," said the friend. "Ooh, yuck!" said Lisa. "And do you know how babies are made?" continued the friend. "No," said Lisa. "The man puts his penis in the woman's vagina," explained the friend. "Ooh, gross," said Lisa. "I'm never having any *French* babies."

Just as having sex is a mandatory part of pregnancy, not only in France, but in Australia, Zaire, and all other countries, experiencing pregnancy sickness is everywhere an inescapable part of pregnancy. Like all aspects of a healthy pregnancy, pregnancy sickness is universal. It's not an idiosyncrasy of any particular culture, but part of human nature.

During the last two centuries many Western writers have romanticized the "state of nature," blaming various afflictions suffered by people in modern industrialized societies on their having lost touch with nature. Since pregnancy and childbirth are natural and salient life events, a number of romanticized notions about them have sprung up, including the fallacies that women in nonindustrialized societies do not suffer pain during childbirth or nausea during pregnancy. Contrary to such notions, women everywhere suffer labor pain and pregnancy sickness.

Pregnancy Sickness in Other Cultures

Pregnancy sickness occurs even among the few remaining hunter-gatherers, whose preagricultural ways of life are remote from our own. In fact, pregnancy sickness is one of the ways that other members of a woman's group realize that she's pregnant. To the Kung! San hunter-gatherers of the Kalahari Desert in southern Africa, for example, vomiting and sudden "unexplained" dislikes for certain foods are telltale signs that a woman is pregnant. In Marjorie Shostak's fascinating book about hunter-gatherer life, *Nisa: The Life and Words of a !Kung Woman,* Nisa's mother-in-law suspects Nisa's pregnancy, saying, "If you are throwing up like this, it means you have a little thing inside your stomach." Efe Pygmy hunter-gatherer women in Zaire also use food aversions as a sign of pregnancy: all of a sudden, food tastes bad. And Aboriginal women of Australia know that vomiting can come with pregnancy. Their groups may even give them certain food taboos during pregnancy to protect the child in the womb, and they believe that a woman who disregards these rules may herself get sick.

Just as women everywhere get pregnancy sickness, it seems that women everywhere have sought remedies to make it more bearable. For example, in many nonindustrialized societies throughout the world pregnant women eat clay (a practice known as geophagy) as a remedy for nausea and vomiting. The apparent reason that this remedy sometimes works is that some clays bind certain types of toxins, preventing the toxins from being absorbed into the bloodstream. The clays, along with the toxins they have bound, simply pass through the digestive tract and are excreted. By eating these clays, pregnant women probably reduce the threat of food toxins to their embryos and, therefore, their need to vomit. "Pica" is the general term for the eating of nonnutritive substances such as clay, chalk, or dirt. Even in industrialized countries, some women in rural communities practice pica during pregnancy. Pica, however, is not necessarily safe. Different clays and dirts consist of different substances, so women practicing pica rarely know just what they're eating. Some clays are considered edible, others are not, and clays vary in their abilities to bind toxins. Someday safe and effective clays may be developed specifically for consumption by first-trimester women, but until such a time, the embryo is probably better off if its mother does not experiment with pica.

"Oh, I Didn't Have Any Pregnancy Sickness"

Virtually all first-trimester women experience some degree of pregnancy sickness. Roughly half of them feel sick enough to vomit. Many women who experience only mild degrees, however, do not subsequently recall their aversions, nausea, or vomiting unless questioned carefully and in detail. Often when a woman insists that she experienced no pregnancy sickness, I "interrogate" her with questions such as the following: In the first trimester, could you drink strong coffee? Did you like the smell of coffee brewing? Could you stand over a stove frying onions and garlic? Did you mind the smell of perfume? Did your partner's breath bother you? Could you barbeque meat? Did you

Women everywhere get pregnancy sickness.

mind opening cans of dog food or cat food? Did you mind the smell of steamed broccoli and Brussels sprouts? Did you mind the smell of leftovers in your refrigerator? Did you ever vomit? Sometimes the partners of pregnant women have more accurate memories of the pregnancy sickness than the women themselves do. When one journalist told me of her plan to poll mothers on the streets of San Francisco to determine the percentage who had experienced pregnancy sickness, I warned her about "pregnancy sickness amnesia." One mother she polled absolutely denied having had any symptoms of pregnancy sickness until her husband interrupted, "But honey, what about all those nights you threw up after dinner?" "Oh that!" she conceded. (When a first-trimester woman tells me she has zero pregnancy sickness, I'm often tempted to ask her to try holding a vial of strong perfume or garlic juice to her nose.) Only a tiny percentage of first-trimester women truly experience no pregnancy sickness (see Chapter 9 for what to do in such cases).

Why Pregnancy Sickness Is Variable

The variability of pregnancy sickness is perhaps its most puzzling feature. Although virtually all pregnant women get it, pregnancy sickness varies in severity from woman to woman and even from pregnancy to pregnancy in the same woman. Some women experience less severe pregnancy sickness with each pregnancy, whereas others experience the reverse. Women carrying twins often experience slightly more severe pregnancy sickness than average.

When women ask me why pregnancy sickness is so variable, usually what they have in mind is two separate questions: First and foremost, what they usually want to know is if pregnancy

PREGNANCY SICKNESS

sickness is so important, why nature didn't give all women the same degree of it. Second, they want to know what specific factors in a woman's pregnancy, genetics, or environment determine the severity of her pregnancy sickness.

To answer the first question, it's important to emphasize that the human body is a "bundle of compromises" (to borrow an expression from evolutionary biologist George Williams). This means that all the different mechanisms in the body impact and infringe on one another. For example, since the mechanisms involved in pumping blood, transmitting neurological impulses, and performing other essential processes that keep the body alive require energy to operate, they necessarily affect the mechanisms designed to acquire sources of energy (food), digest it, metabolize it, detoxify it, and excrete it. Some mechanisms impact others more directly. For example, the immune system's mechanisms that kill viruses, bacteria, and infected cells inevitably end up killing some healthy cells as well.

Operating any mechanism in the body involves trade-offs—costs as well as benefits. Mechanisms, such as pregnancy sickness, that survive for thousands of generations do so only because, on balance, their benefits are greater than their costs. In the case of pregnancy sickness, the benefits are eating fewer teratogens and, consequently, having a better chance of giving birth to babies without defects. The costs are eating fewer nutrients (since avoiding plant toxins necessarily entails avoiding plants, a major source of nutrients) and, consequently, risking malnourishment of the mother and the embryo/fetus.

One reason that nature has permitted pregnancy sickness to vary so much among women may be that the *net* benefit of pregnancy sickness (the benefits minus the costs) is similar for a range of degrees of pregnancy sickness. The amount that pregnancy sickness benefits an embryo and the amount that it costs the mother and embryo both depend directly on how severe the pregnancy sickness is. The more severe the pregnancy sickness, the better it protects the embryo against toxins, but the more it depletes the mother's supply of nutrients, on which the embryo depends. Thus, there may not be one optimal degree of pregnancy sickness, but, rather, an optimal *range* of degrees, all of which would be "normal." The extreme degrees of pregnancy sickness, however—represented at one end by a complete absence of food aversions and at the other end by unrelenting vomiting—would have zero or negative net benefit and therefore would be dysfunctional.

The answer to the second question is that the amount of pregnancy sickness that any given woman experiences depends on many different factors. For example, the variation from pregnancy to pregnancy in the same woman can arise from differences in the hormone levels of different pregnancies. Each embryo is genetically unique, and each placenta, which is formed from embryonic tissue, is also unique, which means that different placentas release somewhat different amounts of hormones into the mother's bloodstream. Assuming pregnancy sickness is hormonally triggered, the degree of pregnancy sickness would be expected to vary with each pregnancy.

One reason that pregnancy sickness varies from woman to woman is that the mechanisms underlying it vary so much. Pick any two nonpregnant women at random, and it is virtually certain that one of them will have a slightly better sense of smell than the other, one will be more easily nauseated, one will be more strongly affected by the same amount of a given drug, and so on. The basic mechanisms for detecting, avoiding, detoxifying, and expelling toxins—such as the senses of smell and taste, the

CTZ, and the detoxification enzymes—vary among individuals. Women who were especially sensitive to odors or susceptible to nausea before pregnancy are probably more likely than other women to experience severe pregnancy sickness.

To some extent the severity of a woman's pregnancy sickness depends on how toxic her particular diet is and on how toxic the air is that she breathes in her home and work environments. (See Chapters 6 and 7 for tips on minimizing one's exposure to toxins and offensive odors during pregnancy.) In addition, a woman's food and odor aversions during early pregnancy are to a large extent affected by her specific food history. Some food aversions may appear to be arbitrary, capricious, and idiosyncratic, but often they result from having had bad experiences with particular foods. If a woman has ever become ill from eating a particular food, for example, then she probably developed an aversion to it and will probably have an even greater aversion to it during early pregnancy. Just because some pregnant women can tolerate a certain food or smell doesn't mean that all should be able to. And if one first-trimester woman is more repulsed by a certain food than another first-trimester woman is, this does not necessarily mean that the food is more harmful for the first woman's embryo.

Constant Nausea and Morning Nausea

If the purpose of pregnancy sickness is to deter women from eating foods high in natural toxins, then it may seem strange—as well as terribly unfair!—that pregnancy sickness isn't limited to times when a woman smells or eats such foods. Why, one may reasonably ask, are some first-trimester women nauseated almost constantly, even when they have not eaten for hours and their diets consist of bland foods low in toxins?

To begin with, I'd like to point out that persistent nausea in the first trimester is not dysfunctional (unless it is extreme), because it causes women to be especially judicious in selecting foods. Women with frequent or constant nausea may find all foods unappetizing, but they find some foods much more unappetizing than others, and these distinctions aren't arbitrary. A nauseated woman is much more likely to choose a meal of applesauce, cereal, and milk than one of fried onions, broccoli, and barbequed fish (see Chapter 7).

How nausea occurs in the absence of food isn't completely understood yet, but for those readers who are curious about it, I'll describe two plausible possibilities. (Other readers may want to skip the next two paragraphs.)

When the brain stem's CTZ senses that pregnancy has begun, which it presumably does by detecting high levels of pregnancy hormones in the bloodstream, it may simply dilate its blood vessels, which are lined with toxin-detectors. This dilation would increase the CTZ's sensitivity to toxins in two ways: first, it would expand the surface area that detects toxins in the CTZ; and, second, it would enable the CTZ to sample a greater volume of blood in a given amount of time. The CTZ is spongelike in appearance, which probably means that it is designed to expand and contract in size, depending on the circumstance—for example, depending on whether it is dilating or constricting its blood vessels in response to hormone levels in the bloodstream. By dilating its blood vessels dramatically, the CTZ might be able to detect tiny amounts of toxins in the bloodstream. Since the bloodstream normally contains at least trace amounts of toxins from foods eaten days or even weeks earlier, pregnancy hormones that caused the CTZ's blood vessels to dilate could trigger a persistent background level of nausea, even when a woman had not eaten for hours.

Alternatively, when the CTZ detects high levels of pregnancy hormones—thereby sensing that pregnancy has begun—it may "automatically" trigger the cascade of neurological signals that cause at least a low degree of nausea, even if it does not detect toxins in the bloodstream. When it does detect toxins, it may simply increase these signals, thereby increasing the nausea.

Some women consistently feel sick upon waking in the morning (hence the term "morning sickness"), even though they have not eaten or smelled food for hours. Digestion slows during pregnancy, so even though meals are usually eaten at discrete intervals, digesting them may take all day and night. This means that throughout the night low levels of toxins may slowly seep into the bloodstream from the digestive tract and stimulate the CTZ. If a woman is nauseated in her sleep, food from her intestines is pushed up into her stomach in preparation for vomiting. Since vomiting is inhibited during sleep to prevent choking, any food that needs to be vomited remains in her stomach until she awakens.

The common remedy for alleviating morning nausea is to eat bland, starchy food, such as soda crackers, before rising. Understanding the function of pregnancy sickness helps to show why this practice makes sense. Filling the stomach with starch dilutes the concentration of toxins there, and lying horizontal (as in bed) slows the rate at which toxins circulate to the CTZ. When the human body changes from a horizontal to an erect posture, the heart and breathing rates increase abruptly, and this increases the rate at which toxins in the bloodstream circulate to the CTZ. So settling the stomach with crackers before getting out of bed may prevent a woman from having to greet each day by vomiting. On the other hand, vomiting usually makes a woman feel better immediately thereafter, and it spares her embryo from the toxins in her digestive tract.

Pregnancy Sickness in Other Mammals

Many women have asked me if their pets also get pregnancy sickness. My guess is that they do. Since pregnancy sickness is so important for embryos, it would be odd if this benefit were "enjoyed" only by people. Although no one has ever bothered to study pregnancy sickness in animals—after all, pregnancy sickness has been assumed to be merely a nuisance in people—sparse anecdotal reports of pregnancy sickness in other animals have appeared in the writings of some observant zookeepers and animal researchers. For example, chimpanzees in the early months of pregnancy sometimes behave as though they have malaise, and their appetites may be unstable. One spider monkey at the Brookfield Zoo in Illinois was reported to vomit during every pregnancy. And some farm animals and domestic pets have been known to alter their food preferences during pregnancy.

I suspect that pregnancy sickness occurs in females of most species of mammal. All mammals have the same basic physiological mechanisms that appear to underlie human pregnancy sickness, such as brain stem CTZs that induce nausea and food aversions in response to high levels of toxins. But I would expect the average degree of pregnancy sickness to vary greatly from species to species, depending on its benefits and costs for females of each species.

PREGNANCY SICKNESS

The benefits of having pregnancy sickness depend on how potentially dangerous a female's diet is for her embryo. Mammals that eat a wide range of plants, experimenting from time to time with new plant species, probably experience the most severe pregnancy sickness, because they expose their embryos to the widest array of toxins. Monkeys that eat both fruits and leaves, for example, may prefer to eat fruit during early pregnancy, because ripe fruit tends to be much less toxic than leaves. Plant-eating mammals with highly specialized diets, such as koalas, probably experience very little, if any, pregnancy sickness, because they are exceptionally well adapted to handle the specific toxins of their narrow food niches, and, in any case, they would be unlikely to specialize in foods that cause birth defects in their embryos. Carnivores (which don't eat plants) would benefit less from pregnancy sickness than would plant-eating mammals, but they may experience some pregnancy sickness, since it would tend to deter them from eating meat contaminated by bacteria. Pet dogs and cats typically are fed meat that is not fresh, and it would not be surprising if, during the period of their embryos' organ formation, they turned up their noses at some of the canned foods that they used to eat with enthusiasm. (Organ formation in dog embryos occurs on days 14–30 of pregnancy, in cat embryos on days 14–26.)

The costs to a female mammal of having pregnancy sickness would depend primarily on how much and for how long it deprived her and her embryo of nutrients. Organ formation lasts a different amount of time in each species, depending in part on the species' gestation length. Organ formation in different species also takes up different proportions of the total pregnancy, depending on whether birth normally occurs when the young are at a relatively mature or immature stage of development. (Some mammals, such as deer, are able to see their surroundings and flee from danger at birth; whereas other mammals, such as cats, are born blind and helpless.) Pregnancy sickness may also have certain costs that are significant for some mammals but not others. For example, the nausea of pregnancy sickness may render females less swift—an especially large cost for prey mammals, which need to be able to flee from danger at any moment.

Humans probably get the most severe pregnancy sickness because they are better able than most mammals to "afford" it. Before they get pregnant, women store a much higher percentage of their body weight as fat than most other female mammals do, giving them calorie reserves that serve as a buffer against the nutritional deprivation caused by severe pregnancy sickness. A physically fit, healthy woman has significantly more body fat, for example, than does a physically fit, healthy chimpanzee. The fact that women have this compensatory mechanism to offset the costs of pregnancy sickness suggests that the human female body has been designed to experience a substantial degree of pregnancy sickness.

PART II

*Managing the
First Trimester*

Chapter Six

~~~
◦~€Ð€~◦
~~~

Preparing for Pregnancy Sickness

Preparing Psychologically and Socially

PEOPLE HAVE many misconceptions (so to speak) about the first trimester. This is not surprising, since people tend to have misconceptions about many aspects of pregnancy. When my South African friends Leon and Frances were a couple of months away from the birth of their second child, their four-year-old daughter Justine pointed to Frances's greatly expanded abdomen and asked, "Mummy, what's that?" "That's a baby," Frances replied. "Where'd you get it?" asked Justine. "Daddy gave it to me," said Frances. Justine trotted up to Leon and asked, "Daddy, did you give Mummy a baby?" "Er, yes, I guess I did," answered Leon. "Well, I don't think you should give her any more," said Justine. "She just eats them."

People find this story funny in part because of its "innocence"; the misconception about pregnancy came from a small child, and it caused no harm. Adults' misconceptions about the first trimester are often no less silly, but they are not funny, because they often do cause harm. Chapter 1 reviewed some of the unfortunate consequences of misconceptions about pregnancy sickness, including guilt felt by pregnant women who were told that

PREGNANCY SICKNESS

their pregnancy sickness stemmed from an attempt at oral abortion, and birth defects that occurred when women tried to suppress pregnancy sickness with the teratogenic drug thalidomide.

A woman should begin preparing for pregnancy sickness as soon as she discovers she's pregnant. This preparation includes understanding the function of pregnancy sickness, having the right perspective on it, knowing what to expect and what to do, and communicating this information to the parenting partner.

No More Guilt About Pregnancy Sickness

Many women with pregnancy sickness experience some guilt about it. They may feel guilty, for example, about throwing up at inopportune moments, not being able to "stomach" cooking dinner for the family, not being able to eat a meal prepared especially for them by their partner, or not being able to stand their partner's breath. But a physiological mechanism that protects the embryo from birth defects should not be a source of guilt. A partner who understands pregnancy sickness should expect a woman suffering from it to be intolerant of such activities as cooking garlic, eating garlic, or smelling garlic on her partner's breath.

Pregnancy sickness is not psychosomatic, nor does it represent a failure to cope with pregnancy and impending motherhood. Many women begin to experience it even before they are aware they are pregnant. In fact, some women who have already been through one pregnancy first realize they're beginning another when they experience the familiar inventory of symptoms. But since the function of pregnancy sickness has been elucidated only recently, it is not yet understood by large segments of the medical and lay populations. If the pregnant woman's parenting partner, relatives, coworkers, and friends cannot make sense of her sudden aversions, nausea, and vomiting, they may end up blaming her for these symptoms. Since pregnancy sickness often starts at about the time the woman finds out she is pregnant, and then it intensifies, her symptoms may seem suspiciously psychosomatic.

I've heard well-educated men say things like, "Oh, she throws up every day—what would you expect from an unathletic woman," or "Everyone told her that she brought morning sickness on herself by going on that weird diet last year, and now she's harming the fetus by being sick all the time." Pregnancy sickness is not a product of low athletic prowess or weird pre-pregnancy diets.

But it's not only men who can lack compassion for a woman who is experiencing severe pregnancy sickness. Some of the most blameful comments I've heard or read about are from women who themselves experienced only mild pregnancy sickness and believe that every woman should "handle" pregnancy as easily. Some of the women authors of the popular pregnancy books alluded to in Chapter 1 embrace the fallacy that severe pregnancy sickness is primarily a psychological maladjustment to pregnancy.

Some husbands of women who experience almost no pregnancy sickness brag about how well their wives handle pregnancy. But these men and their pregnant wives should worry, not brag. A couple of years ago I received a telephone SOS from a woman who had just read about my research in the *San Francisco Chronicle.* She told me that when she was pregnant she had failed to experience any pregnancy sickness, and that even though amniocentesis had not detected any genetic abnormalities, her infant had been born with a suite of birth defects, including major cardiovascular anomalies, a kink in the spine, partial deafness, and a missing facial muscle, among other problems. She was two weeks into her second pregnancy and desperate to learn what she should do to protect her embryo, since she lacked

PREGNANCY SICKNESS

the natural protection of pregnancy sickness. After questioning her carefully to validate her recollection that she had not experienced any pregnancy sickness, I gave her some suggestions (see Chapter 9 for advice on what to do in the absence of pregnancy sickness). Whether or not this woman's lack of pregnancy sickness was the cause of her infant's birth defects is not known, but it may have been. Being able to "handle" the first trimester as though it were no different from pre-pregnancy is cause for concern, as the woman realized the second time around.

People too often assume that someone else's physiological symptoms they don't understand are psychosomatic. The attitude seems to be, "If I can't see the symptoms, he/she must have imagined them," and "If I can't see what caused the symptoms, he/she must have unconsciously willed them." In many cases, mystery symptoms represent genuine illnesses, as exemplified by the famous tombstone in Massachusetts that reads, "I told you I was ill." In certain other cases, such as pregnancy sickness, the symptoms are really adaptations that have not yet been recognized as such. Most aspects of the human body are still mysteries, which is why there are hundreds of biomedical research departments around the world striving to decipher them. Although some symptoms and illnesses of some people are brought on by psychological problems, and some are even imagined, using the psychological diagnosis as a general default for symptoms that aren't easily explained is a cop-out that can do a lot of damage, as in the case of pregnancy sickness.

The Effect of Stress on Pregnancy Sickness

Even though pregnancy sickness is an adaptation, and not under voluntary control, it can still be affected by a woman's psychological state. During periods of psychological stress, the body usually releases higher-than-normal levels of the chemical histamine into the bloodstream, which is one of the chemicals that stimulates the area of the brain that induces nausea. (Antihistamines, which are normally taken to suppress allergic reactions, also are sometimes taken to help suppress nausea and vomiting.) Psychological stress often renders a person more susceptible to nausea and vomiting and, therefore, less tolerant of toxins. The reason the body lowers its tolerance to toxins when psychologically stressed may be that many toxins affect the brain in ways that alter the person's perception of reality, and an accurate perception of reality probably was crucial for dealing effectively with the types of situations that would have stressed our hunter-gatherer ancestors (such as avoiding becoming lunch for hungry lions, avoiding being caught poaching someone else's food or mate, and battling rivals for access to watering holes, fruiting trees, mates, and other resources). Thus, in psychologically stressful situations, our ancestors would have benefited from increased sensitivity to toxins and consequent decreased consumption of them.

It is important to emphasize that pregnancy sickness per se is not a neurotic response to pregnancy. Blaming a woman for getting pregnancy sickness—a suite of symptoms she did not voluntarily summon—is likely to increase her stress, which, in turn, could exacerbate her nausea and vomiting. This type of increase in pregnancy sickness is not good: embryos subjected to high levels of maternal stress hormones may be at higher risk of aborting or developing abnormally (see Chapter 11). For women who feel either guilty about or victimized by pregnancy sickness, discovering that the sudden and seemingly inexplicable symptoms actually serve critical functions may bring great relief and a brighter outlook on pregnancy. Relieving stress through biofeedback or other relaxation techniques may mitigate the severity of pregnancy sickness (see Chapter 9).

Explaining Pregnancy Sickness to Others

The more a pregnant woman "shows"—that is, the farther along she is in her pregnancy—the more sympathy and concern she generally gets from the parenting partner, relatives, friends, co-workers, and strangers. But the reverse would make more sense. Concern for the pregnant woman should be most intense before she is showing, when her embryo is in constant peril. It is important not only that the pregnant woman herself understand the function of first-trimester symptoms, but that she convey this understanding to the people she closely interacts with during the first trimester. Avoiding offensive odors necessarily entails the cooperation of the people producing them—that is, the people who are wearing perfume, brewing coffee, frying garlic, spray-painting furniture, and so on.

If a woman feels that her partner, employer, coworkers, or friends are unsympathetic about her pregnancy sickness, she can proudly announce, "Pregnancy sickness is something I'm doing for my baby," and explain why and how. Some pregnant women, however, do not want to reveal their pregnancies to nonintimates until after the first trimester. A woman who fears jeopardizing her job or her chance for promotion, for example, may want to hide the pregnancy as long as possible. And a woman who plans to undergo fetal testing for genetic defects may not want to reveal the pregnancy until she obtains the results of these tests. If a woman's pregnancy sickness is severe, however, its telltale symptoms will almost certainly be noticed by those around her.

It is especially important that the parenting partner understand the function of pregnancy sickness. Some partners are very

Preparing for Pregnancy Sickness

sympathetic about pregnancy sickness and even claim to experience pregnancy sickness vicariously. But a partner who views the pregnancy sickness of the woman carrying his embryo as psychosomatic is likely to become the target of bitterness, which can fester and resurface later in the relationship. Undercurrents of blame and anger are not healthy for pregnancy or parenthood.

The parenting partner needs to know that the first-trimester woman's requests to help her minimize her exposure to aversive foods and odors are not arbitrary. The pregnant woman is protecting the embryo for *both* parents. Since it's very much in the partner's interest that his embryo develop normally, it's in his interest not to eat foods that make his breath repulsive to her, not to pressure her to cook foods that nauseate her, and not to expect her to do other tasks that expose her to nauseating odors.

When my friend Molly was about twelve weeks pregnant and suffering from extreme pregnancy sickness, I was giving her some tips by phone on what to avoid eating and doing in order to minimize nausea when she interrupted our conversation to call out to her husband, "See, honey, Margie says *I* shouldn't be the one to feed the dogs." One whiff of canned dog food can send a first-trimester woman running to hug the toilet bowl. The division of labor between a woman and her partner usually needs to shift during the first trimester: she endures the nausea; he takes over the tasks that would worsen it.

There are three main reasons why the parenting partner needs to understand the function of pregnancy sickness in order to promote the health of the embryo: to avoid exposing the embryo to unacceptable levels of toxins; to reduce the risk of stress-related harm to the embryo (see Chapter 11); and to avoid depleting the embryo's supply of nutrients (since inflicting odors on the woman could cause her to vomit excessively). If the woman's

PREGNANCY SICKNESS

pregnancy sickness is severe, the first trimester may be an ordeal for her partner as well, since the woman may be bothered even by stimuli unrelated to food and odor, such as noise from the TV and stereo, bright lights, and human touch. The partner may find that he has to actively remind himself that pregnancy sickness is not a form of marital mutiny, spousal manipulation, old-fashionedness, chore avoidance, irresponsibility, melodrama, rejection of motherhood, or failure to cope.

Practical Tips for Preparing
for Pregnancy Sickness

The main pregnancy-related goal during the first trimester is to minimize exposure to toxins, and the main way to accomplish this is to minimize exposure to the foods and odors that trigger or intensify pregnancy sickness. The pregnant woman and her parenting partner can prepare for pregnancy sickness as soon as they find out they are expecting, by arranging their living space, working space, and calendar of activities in ways that minimize the woman's exposure to offensive odors. (Foods, beverages, and cooking are discussed in the following chapter.) Since many common household and office odors are likely to become repulsive during the first trimester, it is prudent to minimize or eliminate them by taking the following steps:

The Kitchen. Clean out the refrigerator. Throw out all odiferous foods, including garlic, onions, fresh herbs, and leftovers. (These foods can be spared if they are kept in truly airtight containers, but most "airtight" plastic bags and other containers leak a small amount of odor, which may be detected by the first-trimester woman.) Wipe up any spills on condiment jars or refrigerator surfaces. Deodorize the refrigerator and freezer by

Preparing for Pregnancy Sickness

placing cartons of baking soda in them to absorb odors that might otherwise contaminate dairy products and other foods.

In the food cupboards, wipe up old spills and throw out moldy foods. Take out odiferous foods, such as bags of onions or potatoes, and store them in a separate room that is seldom used (such as a basement).

Avoiding offensive odors helps to minimize pregnancy sickness.

PREGNANCY SICKNESS

House Cleaning. Clean the house thoroughly of molds and other sources of bad odors—these tend to become increasingly repugnant as the first trimester progresses. (Better yet, have the house cleaned by a professional service or a willing partner.) Use gentle detergents and cleaning products that do not produce strong fumes and that are otherwise low in toxicity. Baking soda, vinegar, or rubbing alcohol can be mixed with water for use as household cleaning solutions. If harsher cleaning fluids are used, do not allow skin contact with them and try not to inhale their fumes. Ways to minimize exposure to cleaning fluids include wearing thick gloves, opening the windows, turning on a fan, and donning a surgical mask. Since even an unopened box of laundry detergent two rooms away may emit a strong enough odor to bother a woman with severe pregnancy sickness, it is best to store detergents and opened containers of harsh cleaning fluids in a place where their odors are less likely to be detected, such as in a basement.

Indoor Air Pollution. Each house has its own distinctive smell because its building materials and contents emit fumes. Wood, paint, upholstery, carpets, and other furnishings emit some of their constituent chemicals into the air, contributing to indoor air pollution. In households that are not well-ventilated, the amount of indoor air pollution can exceed healthful levels. Air out the house often. While at home, leave enough windows open to get crosscurrents of air, if it's safe to do so. If cold weather or concern about crime do not permit this, consider buying a high-quality electronic air filter. Postpone plans to paint or fumigate the house or office until after the first trimester.

Scented Products. Substitute unscented personal care products for scented ones (including soaps, shampoos, laundry detergents, skin lotions, and toilet paper). Refrain from using aromatic personal care products that are not necessary for hygiene, such as perfumes and fabric softener. These suggestions apply to the parenting partner as well, since the first-trimester woman, with her hyperacute sense of smell, can detect fragrances on his hair, skin, and clothes.

Pets. If the household pets eat smelly food, the pregnant woman's partner should take responsibility for feeding them during the first trimester.

Partner's Breath. Unless the woman's pregnancy sickness is extremely mild, her partner should refrain from eating onions, garlic, and other foods that contribute to offensive breath. If the partner eats a meal that contains onions or garlic, he can help stave off offensive breath by swallowing Monjay capsules with the meal, which degrade the odor-causing compounds in the gut before they can be absorbed into the bloodstream and exhaled by the lungs. (These capsules are distributed by Bon Mange, Inc. of Davis, California, telephone 1-800-553-1224.)

Odors in the Workplace (Outside the Home). The woman who works around other people is exposed to their odors. If she is willing to reveal her pregnancy to them, she may need to ask them not to wear perfume or not to smoke in her vicinity. Occupational fumes may also bother the first-trimester woman, and some such fumes are potentially dangerous to the embryo. If the pregnancy sickness is severe and worsened by workplace odors, the woman may need to take a leave of absence for a few weeks or else work at home until the pregnancy sickness wanes.

Public Restrooms. A woman may need to avoid public restrooms whenever possible during the first trimester, because the smell of other people's feces is likely to be more repulsive than usual. The human brain is designed to have strong aversions to the feces of other people because many diseases are transmitted

PREGNANCY SICKNESS

through feces. Billions of bacteria and other rapidly replicating microorganisms colonize even healthy intestines, and they compose about one-third of the nonwater content of feces. Many infectious diseases reach epidemic proportions in countries where the supply of drinking water is contaminated by human feces.

Travel and Entertainment. Traveling may worsen the nausea of a woman with moderate to severe pregnancy sickness, particularly if she was susceptible to motion sickness before pregnancy. Fumes from vehicles may also be nauseating. It makes sense for women with pregnancy sickness to postpone major travel plans until after the first trimester (first-trimester travel is discussed in greater detail in Chapter 11).

It also makes sense to postpone hosting major dinner parties until after the first trimester, since they may end up getting cancelled due to nausea and food aversions.

Chapter Seven

Managing Pregnancy Sickness: Trusting Food Aversions

Natural Cravings and Natural Aversions

CRAVINGS AND AVERSIONS steer us toward some foods and away from others. This chapter ranks different types of foods according to their levels of natural toxins and their palatability to first-trimester women. In order to understand what makes food palatable or repulsive during the first trimester, it's helpful to understand the nature of food cravings and aversions in non-pregnant people.

When modern "health-conscious" people go grocery shopping, they consciously think about foods in a certain self-disciplined way. The natural substances in foods they crave are precisely those they view as "bad." Scanning labels for sugar, fat, and salt, modern health-conscious shoppers try to select foods that are low in these "sinful substances." They struggle not to give in to "temptation," not to satisfy their cravings. On the other hand, they don't give a moment's thought to the natural substances in food that were actually *designed* to be bad—nature's toxins. After all, none of the foods lining the grocery shelves is "poisonous."

PREGNANCY SICKNESS

In the environment of our hunter-gatherer ancestors, by contrast, there was no such thing as being "health-conscious." Sugar came from fruit, not from pastries, candy, or ice cream. On rare occasions, and with great difficulty and risk, hunter-gatherers could steal honey from bees. Fat came from meats, nuts, and vegetables, mostly in small quantities. Wild game is much leaner than even the leanest meats from domesticated animals. Plant oils were not extracted and bottled, so in order to get vegetable fat, people had to eat the vegetables. After they were weaned, at age three or four, our ancestors no longer had access to fat from milk (of course, there was no such thing as butter back then). Salt came only in trace quantities from fruits, vegetables, nuts, and meats. Natural diets were high in natural toxins, so hunter-gatherers were constantly trying to ferret out the most edible foods from the largely toxic array of wild plants. To our hunter-gatherer ancestors, the criterion for eating something they could catch, pick, or dig up was "Will this taste good?" not "Will I get too fat, too many cavities, or hypertension?"

Natural cravings and aversions aren't arbitrary. They evolved to ensure that ancestral humans sought certain essential nutrients and avoided harmful toxins. Since humans were hunter-gatherers throughout almost all of human evolutionary history, our psychology and physiology are adapted to a hunting and gathering way of life, not an agricultural one. The cravings and aversions of our hunter-gatherer ancestors remain embedded in our brains, even though our modern environment differs radically from theirs. The invention of agriculture changed human diets dramatically, enabling people to mass-produce the things that they crave and to eat them in unhealthful quantities.

Managing Pregnancy Sickness: Trusting Food Aversions

Cravings

Three of our strongest built-in cravings are for sugar, fat, and salt. These are important nutrients, but in the ancestral environment none of them was normally obtainable in large, concentrated amounts. Hunter-gatherers eagerly sought sugar, fat, and salt—satisfying their cravings whenever possible. If ancestral humans had not had internal signals telling them to seek and eat these substances, they would not have gone to the trouble of obtaining sufficient amounts of them. In modern environments—where we plant crops, domesticate food animals, and mine minerals—sugar, fat, and salt can be produced cheaply and in great abundance, and the intense cravings for these substances are readily apparent. Witness the enormous popularity of fast-food—a monument to sugar, fat, and salt!

In nature, a high concentration of sugar signifies a relatively nontoxic, easily digested source of calories, and, in the case of ripe fruit, it signifies an excellent source of vitamins. As discussed in Chapter 2, ripe fruit is generally low in toxins and high in sugar so that the plant can attract birds and mammals to eat its fruit and disperse its mature seeds. (The avocado tree appears to use a slightly different strategy: instead of producing a high concentration of sugar to attract animals, it attracts them with a high concentration of fat.) Unripe fruit, on the other hand, is much more toxic and bitter and much less sweet, because the plant does not "want" its seeds to be dispersed before they mature. Some "edible" fruits can even be lethal before they ripen. Several years ago a colleague of mine who was doing research in Africa spied some fruit, which she had seen other people eating some months earlier, dangling from a tree branch; so she picked a

PREGNANCY SICKNESS

piece, but as she started to take her first bite she was knocked to the ground by an African friend, who informed her that this kind of fruit is deadly when not in season.

Fat is a rich source of calories that was difficult for our hunter-gatherer ancestors to obtain. Furthermore, since in nature fat is usually coupled to protein—in the form of meat, eggs, or nuts—the craving for fat also resulted in the consumption of protein and the vitamins that are typically associated with fat.

Salt is an essential nutrient that was much more difficult for our ancestors to obtain than it is for us. We get an overabundance of salt because we can mine it cheaply, but hunter-gatherers had to obtain their salt from food. It has been estimated that ancestral hunter-gatherers consumed, on average, less than one-third of a teaspoon of salt per day from all sources.

In short, cravings for sugar, fat, and salt led ancestral humans to choose as foods the substances in their environment that were relatively high in calories and essential nutrients and low in natural toxins.

Aversions

People have built-in aversions to bitter substances because toxins tend to be bitter. Most of the distinctive flavor of a plant comes from its particular array of toxins. Vegetables, for example, are extremely important sources of nutrients in the human diet, but because their toxins are potentially dangerous, inexperienced humans have a natural aversion to vegetables—as well as to the more pungent plant foods, such as herbs and spices. That is why a young child samples these foods gingerly. Over time, a person's physiological and psychological mechanisms can assess how dangerous these foods are, and they can determine which bitter tastes and pungent odors can be tolerated, and in what amounts. The detoxification enzymes in the liver and other organs are not able to quickly detoxify all toxins, which means that only certain plants can be eaten safely, and then only in certain amounts. In essence, the brain determines whether the food is safe by asking itself: "After eating it, did I feel nausea or vomit?" If the answer is no, then the food can be eaten again.

By adulthood, most people have acquired "tastes" for many bitter but nutritious foods. Most adults will eat spinach, for example, and all the more eagerly if its flavor is enhanced with a spicy curry sauce. Most babies, on the other hand, have to be coaxed to eat any vegetable whose bitterness is not masked by sugar, and almost no baby will eat spicy curry. Babies' natural aversions and limited experience make them hypervigilant to toxins.

In general, aversions override cravings. If a person loves potato chips (full of fat and salt) but is repulsed by onions, the person will be repulsed by onion-flavored potato chips. Aversions are warnings of danger, and so must be obeyed for all foods that trigger them; whereas cravings for the sugar, fat, and salt of any one food can easily be satisfied by a different sugary, fatty, or salty food. Aversions become much more pronounced and dominant during the first trimester.

Food Preferences During the First Trimester

A woman's food preferences usually change dramatically during the first trimester of pregnancy. Her favorite foods may become repulsive to her, and she'll almost certainly prefer a dinner of cereal and milk to one of lamb curry. Many first-trimester women become nauseated just thinking about certain foods or seeing

PREGNANCY SICKNESS

them on TV. Natural aversions to bitter and pungent foods become greatly exaggerated during the first trimester. In many ways, food preferences revert to those of a baby; fruit, cereal, noodles, rice, milk, and yogurt tend to be the foods of choice.

A first-trimester woman retains her natural cravings for sugar, fat, and salt, but to a lesser degree, because they are tempered by her increasing aversions to the bitter and pungent substances, such as spices, that often come with a sugary, fatty, or salty meal. Cravings for specific foods during the first trimester may arise by default. A woman may suddenly crave milk, for example, if most other foods nauseate her. Or she may crave sweet or sour foods, such as fruit, candy, plain yogurt, or vinegar, simply because these foods are not naturally associated with bitterness or pungency. In nature, sweetness is associated with ripe fruit, and sourness with fruit high in citric and other acids.

But what about the idiosyncratic cravings of pregnancy, such as sudden midnight urges for curry or salsa? These tend to occur well after the first trimester and are not consistent among women. Therefore this book does not discuss them in depth. Some people have suggested that food cravings during pregnancy reflect the woman's need for particular nutrients when the fetus is growing rapidly, just as some people have suggested that cravings in nonpregnant people can reflect particular vitamin or mineral deficiencies. But many cravings may simply result from the diminished sense of smell that occurs later in pregnancy. Some third-trimester women may crave spicy foods simply to experience taste/smell sensations that are strong enough to be satisfying. Furthermore, since perceptions of smell and taste fluctuate so much throughout pregnancy, some cravings may merely be by-products of this constant fluctuation. Although most of the idiosyncratic cravings of the third trimester probably have no benefit, they probably are not harmful either, since the third-trimester fetus has defenses against most of the dietary toxins its mother is likely to eat.

The body's main pregnancy-related goal during the first trimester is the proper development of the embryo, and one way that the body accomplishes this goal is by producing aversions to the types of foods that could disrupt organ formation. Thus, the dietary advice of this book focuses on aversions, not cravings. (Since the mother's nutritional status can also affect the developing embryo, the following chapter is devoted to nutrition.) Although having pregnancy sickness generally ensures that a woman avoids eating those foods that she should avoid, a conscious awareness of the types of foods most likely to endanger embryos can enhance her ability to protect her embryo. When a first-trimester woman is thinking about what to eat, she should ask herself not only "Can I stomach eating this?" but "Could this food endanger my embryo?"

Avoiding toxins and managing pregnancy sickness (i.e., making it bearable) go hand-in-hand. Most women should be able to manage pregnancy sickness simply by minimizing their exposure to the foods and odors that trigger it. Because pregnancy sickness serves an important function, women should not try to suppress it with medicine unless it is so severe that they can't hold down any food (see Chapter 9). Medicinal interference would subvert the mechanism that protects the embryo against dietary toxins. Dietary management of pregnancy sickness, on the other hand, promotes rather than subverts the goal of protecting the embryo, and therefore it is safe.

Many foods can be eaten safely during the first trimester, and foods can be prepared in ways that minimize nausea. In general, the best tolerated foods are the least toxic, so a woman usually need only heed her body's warnings to know what to eat and what to avoid. She should be careful, however, not to fool her taste and smell receptors into letting her eat high levels of toxins by masking bitter substances with sugar (examples below).

Cooking and Eating During the First Trimester

Cooking Methods

Different cooking methods generate different levels of toxins and thus affect a first-trimester woman differently. Frying, barbecuing, grilling, and roasting are generally not well tolerated because the fumes rising from the burnt surfaces of foods are toxic (although only mildly so to nonpregnant adults), as is the smoke from the burning charcoal or wood of a barbeque.

Boiling and microwaving are the cooking methods least likely to bother a first-trimester woman because they don't generally burn the food's surface. If a woman boils food on a gas stove, however, the gas fumes may bother her. Baking is likely to be more problematic than boiling, since boiling something doesn't generate as many fumes, but baking may be tolerated if foods are covered tightly before being placed in the oven, since this helps to minimize cooking odors. It is helpful to air out the kitchen during cooking by opening windows and turning on a fan. A woman with severe pregnancy sickness, however, probably should refrain from cooking entirely.

Eating

A first-trimester woman should plan bland meals of very fresh familiar foods and postpone experimenting with new or exotic recipes until the second or third trimester. She should not try

Managing Pregnancy Sickness: Trusting Food Aversions

to force down foods that nauseate her. One mother of a first-trimester woman told me, "Ever since my daughter got pregnant she doesn't like vegetables. She has to force herself to eat *those*." If a first-trimester woman has an aversion to a particular food, she shouldn't eat it (unless the food is bland and her pregnancy sickness is so extreme that she has aversions to all foods). Her body usually knows best.

A food's temperature can have a large effect on a first-trimester woman's ability to tolerate it. Heating food vaporizes some of its toxins, which can then be smelled and absorbed into the bloodstream through the lungs. By contrast, cooling a food to temperatures just slightly above freezing significantly suppresses its odor. A first-trimester woman generally tolerates food much better if it's very cold rather than very hot, but she should be aware that by suppressing a food's odor, she loses important information about its toxin content. Refrigerators are evolutionarily novel. Our hunter-gatherer ancestors had no way of freezing food on a warm day, so suppressing a food's odor by cooling it was not an option for them. Consequently, the body is not designed to detect toxins in very cold food (before it's eaten).

The following sections provide information about specific kinds of foods. Within the subsections "Food and Beverages Derived from Plants" and "Food and Beverages Derived from Animals," common food categories are ranked in order from best to worst for the first-trimester woman. "Best" means generally low toxicity and high palatability; "worst" means generally high toxicity and low palatability. The ratings of palatability are based on what would be palatable to a woman with a *moderate* level of pregnancy sickness. (A woman with extremely severe pregnancy sickness would find virtually nothing palatable, and a woman with extremely mild pregnancy sickness would find virtually everything in her normal diet palatable.)

Foods and Beverages Derived from Plants

Fruits. Ripe fresh fruits are among the best tolerated and least toxic foods, especially if they're peeled (the peel and seeds generally contain the fruit's highest concentrations of toxins). They are also excellent sources of vitamins. Canned fruits, however, often have a "canned" odor that may be nauseating.

If a woman has such severe pregnancy sickness that even fruit nauseates her, she may want to cool the fruit in the freezer before eating it in order to suppress its odor. If a woman is nauseated by fruit juice, she can try diluting it with ice water. She can also suck on ice cubes made from fruit juice (but not while lying down, lest she choke), or she can make fruit juice Popsicles. Fresh-squeezed juice is much more likely to be tolerated than canned juice, which may have a "canned," not-so-fresh odor, so the woman may want to buy a juicer.

Fruit milkshakes and yogurt shakes are nutritious and usually well tolerated during the first trimester. To make one, blend fresh milk or plain yogurt with ice cubes, and add fruit or fruit juice—bananas, peaches, strawberries, and orange juice make good shakes. When Mary Krikorian, the illustrator of this book, was in the first trimester of her first pregnancy, she froze a banana every day, then blended it with fresh milk and ice cubes to make a nutritious and nearly odorless meal.

Grains. Grain-based starchy foods are among the best tolerated and least toxic foods (as long as they do not contain perceptible levels of mold). Cereal, bread, popcorn, crackers, pancakes, rice, and pasta are usually well tolerated. Processed grains are probably better tolerated than whole grains because processing removes the outer husks, which are likely to contain much of the natural toxins of the grains. Plain white and sourdough breads are probably the easiest grain-based foods to tolerate. Eating breads and other starchy grain-based foods often helps to quell nausea, although the reasons for this are not completely clear. It may be that starches slow or inhibit the absorption of some of the toxins released into the gastrointestinal tract by other foods or by the microorganisms that live there.

Rice and pasta can be used as a base food for other ingredients. A first-trimester woman might want to try, for example, a meal of lightly salted rice or pasta with fresh cottage cheese and pieces of boiled fresh turkey swirled in.

Candy. Sugar is not toxic (to a nondiabetic), although anything eaten in excess can have adverse effects in someone, pregnant or not. Sweets are generally very well tolerated during early pregnancy as long as they're not oily. Sucking on hard candy even helps some women relieve nausea. But unlike fruit (nature's sweets), most candy has no nutrients except calories.

Chocolate is made from the very bitter cocoa bean and is less likely to be tolerated than hard candy. Many of us vividly remember as children sneaking into Mom's kitchen cupboard and taking a bite out of unsweetened baker's chocolate—only to recoil in dismay at its terrible taste. If chocolate is mixed with enough sugar, it does not taste bitter, but toxin-detectors in the gut and brain stem may still recognize it for what it is and trigger vomiting. Although cocoa powder does not appear to cause birth defects in rats (in studies done so far), whether it does so at some dose in humans is not known. It's possible that moderate amounts of chocolate pose no danger to human embryos, but to play it safe, it's best to avoid or at least minimize chocolate consumption during the first trimester. The extreme bitterness of unsweetened chocolate is a warning of its natural toxicity.

Other dessert flavorings that require sugar to make them palatable, such as vanilla and mint, should also not be eaten in large amounts during the first trimester.

Nuts. Much of the natural bitterness and toxicity of nuts has been bred out of domesticated varieties—the kind one buys at the grocery store—but nuts still can be somewhat bitter (indicating toxins) and, if ground into a spread (like peanut butter), slightly pungent. Wild nuts—such as the ones growing on the backyard walnut tree—are usually edible for squirrels, but too bitter and toxic for people. It's probably safe for a first-trimester woman to eat a modest amount of domesticated nuts as long as she can't see, taste, or smell any mold on them. Nuts can be chopped up and mixed with rice or cereal.

Vegetable Oils. Oily foods, which tend to be more difficult to digest than nonoily foods anyway, generally are not well tolerated during the first trimester. Some possible reasons for this include the following. Oils can become mildly toxic when they turn rancid or are heated to high temperatures (as in frying). Also, vegetable oils may contain some of the vegetable's toxins. Furthermore, oils may enable fat-soluble toxins to be absorbed more easily into the circulation. To minimize nausea, eat dry starchy foods in lieu of oily ones. Oils used in baking (rather than frying) probably do not pose much, if any, danger, as long as the food doesn't seem greasy.

Vegetables. After a lifetime of hearing "Eat your vegetables," it may seem odd to be told, "Be wary of eating vegetables." But vegetables tend to be bitter, a signal of their toxicity. Most vegetables are not well tolerated during the first trimester, and women with pregnancy sickness almost invariably prefer to get nutrients from fruits rather than vegetables. If a first-trimester woman decides to eat vegetables, she should avoid the most unpalatable ones—that is, the pungent, more bitter ones—such as broccoli, Brussels sprouts, bell peppers, onions, and garlic. Instead, she should choose the most palatable ones—that is, the less bitter ones.

I don't provide a list of recommended vegetables for the first trimester because I can't give a definitive "green light" to any of them. We know that all vegetables contain many natural toxins, but we don't know just which of these toxins—or which vegetables—can harm embryos. A first-trimester woman who chooses to eat vegetables should eat them only in small amounts at any given meal. It may turn out that some vegetables, even in large quantities, are harmless to embryos, but until we know which ones, all vegetables should be treated with caution during the first trimester. Peeling vegetables helps to reduce their toxicity and bitterness, because peels contain especially high concentrations of toxins.

First-trimester women generally tolerate cooked vegetables better than raw ones, although the odor of vegetables cooking may be nauseating. Vegetables can be made into soups, but the soups should be kept as bland as possible, rather than flavored with onions, garlic, spices, or herbs. For example, one way to make soup is to boil carrots or butternut squash until tender; drain and blend finely in a food processor or blender; dilute the mixture with hot water or milk and add salt to taste; stir, then add a swirl of fresh cream or yogurt (if desired).

Potatoes are tolerated better than many vegetables by many first-trimester women, but, as discussed in Chapter 3, in the amounts that many people eat, they may be a risk factor for spina bifida and other neural tube defects. Until more information is available, it is probably best to avoid them—especially the skins—during the first trimester (particularly during the first five weeks after conception) and, if possible, during the several months preceding conception. The green parts of potatoes and the sprouts are especially toxic and should never be eaten, even by nonpregnant people.

Hot peppers are also tolerated by some first-trimester women; nevertheless they should be avoided during the first trimester. The ingredient that makes hot peppers "hot" is the toxin capsaicin. One reason that women do not always have sufficiently strong aversions to it is that the sensation of "hotness" can overwhelm the sensation of bitterness. Thus, when hot peppers are added to other ingredients, as in hot and sour soup, the "hotness" can mask the bitterness not only of the peppers, but of the toxins in the other ingredients as well.

Spices and Herbs. Spices and herbs contain very high concentrations of toxins, which is why they have such strong flavors. Fresh basil, for example, contains very high concentrations of the toxin estragole; in fact, this toxin constitutes more than 7 percent of the weight of the dried plant. Fresh nutmeg contains very high concentrations of the related toxin safrole. It also contains myristicin, a hallucinogenic chemical that made nutmeg a popular recreational drug with sailors a few centuries ago (even though the hallucinations were frequently accompanied by nausea and vomiting). These are precisely the sorts of chemicals that pregnancy sickness was designed to protect against.

It's easy to appreciate how toxic spices and herbs are if one imagines eating an entire plateful of them at one sitting—even assuming that one is not pregnant. Eating a plateful of apples, cantaloupe, or other fruit would be just fine, and eating a plateful of salad or green beans would be considered a very "healthy" thing to do; but eating a plateful of basil, oregano, black pepper, or nutmeg would be not only extremely unappetizing, but very dangerous. A person would be lucky to vomit, and could even die. A physician I knew who worked in a hospital in Germany told me about one of his most heartrending cases, in which a mother who was angry at her five-year-old daughter punished her by forcing her to eat an entire jar of black pepper. The girl was rushed to the emergency room, where she died.

Spices taste delicious to a nonpregnant person, in very small doses, but they're potentially lethal in large doses, and many of them are probably dangerous to embryos even when used as seasoning.

Mushrooms. Mushrooms are loaded with toxins—most notoriously with those known as hydrazines—which is why so many mushroom species are poisonous. Whether edible mushrooms can cause birth defects in humans is not known, but during the first trimester it's best to err on the side of caution and avoid them.

Condiments. Mustard, horseradish, and other pungent condiments have high levels of toxins, which is why they're poorly tolerated during early pregnancy. Mustard and horseradish come from the same family of plants as cabbage, Brussels sprouts, and broccoli, but they contain much higher concentrations of natural toxins. Up to 7 percent of dried brown mustard seeds, for example, is made up of the toxin sinigrin. Pungent condiments should be avoided during the first trimester.

The less pungent condiments are less toxic and more likely to be tolerated, but most are still not likely to be well tolerated. Catsup may be too concentrated to appeal to a first-trimester woman, and many brands are spiced and so should be avoided. Mayonnaise is too oily to be well tolerated by most first-trimester women, and commercially prepared mayonnaise (the kind from a jar) is not fresh and almost certainly will not smell fresh to most first-trimester women. White wine vinegar, on the other hand, usually just tastes sour, so it is likely to be tolerated, whereas red wine vinegar usually contains many of the tannins of red wine, which are natural toxins that are best avoided during the first trimester.

Coffee, Tea, Other Caffeinated Beverages, and Herb Tea. Coffee is one of the most poorly tolerated beverages during the first trimester. Roasted coffee contains more than 1,000 different toxins, caffeine being just one of them. Caffeinated and noncaffeinated teas and herb teas contain their own large spectra of natural toxins. It's important to realize that herb teas are herbs, and as such contain high concentrations of toxins. A number of books advocate herbal tea remedies for various ailments of pregnancy, including pregnancy sickness, but the medicinal effects of these herbs, if any, derive from their toxins. If medications are needed during the first trimester, they should be discussed with one's OB/GYN, not sought in herbal teas.

The verdict isn't in on whether high doses of caffeine or other ingredients of coffee can cause birth defects in humans. In rodents, high doses of caffeine (the human equivalent of about twenty-five cups of a caffeinated beverage per day) can cause birth defects, including cleft palate and missing digits. This dose of caffeine is substantially higher than that consumed by most women, but it's not outside the realm of possibility. Some human studies, but not others, show that drinking large amounts of caffeinated coffee—roughly twelve or more cups per day during

Managing Pregnancy Sickness: Trusting Food Aversions

early pregnancy—increases the risk of various birth defects, including missing fingers and toes.

It's prudent for first-trimester women to consciously halt or at least strictly limit their intake of coffee, tea, and herb tea if pregnancy sickness does not do it for them. If a woman does drink these beverages during the first trimester, she should brew them much weaker than usual.

In cola-type soft drinks, the natural bitterness of caffeine and other toxins of the kola nut is masked by sugar. In nature, high concentrations of sugar are not associated with toxins in the same plant parts, and, therefore, sweetness is not naturally associated with bitterness. As a fruit ripens, for example, its transition time from bitter to sweet is very short—there simply isn't much of an in-between state of bittersweet. Our hunter-gatherer ancestors thus did not need to be able to detect toxins lurking in sweet foods, and we are not adapted to do so. That's why our toxin-detecting taste mechanisms can be so easily fooled by concentrated sugar. It's prudent for first-trimester women to strictly limit their intake of such soft drinks.

Any Food That Smells or Tastes of Mold. Molds commonly contaminate fruits, grains, nuts, dairy products, and other foods. Some common food molds produce potent toxins that can cause birth defects in mammals. If foods smell or taste even slightly moldy, don't eat them, even if the mold is not visible. Popcorn, strawberries, and bread, for example, are just some of the common foods that can easily become contaminated by molds that are detectable by smell or taste at levels too low to be detected by sight.

Alcohol. As discussed in detail in Chapter 10, it's important to strictly limit alcohol consumption during the first trimester.

Large, frequent intakes of alcohol during pregnancy can cause mental retardation and other birth defects in humans.

Foods and Beverages Derived from Animals

Dairy Products. Fresh milk, yogurt, and cottage cheese generally are free of toxins and are well tolerated, but bacteria contaminate them rapidly, especially if they're not refrigerated. Check the dates on dairy product containers, buy the freshest available, and keep them very cold.

Dairy products can be contaminated, however, by the toxins of plants that the dairy animal grazed on. Abe Lincoln's mother died from drinking the milk of a cow that had grazed on poisonous snakeroot. Some toxins that end up in milk can cross the placenta and harm the embryo, as in the case of "crooked calf syndrome," discussed in Chapter 3.

There is a memorable scene in the nineteenth-century novel *Tess of the D'Urbervilles* by Thomas Hardy in which the heroine Tess has taken a job as a milkmaid on a dairy farm and is urgently summoned one morning because the butter churned the previous day tastes of garlic. Tess, along with her coworkers, search frantically until dusk to locate and uproot the small patch of garlic their cows had grazed on. Nowadays, large commercial dairy farms monitor their cows' diets, and the risk of consuming dangerous (or even annoyingly unpalatable) levels of plant toxins from their dairy products is probably negligible. But drinking milk fresh out of the family farm animal may not be prudent during the first trimester. To be as safe as possible, stick to pasteurized milk from the supermarket.

Recently there was a public outcry against milk from cows treated with synthetic bovine growth hormone, which is used to increase milk production. This outcry seems to have stemmed more from a generalized fear of modern technology than from any well-grounded reason to fear this hormone. When consumed orally (as in drinking a glass of milk), bovine growth hormone is not "biologically active"—which means that it has no apparent effect on the human body—presumably because it is broken down by the intestines before it can be absorbed into the blood-stream. There does not seem to be a good theoretical reason to suspect that this hormone is capable of harming people who consume it, but to my knowledge no studies have been done to determine whether there are any risks to human embryos. Most likely, it is just as safe for a first-trimester woman to drink milk from a treated cow as from an untreated one.

Milk and yogurt can be blended with fruit, vitamin powder, or protein powder. Drink/eat them very cold. It's important to keep the refrigerator as odor-free as possible because milk, cream, and butter rapidly absorb the flavor/odor molecules (such as volatile toxins) that are emitted from other foods in the refrigerator, particularly pungent ones like onions and garlic.

Cheeses (excluding cottage cheese) generally are pungent and not well tolerated during early pregnancy. The least pungent and best-tolerated cheeses probably are fresh ricotta and mozzarella. Mold cheeses, such as blue cheese, tend to be pungent and not well tolerated during the first trimester. It is not known if the types of molds contained in these cheeses, at levels that are normally consumed, produce toxins that are potentially harmful to embryos.

Fresh butter from pasteurized milk does not contain toxic chemicals (unless it turns rancid or is heated to high temperatures), but since oily foods tend not to be tolerated well during the first trimester, limit the amount of butter to a level that does not make food seem greasy. If butter exacerbates nausea, eliminate it from the diet.

Meat and Poultry. Extremely fresh meat and poultry usually don't contain toxins, but bacteria contaminate them rapidly, causing them to acquire increasingly pungent, unpleasant odors (indicating spoilage). A first-trimester woman will detect the odor of spoilage long before a nonpregnant person will, so she should buy the freshest meat and poultry available. Packaged hot dogs and lunch meats are less likely to be tolerated because they are not fresh and because many of them contain spices and other pungent seasonings, such as garlic.

As discussed above, frying or barbequing meat frequently triggers nausea in pregnant women and should be avoided, as should smoked meat. Covering the meat while microwaving or baking it helps to reduce cooking odors and to prevent the meat's surface from being burned. If baked meat is too nauseating, try boiling or microwaving small pieces and mixing them with rice or pasta.

Probably the best tolerated meat/poultry during the first trimester is the white meat of turkey. Chicken, on the other hand, repulses many first-trimester women. This is not because chicken meat per se is harmful, but because it spoils easily and usually is not eaten very fresh. Chicken that has been sitting in a delivery truck or grocery store for a few days after slaughter is very likely to have picked up some bacteria, and the faint odors of the beginnings of spoilage are greatly amplified in a first-trimester woman.

Eggs. Unless they're very fresh, eggs have a sulfurous aroma that may not be tolerated during early pregnancy. Eggs are very nutritious, however, and generally do not contain toxins (if cooked). To eat eggs without having to smell them, use them as an ingredient in waffles, pancakes, souffles, egg noodles, breads, cakes, or other foods. Since raw eggs occasionally are contaminated by salmonella bacteria, it's best to avoid them during pregnancy.

Fish. Fish is not usually well tolerated during early pregnancy. It spoils easily, acquiring an unpleasant "fishy" odor. Unless the fish has been caught the day it's to be eaten, it probably will have at least a faint fishy odor, which will be detected easily by a first-trimester woman. Even thinking about eating fish may be unpleasant, because most people's memories of eating fish include the fishy smell and taste of the fish they typically eat.

Although fresh fish usually isn't toxic, some parts of the fish can be contaminated by toxin-producing plankton, especially if caught during red tide. Some fish that are caught in polluted waters contain high levels of pollutants, such as mercury, which at high levels can cause neurological defects in humans and other animals (see Chapter 10). A first-trimester woman who eats fish should make sure that it is very fresh—or that it was very fresh when frozen—and that it comes from relatively unpolluted waters. To play it safe, a first-trimester woman should probably avoid raw fish because of the risk of bacterial contamination. Instead, she should either microwave it or bake it in a covered dish.

Food Colorings, Artificial Sweeteners, and Other Additives

Food additives include preservatives, flavorings, coloring agents, sweeteners, thickeners, and many other types of natural and synthetic chemicals. Of the several thousand additives on the market, only a small percentage have been tested for their capacity to cause birth defects in animals, and most of these were tested at very high doses that don't reflect plausible human exposures. The effect of food additives on human embryos is not known, but most are probably safe in small doses. To err on the side of caution, it is prudent for a first-trimester woman to avoid consuming large amounts of any single additive, such as an artificial sweetener. Women who drink diet soft drinks daily, for example, should consider strictly limiting their consumption during the first trimester. Although the common artificial sweeteners do not appear to cause birth defects in rodents, their effects on human embryos have not been carefully investigated, and some anecdotal reports have linked behavioral and physical anomalies in children to their mothers' consumption of large amounts of them during pregnancy (although this does not prove a cause-and-effect relationship).

What Not to Worry About

Synthetic Pesticide Residues. Some toxic compounds are not worth worrying about during pregnancy because the doses encountered are too tiny to pose a significant risk of birth defects. Synthetic pesticide residues on the fruits, vegetables, and grains found in most U.S. supermarkets probably belong in this category. (Exposures to *high* doses of synthetic pesticides, as sometimes occur occupationally, however, may endanger human embryos.) Pesticides are sprayed on crops in order to ward off insects and fungi, which would otherwise wipe out a large percentage of crops and dramatically increase the cost of food. The amounts of synthetic pesticide residues on fruits or vegetables in a typical U.S. supermarket are miniscule compared to the amounts of natural toxins contained in these plant foods. In fact, if one were to extract all the toxic compounds in a commercially grown vegetable and divide them into two piles—natural and synthetic—the natural pile would weigh, on average, several thousand times as much as the synthetic one. The body's detoxification enzymes can't distinguish between natural and synthetic pesticides and therefore work to protect us against both.

A first-trimester woman should not switch to "organic" produce just to protect her embryo. "Natural" does not mean "safe." Some "organic" vegetables contain much higher levels of natural toxins than their ordinary supermarket counterparts. For example, in the 1980s a strain of potato was developed that was naturally insect-resistant; but this was accomplished by selective breeding for very high levels of the natural toxins solanine and chaconine. This strain of potato, which was so toxic that most insects left it alone, had to be withdrawn from the market after its toxins caused many people who ate it to become ill.

Furthermore, "organic" farming does not necessarily mean that the crops are free from pesticides; it simply means that any pesticides used on the crops are of natural origin. For example, the toxins known as pyrethrins, which come from chrysanthemums, are sprayed on a variety of "organic" produce to ward off insects. Few of these natural pesticides have been tested for their effects on humans or other mammals.

By using low levels of synthetic toxins to defend plants against local pests, farmers can breed strains of plants containing greatly reduced levels of natural toxins. This lowers the total level of toxins that people consume when eating fruits and vegetables. If a first-trimester woman is still worried about synthetic pesticide residues, she can peel all fruits and vegetables before eating them, although some residues may persist in the flesh of the fruits and vegetables.

PREGNANCY SICKNESS

To err on the side of caution, a first-trimester woman should scrub fruits and vegetables thoroughly before eating them. Since the aim of using synthetic pesticides is to kill insects, but not necessarily to warn them first, many synthetic pesticides may not have the same taste and smell cues that natural toxins typically do. Although a first-trimester woman may not be able to detect synthetic pesticide residues on fruits and vegetables, she should, nonetheless, be able to avoid most of them through food hygiene.

Genetically Engineered Food. A first-trimester woman should not fear a fruit or vegetable simply because it is "genetically engineered"—that is, simply because a gene has been inserted into its DNA to keep it from freezing easily or spoiling quickly. Foods that have been irradiated to kill their bacteria or other parasites are also highly unlikely to increase the risk of harm to embryos. A first-trimester woman has a lot more to fear from nature than from modern food technology. Plant nature is designed to cause us harm. Human food technology is not.

Food Contaminants

Foods can contain a number of other "invisible" ingredients— that is, ingredients that can't be smelled or tasted and that aren't listed on the food labels. Crops can be contaminated by water and soil pollution, but pollution and crop import regulations in the United States and other technologically advanced countries are probably strict enough to prevent any significant risk of birth defects from contamination of commercially grown food. Almost all well-documented reports of birth defects caused by food contaminants involve infants born in countries that are much less technologically developed than the United States, such as Japan in the 1950s or Iraq. If a first-trimester woman travels to a country with significantly less stringent pollution standards, she risks inflicting greater levels of food contaminants on her embryo. In the United States, a few preliminary reports have linked pregnant women's consumption of fatty fish from polluted waters to mild neurological problems in their children. Since some chemical pollutants persist in fatty tissues, fatty fish, such as salmon and swordfish, can accumulate fairly high levels of pollutants. To err on the side of caution, women may want to avoid eating fatty fish during the first trimester, unless they are sure it comes from very clean waters. Currently in the United States, however, there is only scant evidence linking birth defects to pollution-contaminated food.

Creating Recipes

It's a challenge for a first-trimester woman to come up with recipes when she's restricted to using bland ingredients. Even though a meal lacks spices, herbs, and condiments, it can still be made appetizing with interesting combinations of tolerable ingredients. If pregnancy sickness is severe, however, the woman probably will not want to eat anything more complicated than cereal, fruit, or rice.

The specific food aversions that are part of pregnancy sickness are to some extent idiosyncratic, because each person has a unique food history, and a woman's previous food dislikes are likely to be amplified during the first trimester. Although the range of variability in food preferences among first-trimester women may seem to be great, it is actually quite limited, considering all the possible sources of nutrients in the world. Although a particular woman might not be crazy about bananas, for example, whereas another loves bananas but not cantaloupe, virtually all women like fruit in general and prefer it to vegetables during the first trimester, since fruit is so much lower in natural toxins than vegetables are.

In planning meals, a first-trimester woman should think about each ingredient and decide whether or not it appeals to her. If it does, she'll probably tolerate it well; if it doesn't, she should avoid it if there are more appealing nutritious alternatives. In some recipes, the substitution of one ingredient for another—such as a fruit one likes for a fruit one doesn't like in a fruit cobbler recipe—may turn an unappealing dish into an appealing one. A first-trimester woman who concocts her own recipes should use this chapter's guidelines when selecting ingredients.

Quick Review List of Which Foods Can Be Eaten and Which Should Be Avoided

Best Foods to Eat During the First Trimester

- Fruits and fruit juices
- Milk and plain yogurt; milk products flavored with fruit and/or sugar
- Processed grains made into bland breads, pastas, and other starchy foods
- Cooked fresh eggs—best tolerated as an ingredient in breads, cakes, noodles, waffles, or pancakes
- Fresh meat that is boiled or microwaved

Foods to Be Cautious About During the First Trimester— Eat Only in Small Amounts

- Vegetables that are not especially bitter or pungent, such as green beans, carrots, tomatoes, and peas

Managing Pregnancy Sickness: Trusting Food Aversions

- Oils and oily foods
- Dessert flavorings derived from bitter or pungent plant parts, including chocolate, vanilla, mint, and ginger

Worst Foods to Eat During the First Trimester— Avoid Them

- Particularly pungent or bitter vegetables, such as broccoli, Brussels sprouts, and peppers
- All spices and herbs, including basil, bay leaves, black pepper, cinnamon, coriander, cumin, dill, fennel, marjoram, mint, nutmeg, oregano, rosemary, sage, tarragon, and thyme (salt is not a spice or herb; it can be eaten by healthy first-trimester women in normal amounts)
- Other pungent or bitter plants used to flavor foods, such as onions, garlic, hot peppers, and mustard
- Mushrooms
- Potatoes
- Barbequed or burnt foods
- Beverages derived from bitter plant parts, including coffee (whether caffeinated or decaffeinated), tea, herb teas, and colas

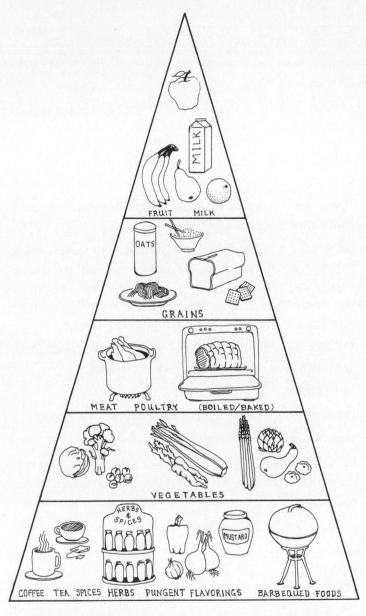

Foods for the first-trimester woman can be ranked from least toxic/most palatable (top) to most toxic/least palatable (bottom).

Chapter Eight

⚜

Balancing Good Nutrition and Pregnancy Sickness

GETTING GOOD NUTRITION usually entails consuming a lot of natural toxins. It is crucial that pregnant women understand this fact before embarking on a nutrition plan for the first trimester. (It is also crucial that people who counsel pregnant women understand it before dispensing nutritional advice.) But all pregnancy books currently available to the general public—although full of dietary and nutritional advice—make a critical mistake: they fail to appropriately differentiate the first trimester from the rest of pregnancy. Instead, they offer "generic" nutritional advice for pregnant women, and, consequently, they fail to properly guide women who are nurturing vulnerable embryos. Some of the well-meaning advice given in these books is potentially dangerous to embryos. For example, a typical recommendation is "When you find out you're pregnant, be sure to eat lots of vegetables every day—try cabbage salad, for instance." This advice differs by 180 degrees from what the mechanism designed to protect embryos—pregnancy sickness—is telling the pregnant woman: "Be repulsed when you smell, taste, or even look at cabbage." Pregnancy sickness is supposed to alter a woman's diet radically. What's good advice for a nonpregnant or third-trimester woman can be very bad advice for a first-trimester woman.

An ancestral hunter-gatherer woman did not need nutritional advice during pregnancy or at any other time. She was as unaware of the concept "good nutrition" as all lean, well-nourished wild animals are. Her natural cravings and aversions ensured that when she wasn't experiencing the first trimester of

The typical modern diet differs vastly from
the ancestral hunter-gatherer one.

pregnancy she sought good nutrition, and that when she was experiencing the first trimester she balanced good nutrition with avoidance of toxins. In fact, if some future human being were able to go back in a time-machine and inform an ancestral hunter-gatherer woman about "good nutrition," she probably would fare no better in nourishing herself and her embryo. The reason that we who live in modern industrialized societies need nutrition advice at all is that our natural cravings and aversions (discussed in the previous chapter) are designed to optimize nutrition in the natural hunter-gatherer environment, not in the modern environment we've created.

This chapter prefaces its nutrition advice by discussing the relationship between pregnancy and nutrition: how a woman's nutritional status affects her ability to become pregnant and how pregnancy affects her nutritional status. It discusses how the body, which is adapted to a hunter-gatherer environment, gauges whether or not a woman is nutritionally secure enough to undertake pregnancy, and how a typical modern diet can "fool" the body into assuming it has acquired enough nutrients to ensure a healthy pregnancy. This chapter then provides information on vitamins and minerals that are known to affect the health of embryos, as well as information on medical conditions of the mother that can interfere with her nutrition and, consequently, her embryo's development.

The Costs of Pregnancy and the Costs of Pregnancy Sickness

Everyone intuitively understands that pregnancy costs a woman something. She has to supply all the calories and nutrients for the tissues and fluids that go into having a healthy baby, including all the tissues of the fetus; the placenta; amniotic fluid; extra breast tissue (to prepare for nursing); extra fat stores (to prepare for reduced food intake caused by pregnancy sickness or food shortages); and extra blood (to transport oxygen and nutrients to the fetus). These extra tissues and fluids cost energy to build and maintain. As pregnancy progresses, energy costs increase: the daily costs of pregnancy during the second and third trimesters are about four times as much as they are during the first trimester. Pregnancy would have been especially costly for ancestral hunter-gatherer women, because the extra calories and nutrients that went into producing a healthy baby were often very hard earned.

Pregnancy sickness is an additional cost of pregnancy, in that it prevents a woman from consuming as many nutrients (and often as many calories) as she otherwise would. Not only is she apt to be repulsed by many of the best sources of nutrients— vegetables; she is likely to vomit some of the nutrients that she worked hard to get. For three months pregnancy sickness deprives her of an optimal intake of food, and it commonly causes her to lose weight during the first trimester. Ancestral hunter-gatherer women were probably even more prone to lose weight during the first trimester than are women in modern industrialized societies because they did not have easy, consistent access to large quantities of low-toxin foods, such as cereals, breads, and yogurt. Their foods consisted primarily of fruits, vegetables, and meats cooked over an open fire, and foods in the latter two groups would have triggered significant aversions. In sum, pregnancy is costly because it requires a lot of calories and nutrients, and pregnancy sickness is costly because it often reduces the intake of calories and nutrients.

What the Body Does to Buffer These Costs

A woman needs energy reserves to nourish her baby-to-be, and if she depletes these reserves early in pregnancy, she may face a shortage later in pregnancy or when she is nursing. The body, however, has ways of buffering itself against the nutritional hardships of pregnancy before conception occurs, before a fertilized egg implants, and throughout pregnancy.

Before Conceiving

Human bodies, like those of other mammals, are very sensitive to cues from their environment telling them when it is a good time to reproduce and when it isn't. (The body's ability to detect and interpret these cues isn't perfect, however, and mistakes are sometimes made.) Pregnancy generally can't occur if the body senses that it would be too great a nutritional hardship. For example, ovulation is suppressed if a woman's body senses that there is not enough food in her current environment to ensure a reasonable chance of nourishing an embryo, then a fetus, then an infant. The body can't know for certain what the future holds, of course, but it can use current environmental cues to predict future conditions. It appears to do this by determining at least two things: whether the woman has accumulated a certain threshold of "reproductive" fat—which refers to fat that is deposited primarily on the hips and thighs; and whether she has recently maintained a stable weight. Since human bodies are adapted to a hunter-gatherer environment, if a woman becomes extremely lean or suddenly starts losing weight, her body will interpret this to mean that food has become scarce and that she cannot afford pregnancy at this time. As a solution, it temporarily halts ovulation until it senses that food is more abundant.

Because fat is an efficient way for the body to store calories, the fat reserves of ancestral hunter-gatherer women entering pregnancy provided a buffer against the deprivation of calories caused by pregnancy sickness. In the natural environment, furthermore, fat reserves would have signified to the body that a woman had ample vitamin and mineral reserves. To accumulate enough fat to become pregnant, an ancestral hunter-gatherer woman would have had to have eaten (and stored) a lot of vitamins and minerals, because sources of fat in the natural environment were generally also excellent sources of these nutrients. Fat was not easy for our ancestors to obtain in large quantities because the main sources were vegetables—most of which contain but tiny amounts of oil—and wild animals—which contain, on average, only about one-tenth of the fat that meat from domesticated animals contains. Thus, a woman whose diet consisted of a moderate amount of fat "automatically" consumed enough vitamins and minerals to have sufficient stores of them to buffer her against the nutritional deprivation caused by first-trimester food aversions.

Not only did an ancestral woman who accumulated enough fat to conceive generally eat a large quantity of nutrients; she also ate a wide diversity of nutrients. Humans need to eat diverse foods in order to get the full spectrum of nutrients that they can't manufacture themselves (unlike animals that eat highly specialized diets and can manufacture the vitamins that don't come preformed in their food). Since ancestral hunter-gatherers foraged and hunted whatever was edible in their environment, rather than planting and herding just a few species, their diets, at least over an annual cycle, would have been extremely diverse. Even contemporary hunter-gatherers of the Kalahari Desert eat an enormous range of plants and animals, despite the fact that they live in a region so desolate that it would be considered by most people to be uninhabitable. The great diversity of ancestral hunter-gatherer diets would have ensured a healthy diversity of vitamins and minerals. In sum, a woman's body interprets her fat reserves as a cue that environmental conditions are favorable for reproducing and that she very likely will be able to nourish an embryo/fetus/infant.

Before the Fertilized Egg Implants

If the body senses that a particular month isn't the optimal time to get pregnant, it doesn't have to resort to shutting down ovulation. It can prevent a fertilized egg from implanting in the uterus. Infertility investigator Sam Wasser of the University of Washington, Seattle, has shown that the week following ovulation is a critical decision-making time: the body evaluates various cues to determine whether to allow or to suppress pregnancy. One major cue favoring suppression is stress. The body apparently "listens" for stress hormones. If it senses that levels are high, it may cause "luteal phase deficiency," a fairly common syndrome in which lower-than-normal levels of progesterone are produced. When progesterone levels are insufficient the uterine lining does not mature enough to support successful implantation, and menstruation occurs about a week earlier in the cycle than usual, making it impossible for an embryo to implant. Baboons and certain other mammals also experience this syndrome when living in stressful social situations.

The body may try to prevent or thwart pregnancy during acute periods of stress for two reasons. First, high levels of stress often indicate that the individual is in an unstable social or economic situation (in terms of resources, not money per se), which is generally a bad time to have a baby. Infants whose mothers lack social and economic supports rarely fare as well as infants whose mothers have such supports. In an ancestral environment, where there was no government "safety net," completing pregnancy during periods of great stress meant investing a lot of time and energy in a baby whose survival chances probably were slim. Among many mammals that live in social groups—such as baboons, rhesus monkeys, and elephants—infants of females that are socially stressed—for example, from being bullied by higher-ranking animals in their group—are much less likely than other infants to survive. Second, stress itself appears to increase the embryo's risk of birth defects (as discussed in more detail in Chapter 11). The reason for this isn't known for certain, but it is thought that high levels of the hormones released during stress can directly or indirectly perturb some processes of embryonic development. Thus, the body chooses the option of delaying pregnancy or inducing very early miscarriage, rather than "squandering" its scarce resources by producing an infant who will be at increased risk for malformation or early death.

After Getting Pregnant

Once pregnancy has begun, the body has ways of coping with the nutritional costs of creating a baby and having pregnancy sickness. If a woman's body senses that she is not getting enough to eat during pregnancy or that she does not have ample stores of fat, it apparently lowers its basal metabolic rate, which is the rate at which energy is expended on basic body maintenance. Different species of mammals have different basal metabolic rates: small mammals, such as rats and mice, usually have very high rates; whereas large mammals, such as humans, tend to have much lower ones. But an individual's basal metabolic rate is not a set, absolute value; rather, it can be adjusted (within limits) to different circumstances, such as pregnancy or famine.

The change in basal metabolic rate during pregnancy varies greatly among women, depending, in part, on a woman's fat stores and caloric intake. Among well-nourished women in industrialized societies, for example, basal metabolic rate usually increases gradually throughout pregnancy, particularly during the second and third trimesters, reflecting the demand of the growing fetus on the mother's energy resources. But among women who are only marginally nourished—as in many rural parts of Africa—the basal metabolic rate usually decreases during the first trimester and then increases only slightly during the second and third trimesters. This means that when pregnancy inflicts a nutritional hardship, a woman's body compensates by sparing energy wherever it can.

One might ask why the body doesn't permanently maintain a lower basal metabolic rate, thereby sparing more energy all the time. The reason is that all bodily processes entail trade-offs (a major theme of Chapter 5), and the standard human basal metabolic rate is, on balance, the optimal rate for the human body to perform its necessary functions. When the body lowers its basal metabolic rate in response to pregnancy or starvation, it must temporarily "shortchange" some of its systems.

In sum, the woman's body only undertakes pregnancy if it senses that it can cope with the nutritional costs.

The Nutritional Difference Between Ancestral and Modern Pregnant Women

People giving nutritional advice to women who plan to conceive generally have two main concerns: First, has the woman been eating enough calories to have a healthy pregnancy? And second, has she been obtaining roughly the optimal amount of each essential vitamin and mineral? In the ancestral hunter-gatherer environment, a yes in answer to the first question generally would have meant an automatic yes to the second. Women who had enough fat reserves to conceive generally would have had adequate stores of essential nutrients to carry their embryos safely through the period of pregnancy sickness. The nutritional deprivation caused by normal pregnancy sickness would not have harmed the embryo or taken a serious toll on the woman's health.

But in modern industrialized societies, fat is often decoupled from nutrients. A woman can consume a bottle of vegetable oil without eating any of the rest of the vegetable. Therefore, a woman can become downright plump, yet still lack an adequate store of essential vitamins and minerals. It's easy for her to acquire enough fat to "trick" her body into thinking that it has sufficient nutrient stores to support an embryo/fetus, even if it doesn't. Because of this key difference between ancestral and modern diets, first-trimester women living in modern industrialized societies need to be consciously alert to what does and does not constitute "good nutrition."

Vitamins and Minerals— What Are the Right Amounts?

Vitamins and "essential" minerals are small but necessary constituents of our bodies. Vitamins are certain organic compounds (that is, they contain the element carbon) that our bodies need in order to function properly but can't synthesize. Instead, we must obtain vitamins preformed in our diets. (Vitamin D is a partial exception, in that our skin synthesizes it from a precursor when exposed to sunlight; but some people—particularly infants—depend on diet for much of their vitamin D, which they obtain primarily from milk.) Plants need many of the same vitamins we need, but they are able to synthesize them from elements they absorb from soil, water, and air (most plants don't have the option we do of obtaining vitamins preformed by other organisms). Animal meat and blood also contain many vitamins because animals eat plants, eat other animals that eat plants, or synthesize vitamins themselves.

The essential minerals—such as potassium, calcium, sodium, chlorine, magnesium, iron, copper, iodine, manganese, selenium, and zinc—are elements that must also be obtained through diet. Plants obtain minerals directly from the soil and water. People obtain minerals by eating plants, animals that eat plants, and soil residues on unwashed foods, as well as by drinking water.

Different plants, plant parts, animals, and animal parts contain different amounts of any given vitamin or mineral. The juice of an orange, for example, is a good source of vitamin C and folate (folic acid), but a poor source of vitamin B-6 and iron. So in order to obtain the full spectrum of nutrients that our bodies require to function optimally, we must eat a diversity of foods. (Animals whose diets are highly specialized can get away with a lack of dietary diversity because they have the abilities to synthesize some of the vitamins that we can't.)

Vitamin and Mineral Deficiencies and Excesses

A person's intake of vitamins and minerals fluctuates from day to day and from season to season, so in order to prevent deficiencies and excesses, the body has mechanisms to store vitamins and minerals, as well as mechanisms to eliminate them. But not all vitamins and minerals are stored or eliminated with equal ease. Some can be stored in the liver and in cells of various other tissues in such large quantities that they don't need to be replenished as frequently as others do. Fat-soluble vitamins, such as vitamins A, D, and E, readily permeate fatty membranes and thus are more likely to be stored for a while, rather than rapidly eliminated, if they are not immediately utilized. On the other hand, water-soluble vitamins, such as the B vitamins and vitamin C, tend to be excreted in the urine if not immediately utilized or actively pumped into specialized storage compartments. Some minerals, such as iron, cannot be eliminated from the body easily (because of certain biochemical constraints), and if absorbed in excess they will reach dangerous levels in bodily tissues and in the bloodstream. Many other minerals are flushed from the body more rapidly.

Some people have deficiencies or excesses of particular vitamins or minerals. Deficiencies can arise from a variety of situations: eating a diet that is not sufficiently diverse; eating only plants grown in soil that is deficient in a particular mineral; having a genetic or acquired malfunction in the mechanisms that absorb or metabolize a particular vitamin or mineral; or eating too much of a particular vitamin or mineral that happens to interfere with the ability of another vitamin or mineral to be absorbed or to perform its function. Excesses also can arise from a variety of situations: consuming megadose vitamin/mineral supplements (some vitamins and minerals can safely be eaten in megadoses, but others cannot); eating liver that contains too large a store of vitamins or minerals (fatal vitamin A overdoses have occurred this way); storing food or frequently cooking it in metals that are absorbed by the food (some Bantu men have developed iron overload from brewing beer in iron casks); or inhaling metal particles (which is a hazard of certain occupations).

Vitamin and Mineral Doses for Embryos

Too little or too much intake of certain vitamins and minerals can cause birth defects. For example, vitamin A is essential for an embryo to develop normally, and a deficiency of it in the first trimester causes serious birth defects, such as blindness and nervous system disorders. But an excess of vitamin A causes equally serious birth defects, such as major eye and ear deformities. The dilemma is that although we know that embryos need the "right amounts" of vitamins and minerals, no one really knows exactly what the right amounts are. Trying to estimate the optimal intake of vitamins and minerals for a first-trimester woman is tricky, for a variety of reasons.

First, although vitamin and mineral charts for pregnant women have been devised by the National Nutrition Consortium, which assigns a U.S. RDA (Recommended Daily Allowance) to each vitamin and mineral, and by the National Research Council, which assigns its own RDA (Recommended Dietary Allowance), these recommendations are only estimates, or, in some cases, "guesstimates," with a significant degree of arbitrariness. The recommendations also tend to be conservative, and often they don't reflect the latest scientific findings. Although the RDA for healthy adults will prevent an acute deficiency syndrome, it is not necessarily the optimal vitamin or mineral intake.

For example, the U.S. RDA of vitamin C is 60 milligrams— roughly the amount contained in a medium-sized orange— which is enough for vitamin C to perform its function of helping to synthesize the protein collagen (a structural component of bone, muscle, cartilage, and blood vessels), thereby preventing outward signs of deficiency, such as scurvy. But the U.S. RDA for vitamin C is not sufficient for vitamin C to perform its function as an antioxidant. Vitamin C is one of the body's first lines of defense against "oxygen radicals"—toxic by-products produced by the body as it performs its many biochemical tasks. Oxygen radicals can rip through DNA and mutate it. Without sufficient levels of vitamin C, DNA mutations accumulate at a higher rate, apparently increasing a person's risk of cancer and probably of various other degenerative diseases. The amount of vitamin C recommended by many of the scientists who study its antioxidant properties is 250 milligrams per day—well above the U.S. RDA. For people who consume this much vitamin C in their diets, the cancer risk appears to be significantly reduced. Although acute deficiency diseases, such as scurvy, usually can be reversed easily by consuming a lot of vitamin C, chronic degenerative diseases, such as cancer, generally cannot. Prevention of diseases is often our best defense against them. RDAs provide a framework for thinking about nutrition, but it's important to realize that these recommendations are tentative and that research is still being conducted to determine the optimal amounts of various vitamins and minerals.

Second, the embryo's nutritional needs differ from its mother's; the dose of a vitamin or mineral that is adequate for the health of a pregnant woman may not be adequate for her embryo. Although almost any vitamin or mineral deficiency that is severe enough to visibly affect the mother puts her embryo at greater risk for birth defects, vitamin deficiencies capable of harming an embryo aren't necessarily apparent in its mother. Whereas the mothers of infants born malformed because of vitamin A deficiency tend to be so deficient in vitamin A that they have readily discernible disease, such as blindness, the mothers of infants born malformed because of folate deficiency often exhibit no outward signs of deficiency. This type of "silent" deficiency in a woman of reproductive age is cause for concern.

Third, different women vary in their abilities to absorb, utilize, and excrete different vitamins and minerals. Some people, for example, absorb riboflavin poorly, whereas others absorb it readily. Some vitamins and minerals must be actively pumped across the intestinal lining in order to be absorbed into the bloodstream, and some people have better pumping mechanisms for certain vitamins and minerals than other people do. Furthermore, different vitamins and minerals interact with each other, which means that high levels of one can affect the way that another is absorbed, transported, metabolized, or excreted. For example, iron inhibits zinc absorption, zinc inhibits copper absorption, and calcium inhibits both iron and zinc absorption. This means that the "right amount" of a vitamin or mineral for a given woman depends on the amounts of other vitamins and minerals she is consuming, so that the "right amount" varies from woman to woman. We don't yet have a good way of tailoring RDAs to specific individuals.

Fourth, vitamin guidelines for pregnant women usually fail to distinguish the first trimester from the others. Vitamin and mineral requirements are different for different trimesters. The amount of iron a woman needs in order to transport oxygen to a 5-pound fetus, for example, differs from the amount she needs to transport oxygen to a 1/2-ounce embryo. During the first trimester the body alters its rates of absorption and excretion for some vitamins and minerals; after the first trimester it again alters these rates for some vitamins and minerals, adapting to the specific requirements of the different stages of pregnancy. Guidelines for vitamin and mineral consumption during pregnancy should be tailored to the stages of pregnancy and the changing needs of the baby-to-be.

PREGNANCY SICKNESS

Vitamin and Mineral Supplements

Given that we don't really know the optimal vitamin and mineral intake for first-trimester women, how can a woman trying to conceive or beginning her pregnancy determine whether her nutritional intake has been adequate or whether she's likely to be mildly deficient in one of the vitamins or minerals? One way she can try to gauge her nutritional status is by comparing her diet with the kind of diet that a healthy hunter-gatherer woman is likely to have had—that is, a diet that included a wide diversity of plants and animals. Of course, we don't have a photographic or written record of our ancestors' diets, but we can infer what they were like from our knowledge of the ancestral environment, the diets of contemporary hunter-gatherers, and the kinds of built-in cravings and aversions that humans do and don't have.

From this perspective, a first-trimester woman should be particularly concerned about her nutritional status if her diet during the six months before conception did not include a daily average of at least five servings of different fruits and vegetables (1 serving = one medium-sized apple or one average portion of broccoli) and a modest serving of animal products (meat, poultry, fish, milk, or eggs). If a woman's diet is typical of that of most women in modern industrialized societies—that is, low in fresh fruits and vegetables—she should consider taking vitamin/mineral supplements, after consulting with her obstetrician/gynecologist (OB/GYN) or other health care provider, especially if her pregnancy sickness is so severe that she is averse to even very low toxin sources of nutrients, such as milk and fresh fruit. (As discussed below and in Appendix A, a woman should consider starting vitamin/mineral supplementation several months before conception.)

Balancing Good Nutrition and Pregnancy Sickness

Any woman whose diet has been very restricted for a long period of time and who does not take supplements is at risk for a serious vitamin and mineral deficiency, which means that she should consult with an OB/GYN or other health care provider before she gets pregnant, or as early in pregnancy as possible, to find out whether or not she has a detectable deficiency. In experiments with pregnant animals, a severe deficiency in almost any vitamin or essential mineral causes major birth defects in embryos, and it's prudent to assume that severe deficiencies cause defects in human embryos, too.

The question of whether or not all pregnant women should take supplements has polarized the "experts"—including vitamin biochemists, public health researchers, nutritionists, and OB/GYNs. Some strongly advocate supplements for all pregnant women and women planning to conceive in order to compensate for any hidden deficiencies. Others, however, believe that unless a woman exhibits overt signs of a deficiency, supplements of most vitamins and minerals are unnecessary and potentially harmful, because of the risk of overdoses to the embryo; their attitude seems to be that until vitamin/mineral supplements are proved beyond a shadow of a doubt to enhance the health of embryos and fetuses, they should be avoided by most pregnant women.

Personally, I think that vitamin/mineral supplementation for first-trimester women and women planning to conceive is a very good idea, but I also think it's prudent to be wary of certain vitamins and minerals and to avoid megadose supplementation during pregnancy. Although it's rare to find women in modern industrialized societies with severe vitamin and mineral deficiencies, mild deficiencies are common, and the evidence is very strong that some of these increase the embryo's risk of birth

PREGNANCY SICKNESS

defects. Dozens of studies over the past few decades have shown that vitamin and mineral supplements taken around the time of conception and early in pregnancy help to prevent certain birth defects. Women who have given birth to one infant with neural tube defects or cleft palate, for example, significantly decrease the risk that their second infant will have the same defect if they take prenatal vitamins before conceiving (as discussed below).

Even if she doesn't realize it, a first-trimester woman is constantly making nutritional decisions for her embryo by choosing what to eat and what not to eat. No matter how conscientious a woman is about nutrition during early pregnancy, she has to make decisions based on incomplete information. She can't wait to decide about supplements until definitive studies on the relationships between supplements and birth defects have been completed. If there is good preliminary evidence that supplements can decrease her embryo's risk of birth defects, a first-trimester woman may want to take advantage of this information.

Many scientists and physicians emphasize that it's generally better to get one's vitamins and minerals through a good diet than through pills. But during the first trimester it's best to avoid many of the excellent sources of vitamins and minerals—that is, most vegetables—because they are also sources of natural toxins. Taking supplements is a way to obtain many nutrients without the toxins, an option that wasn't available to our hunter-gatherer ancestors. Although our ancestors often were able to obtain adequate nutrition during the first trimester while avoiding teratogens (otherwise we wouldn't be here), we may be able to improve our embryos' chances of developing without defects by supplementing bland, low-toxin diets with vitamin/mineral pills. A supplement can be a prophylactic against mild deficiencies caused by subtle abnormalities in the way a particular woman metabolizes certain vitamins and minerals.

Instead of trying to devise a new RDA chart for first-trimester women (since we really don't know the optimal vitamin and mineral intake for anyone, let alone a first-trimester woman), I'll discuss the several vitamins and minerals for which supplementation seems most relevant to women living in industrialized societies. Some vitamin and mineral deficiencies and excesses are much more likely than others to increase the risk of birth defects, and some are much more likely than others to occur in women who live in industrialized societies. The information presented here is necessarily incomplete because we still don't understand the role most vitamins and minerals play in embryonic development. Anyone purporting to be an authority on the optimal intake of vitamins and minerals for first-trimester women is guilty of misrepresentation. I'm baffled when I read pregnancy books whose authors give advice about vitamins and minerals with a tone of certainty and authority. In the near future many more studies to assess the nutritional needs of first-trimester women and their embryos probably will be done, and new recommendations by health organizations inevitably will follow. For now, the best we can do is to make educated guesses.

Vitamins of Special Importance Near Conception and During the First Trimester

Folate. Folate (also called "folic acid") is vital for embryonic development. Insufficient levels of folate lead to breaks in the strands of DNA, which often lead to genetic mutations—risk factors for genetic defects in embryos. About one dozen large-scale studies in North America, Europe, and Australia have confirmed that women who take folate supplements near the time of conception and during early pregnancy are significantly less likely to deliver infants with neural tube defects (spina bifida or anencephaly). Since the neural tube forms so early in pregnancy—the fourth week—it's extremely important that the mother build up her folate levels *before* or immediately following conception. Unfortunately, many women don't find out that they're pregnant or that folate is important until it's too late for them to help prevent neural tube defects in their embryos. For this reason, some countries now fortify many breads and cereals with folate.

The RDA and U.S. RDA of folate for pregnant women are 400 and 800 micrograms, respectively; many prenatal vitamin supplements supply 800 micrograms. Since women vary in their abilities to absorb and metabolize folate, however, the RDAs may be insufficient for certain women and their embryos. Neural tube defects occur in about 1 out of every 1,000 newborns; but women who have given birth to an infant with neural tube defects have about a 1 in 25 chance that their next infant also will have these defects. It is believed that many of these women have a flaw in their physiological mechanisms designed to absorb or metabolize folate, requiring them to consume relatively massive amounts of the vitamin in order to achieve the same benefits that most women get from the RDA. Many researchers recommend, therefore, that women who have delivered one infant with neural tube defects and who want to conceive again take a daily supplement of folate ten times the RDA—4 milligrams—for several months prior to conception and during early pregnancy. Women who do so reduce the risk of neural tube defects in their second infant by about 70 percent.

It might seem puzzling that a vitamin deficiency with such devastating consequences is so common among women in modern industrialized societies who are generally so well fed. However, many women have low stores of folate at the start of pregnancy because their pre-pregnancy diets did not include sufficient amounts of fresh fruits and vegetables. Most ancestral hunter-gatherer women, by contrast, would have had adequate stores of folate before getting pregnant because their diets included so many plants. (Foods high in folate include romaine lettuce, pinto beans, lima beans, kidney beans, orange juice, cantaloupe, spinach, cabbage, broccoli, okra, avocados, asparagus, egg yolk, liver, various cereals, and brewer's yeast.) Once pregnancy sickness begins, a first-trimester woman develops aversions to many of the foods that are rich in folate, and thus her folate levels are at risk of decreasing. But if a woman's pre-pregnancy diet includes ample amounts of folate, then her body generally stores enough folate to buffer her against the short-term deficiency that can take place between onset of her pregnancy sickness and formation of her embryo's neural tube about a week later.

Vitamin B-12. In order to perform its function, folate requires vitamin B-12. Therefore, a first-trimester woman may want to adjust her B-12 intake to her folate intake. The RDA and U.S. RDA of vitamin B-12 for pregnant women are 2.2 and 8 micrograms, respectively. Women who have been advised to take especially large amounts of folate before conception or during early pregnancy may also be advised to take proportionally large amounts of vitamin B-12. Since the major sources of B-12 are animal products, vegetarians who refrain from eating all animal products may want to get their B-12 levels measured before conception or during early pregnancy and to take a B-12 supplement if a deficiency is detected.

Vitamin C. The link between vitamin C and the embryo's health is less direct and more ambiguous than is the case with folate. Although studies thus far have not found that vitamin C protects against birth defects, scientific discoveries during the last couple of decades suggest that ample levels of vitamin C in the mother during the first trimester and in the father before conception may enhance the health of the embryo. Vitamin C appears to play a crucial role in preventing excess DNA damage from oxygen radicals—which means that it may also help prevent damage to the DNA of sperm, eggs, and embryos. An embryo's cells divide rapidly in order to generate enough new cells to form a whole person. But when cells divide, their DNA is particularly vulnerable to damage by oxygen radicals (DNA is more "exposed" during cell division). It is possible that ample levels of vitamin C in the father help to prevent damage to the DNA of his sperm and that ample levels of vitamin C in the mother help to prevent damage to the DNA of the embryo.

One way that vitamin C can become depleted in the bloodstream is by smoking, which bombards the body with so many oxygen radicals that it uses up the spare vitamin C, leaving DNA underprotected. Although the mother's egg cells have other good defenses to protect their DNA from oxygen radicals, sperm cells apparently do not have such good defenses. At the University of California, Berkeley, Bruce Ames and his associates have found that the sperm of men who consumed adequate amounts of vitamin C (at least 250 milligrams per day) have less DNA damage from oxygen radicals than the sperm of men who do not. This may be why embryos whose fathers are moderate or heavy smokers are at much greater risk for at least one serious birth defect (cleft palate). Embryos whose mothers are mildly deficient in vitamin C are not known to suffer an increased risk of birth defects, but it's possible that DNA damage in embryos resulting from low levels of vitamin C in the mother can show up later in life in more subtle ways.

Balancing Good Nutrition and Pregnancy Sickness

A preconception nutrition plan for women and their parenting partners should include ample levels of vitamin C, especially if they smoke. Although the RDA and U.S. RDA of vitamin C for pregnant women are only 70 and 60 milligrams, respectively, many scientists who study the physiological effects of vitamin C recommend a daily intake of 250 milligrams (but smokers may need much more than this). Before pregnancy, it is possible to obtain this amount of vitamin C through a good diet, since natural sources include not only citrus fruits, but a wide variety of fresh fruits and vegetables. During the first trimester, vitamin C can be obtained through fruits and vitamin supplements. Many people regularly consume 1,000–2,000 milligrams of vitamin C per day, and what the body doesn't need for immediate use or storage it simply excretes in the urine. However, even though such large quantities of vitamin C are not known to harm adults or embryos, during the first trimester it is prudent to be wary of consuming megadoses of any vitamin or mineral.

Vitamins and Minerals to Be Cautious About During the First Trimester

Vitamin A. Vitamin A in large doses is a potent teratogen. Women who take megadoses of it during the first trimester greatly increase their risk of delivering babies with a suite of defects. Two prescription drugs on the market are synthetic analogs of vitamin A, and they are teratogenic, even when taken at their prescribed doses. These drugs are isotretinoin (brand name Accutane), which is used to treat severe acne, and etretinate (brand name Tegison), which is used to treat psoriasis. Infants born to mothers who take these drugs during the first trimester are at very high risk of suffering facial malformations, heart problems, and mental retardation. Both drugs come with clear warnings on their packages and package inserts about the dangers they pose to embryos. Women of reproductive age who are taking Accutane are advised to use two methods of birth control to make absolutely sure that they do not get pregnant while on the drug and to wait at least one month after stopping the drug before they try to get pregnant (more cautious women may want to wait more than one month). Women taking Tegison, however, need to wait much longer after discontinuing the drug and before trying to conceive because it is eliminated from the body extremely slowly. Women taking either drug and planning to conceive should consult with their OB/GYN about a safe waiting period.

Vitamin A, however, is essential for an embryo's development. Therefore, it's important that a first-trimester woman consume the right amount of it. (Vitamin A deficiency is rare in the United States and other industrialized countries.) Many fruits, vegetables, fish, and liver contain vitamin A and/or beta-carotene (the body converts beta-carotene to vitamin A when needed). Since beta-carotene and vitamin A differ in potency, their amounts are not expressed in units of weight but are converted to units of common potency known as retinol equivalents (RE) or "international units" (IU). The RDA of vitamin A for pregnant women is 800 RE, and the U.S. RDA is 8,000 IU (which equals 2,400 RE when the source is pure vitamin A rather than beta-carotene). Whereas large doses of vitamin A are not considered safe for adults or embryos, large doses of beta-carotene are thought to be relatively safe. Thus, a first-trimester woman who eats plenty of vitamin A and also wants to take a multivitamin supplement may want to choose one whose main source of vitamin A is beta-carotene rather than preformed vitamin A. Liver often has such high levels of vitamin A that it probably should not be eaten regularly by a first-trimester woman (although it's extremely unlikely that she could stomach it in the first trimester anyway).

Iron. "Anemia" takes on a different meaning during early pregnancy. Iron levels in a woman's bloodstream almost always drop during the first trimester, even though the tiny embryo is taking very little iron from its mother. There are at least two reasons for this drop: during the first trimester the intestines, which regulate iron absorption from the diet according to the body's needs, significantly decrease the percentage of iron they absorb; and during the first trimester the number of red blood cells, which contain most of the iron in a woman's body, decreases. This consistent first-trimester drop in iron levels is unlikely to represent some fluke of pregnancy or sudden deficiency; rather, it appears to be an adaptation.

There is now a large body of scientific evidence from studies pioneered by Eugene Weinberg of Indiana University that one of the body's defenses against infectious microorganisms is to withhold iron from them. Iron is essential for many fundamental physiological processes; our cells couldn't function without it. But almost all bacteria, viruses, and other kinds of infectious microorganisms also depend on iron (either directly or indirectly) in order to reproduce and successfully infect their hosts. Humans and other animals therefore have evolved defenses to prevent microorganisms from obtaining iron. When the body recognizes that it is being infected, it triggers these defenses. For example, immune cells known as macrophages start taking up iron from the bloodstream at a fast pace and sequestering it— that is, "hiding" it from the invaders.

The probable reason that bloodstream iron levels decrease during the first trimester is, as suggested by Patricia Stuart-Macadam of the University of Toronto, to reduce the mother's

PREGNANCY SICKNESS

vulnerability to infection at a time when her embryo is very susceptible to harm from infection. A mother's infection can harm her embryo directly, if the microorganisms infect the placenta or cross it and infect the embryo, or indirectly, if her body induces a fever to combat the infection (Chapter 11 discusses the link between fever and birth defects). Thus, decreasing the bloodstream iron levels during the first trimester may be one of the body's prophylactic measures against birth defects.

This means that the optimal iron level is lower for a first-trimester woman than for a nonpregnant woman. (Bloodstream iron levels during the second and third trimesters also are low, but for a different reason: the volume of blood plasma—the liquid part of blood—increases by about 50 percent, thereby diluting the concentration of iron in the blood.) Just because a woman's iron levels decrease during pregnancy doesn't necessarily mean she's anemic. Yet many OB/GYNs, midwives, and popular pregnancy books routinely recommend iron supplements for pregnant women, often beginning in the first trimester. It is counterproductive to dump extra iron into the body just when the body is trying to lower its bloodstream iron levels, so a first-trimester woman who does so may be defeating one of her defenses against infection-induced birth defects.

If a woman was anemic before getting pregnant, however, she may need to take iron supplements during the first trimester. True iron deficiency compromises her immune system's ability to fight off infections, since her immune cells need iron in order to proliferate. Women who are vegetarians are especially at risk for being anemic, since red meat is one of the major sources of iron in the human diet.

If a woman is advised by her OB/GYN or other health care provider to take iron supplements during the first trimester, she may want to alert her or him to the function of the body's iron-withholding defense. Unless the health care provider offers a compelling reason to take them, a healthy woman should consider avoiding iron supplements *during the first trimester.* It should be emphasized, however, that during the second and third trimesters, adequate iron intake is very important for the health of the fetus (although excess iron is harmful).

The body's natural defense of iron-withholding is often mistaken for anemia in other circumstances as well. When a woman gets sick from a bacterial or viral infection, her body defensively sequesters much of its iron so that it is not freely available in the bloodstream. But if she visits a physician to find out why she's sick, a blood test is likely to reveal that she's "anemic," for which she then takes iron supplements, which just end up fueling the invaders that sent her to the physician's office in the first place. Following illness, a person doesn't usually need to consciously replenish iron levels, because iron is simply released from its "hiding places" back into the bloodstream. In fact, the body is unable to eliminate iron easily once it is absorbed by the intestines; only tiny amounts of it are eliminated daily through feces, urine, sweat, and the shedding of skin cells (menstruating women eliminate more iron because some iron is shed with menstrual blood and tissue). Most of the iron in the body is simply recycled indefinitely.

Megadoses in General. Megadoses of vitamins and minerals are not considered safe for embryos. Although vitamin A is the only vitamin that is known with certainty to cause severe birth defects when consumed in megadoses, there are isolated reports that megadoses of some other vitamins and minerals can harm embryos. "Megadose," however, does not have a consistent definition for all vitamins and minerals. Whereas a megadose of pure vitamin A (not beta-carotene) might mean three times the U.S. RDA for pregnant women, a megadose of vitamin C might mean twenty or thirty times the U.S. RDA.

Special Nutritional Warnings
for Women with Medical Conditions

Medical conditions that cause nutritional abnormalities in a woman are risky for her embryo and sometimes result in birth defects, miscarriage, or infant death. These conditions may be genetic or the result of lifestyle or surgery. If a woman who is pregnant or planning to conceive is aware of any condition that affects her body's ability to absorb, transport, metabolize, or utilize a particular nutrient—whether it be sugar, an amino acid, or a certain vitamin—she should alert her OB/GYN immediately. The following medical conditions are known to be risky to embryos and should be treated before pregnancy, or as early in pregnancy as possible.

PKU. There are a number of genetic disorders known as "inborn errors of metabolism," one of which is "*phenylketonuria*" (PKU). It affects about 1 in 16,000 people in the United States. People with PKU cannot metabolize the amino acid phenylalanine at the proper rate. Consequently, phenylalanine—a constituent of all naturally occurring proteins—reaches abnormally high levels in the bloodstream. If a woman with PKU does not severely restrict her dietary intake of phenylalanine throughout pregnancy her infant has an extremely high chance of being mentally retarded and suffering other developmental defects, such as congenital heart disease. This is true even if her infant doesn't inherit the disorder: to develop normally, the embryo/fetus requires a normal nutritional environment.

Balancing Good Nutrition and Pregnancy Sickness

PKU is to some extent treatable by dietary intervention, so it is very important that women with PKU who are planning to conceive consult with an OB/GYN or other health care provider about reducing phenylalanine levels before pregnancy. (If a woman was treated for PKU as a child, she still has the disorder, even though it does not adversely affect her in adulthood.) By almost completely avoiding foods that contain large amounts of phenylalanine—including animal products and legumes—a woman greatly improves her chances of delivering a healthy infant (although the risk that her infant will be retarded is still significant). Infants who survive life in the womb unscathed but who inherit the disorder must be kept on restricted diets throughout childhood if their brains are to develop normally.

Diabetes. Infants of diabetic women (whose diabetes began before pregnancy) have about three times the risk of serious birth defects. The diabetic mother provides an abnormal metabolic environment for her embryo, but just how this environment causes malformations is still a mystery. Simple genetics is not the explanation, because diabetic fathers are not at increased risk of producing children with birth defects. It appears that the more severe the mother's diabetes, the greater the risk that her baby will have birth defects. Diabetic women who are insulin-dependent are at greater risk than those who are not insulin-dependent for giving birth to babies with defects. However, women with "gestational diabetes"—that is, whose diabetes begins during pregnancy—do not appear to be at increased risk.

It is very important that the mother get her diabetes under control before her embryo's organs begin to form. Studies have shown that diabetic women who carefully control their hyperglycemia before conception and throughout the first trimester greatly reduce the risk that their embryos will be malformed.

Obesity. Pregnant women who are very obese—even if not diabetic—run an increased risk of delivering an infant with spina bifida or other major birth defects. The reason for this association isn't known, but many obese women probably have metabolic abnormalities that either cause or result from the obesity. Obese women who become pregnant or who are trying to conceive may want to make sure they do not have any measurable vitamin or mineral deficiencies.

Another reason maternal obesity is a risk factor for birth defects may be that obese women are likely to accumulate higher-than-normal levels of dietary toxins in their fat. Many dietary toxins are fat-soluble, which means that they can penetrate fatty tissue easily and be stored there for some time before being released back into the bloodstream and eliminated by the liver and kidneys. An obese woman may have accumulated an abnormally large amount of dietary toxins, which, when released into the bloodstream from fatty tissues, can cross the placenta and harm the embryo.

Gastric Bypass. To help curb their obesity, some people elect to have "gastric bypass" surgery, in which a large part of their stomach is tied off and rendered unusable in order to limit the amount of food they can eat. This operation, however, dramatically decreases the surface area for absorbing nutrients, thus creating serious nutritional problems for some women and their embryos. Women who have had a gastric bypass appear to be at greater risk for giving birth to an infant with neural tube defects. If a woman who has had a gastric bypass is planning to conceive, it is extremely important that she consult an OB/GYN, midwife, and/or nutritionist about ways to obtain adequate levels of vitamins and minerals before and during pregnancy.

Addictions and Medications. Habitually smoking tobacco or drinking alcohol can interfere with the body's metabolism of various nutrients. For example, alcohol can interfere with zinc metabolism, so that women who drink heavily on a regular basis before conception may be seriously deficient in zinc, and severe zinc deficiency is believed to increase the risk of neural tube defects in embryos. Women who are addicted to cigarettes or alcohol should get help to curb their addiction before conceiving. If their smoking or drinking was heavy prior to conception, and especially if they continue to smoke or drink after conception, they may need to take vitamin and mineral supplements to improve their nutritional status. It's best if these women speak openly about their smoking and drinking habits with their OB/GYNs and other health care providers, who may want to check some of their nutrient levels for possible deficiencies.

Some drugs interfere with the body's metabolism of certain vitamins and minerals and consequently can cause birth defects. Some of the anticancer drugs, for example, inhibit the action of folate in order to suppress the growth of tumors and therefore greatly increase the risk of birth defects. As emphasized in Chapter 10, if a woman is on chronic medication she should consult an OB/GYN before conceiving, or as early in pregnancy as possible, about the potential effects of the medication on her embryo. Women taking certain medications or addictive drugs may need to take large doses of certain vitamins or minerals to offset adverse nutritional effects.

Should a First-Trimester Woman Worry About Weight Changes?

The topic of weight gain during pregnancy has received a lot of attention recently from OB/GYNs, midwives, public health researchers, and the popular media. The current recommendation is that women whose weight is in the normal range for their height should gain 25–35 pounds during pregnancy, lean women 28–40 pounds, overweight women 15–25 pounds, and obese women at least 15 pounds. For women of normal weight, the current recommendation is essentially double that of the 1930s, when pregnant women were encouraged to restrict their weight gain to about 15 pounds. Although pregnancy weight gain primarily concerns the second and third trimesters, rather than the first, a first-trimester woman's diet and pregnancy sickness do affect her weight, so I'll discuss this topic briefly. A first-trimester woman is likely to have two main questions about weight gain: First, why all the fuss about making sure to gain a lot of weight during pregnancy, when most people in our society are already overweight? And second, what do recommendations about pregnancy weight gain mean for the first-trimester woman, whose pregnancy sickness tells her to avoid most foods and sometimes to vomit them?

Weight gain recommendations for pregnant women are based on studies showing that weight gain influences infant birth weight, and that infants deemed "low birthweight" (less than 5 pounds 8 ounces) are less healthy, on average, than infants of normal birth weight. After viewing media images of low birthweight babies lying in hospital incubators, some pregnant women undoubtedly are persuaded to maintain a high food intake throughout pregnancy. Although every pregnancy researcher seems to agree that a healthy pregnancy requires some minimum weight gain, it's not yet clear what that minimum is or what the optimum weight gain is.

Among women who gain at least 15 pounds during pregnancy, a clear cause-and-effect relationship between additional maternal weight gain (that is, a gain above 15 pounds) and infant health has yet to be demonstrated. Although mothers who gain about 30 pounds during pregnancy have less risk of giving birth

Balancing Good Nutrition and Pregnancy Sickness

to an infant with low birthweight than mothers who gain only 15 pounds, the various factors influencing the mother's pregnancy weight gain and the infant's health and birthweight still need to be disentangled. Many low birthweight newborns are underweight because they are premature, malformed, or have mothers who smoke. In some malformed fetuses, for example, the mechanisms that take up nourishment from the mother probably do not function properly, and the fetuses consequently fail to grow at normal rates. In mothers who smoke, the arteries nourishing the placenta are more likely to be abnormally constricted, consequently making it more difficult for some fetuses to obtain adequate nourishment. In both cases, the fetuses may be making lower-than-normal nutritional demands on the mother, which means that the mother's appetite may not increase as much as it would in a normal pregnancy, and she therefore gains less weight. But had she forced herself to eat more during pregnancy and to gain more weight, her infant would not necessarily have turned out larger or healthier. (Prematurity in infants is discussed below.)

Unless the mother is severely undernourished during pregnancy, her embryo/fetus is usually able to "siphon" ample calories from her bloodstream. As explained with many illuminating examples by David Haig of Harvard University, embryos/fetuses are not passive participants in pregnancy; rather, they exercise a lot of control in extracting nutrients from their mothers. (This means, of course, that mothers and their embryos/fetuses don't have perfectly harmonious relationships.) Even rural African women who are lean, work hard physically throughout pregnancy, and gain only 15 pounds by the final weeks of pregnancy generally deliver infants of healthy weight.

Mothers aren't entirely at the mercy of their fetuses, however; they, too, have some control. If a pregnant woman's nutritional status declines sharply, such as during a period of famine, her body may sharply limit the amount of nutrients allocated to the fetus, even if by doing so the fetus suffers irreversible damage. One reason that weight loss during the second and third trimesters is detrimental to the fetus's health may be that it signals to the body that food is in short supply and that the body must conserve its resources in preparation for famine conditions.

In addition, if a pregnant woman's social and economic situation is not conducive to rearing a child, her body may not only withhold nutrients from the fetus, but try to abort it. One of the biggest risk factors for delivering a premature, low birthweight infant is being unwed—that is, lacking strong support from the infant's father. (Sam Wasser points out that very premature infants are actually late miscarriages; with the intervention of modern medical technology, some of these infants survive— although often with some mental or physical impairment.) If the woman's body uses the stress of being pregnant yet unwed (and lacking male support) as a cue not to invest too many resources in that particular fetus—that is, to limit nourishment to the fetus or to abort it—then low pregnancy weight gain is a likely consequence.

Although it's important to emphasize that the fetus needs good nourishment, it's also important to emphasize that bigger isn't necessarily better. A newborn needs a certain minimum weight to have a good chance of surviving in the outside world, but a 9-pound newborn is not necessarily healthier than a 6 1/2-pound one. The growing fetus is eventually going to try to emerge through a relatively narrow cervix and vagina, and extra-large babies have much greater difficulty doing so. Women who gain a lot of weight during pregnancy are at much greater risk of having extra-large babies and of needing cesarean sections. An extra-large baby also is at risk for other complications involving the birth process, such as needing oxytocin-induced delivery or resuscitation with an oxygen mask. And many women who gain a lot of unneeded extra weight during pregnancy are never able to lose it afterward, which often hurts their long-term health and self-image. Bigness entails costs. I've heard a number of mothers of big babies and toddlers announce with pride that their child is "off the charts" in height and weight. But girls who are big for their age throughout childhood usually start to menstruate earlier, which puts them at greater risk for cancers of the breast, uterus, and ovaries for the rest of their lives.

The large weight gains currently being recommended for pregnant women almost certainly did not characterize human pregnancy in the natural environment. Ancestral hunter-gatherer women are extremely unlikely to have averaged anywhere near the 30- or 34-pound average gain recommended for normal-weight or lean women, respectively. Contemporary hunter-gatherers appear to gain about 14–20 pounds during pregnancy. Compared to most women in modern industrialized societies, ancestral hunter-gatherer women would have been lean at conception, which means that they stored less fat before pregnancy to buffer them against the nutritional deprivation caused by pregnancy sickness.

We don't know yet whether the "natural" average weight gain during pregnancy (that is, the weight gain of humans who lived in the natural environment) is the optimal one or merely an adequate one. If the latter, then we can improve the chances of having a healthy infant by gaining more weight during pregnancy than did humans in the natural environment (just as we can improve the chances of having a healthy infant by consuming more folate than did humans in the natural environment). But until more studies are done to determine the relationship between the mother's weight gain during pregnancy and her infant's health, recommendations about pregnancy weight gain will continue to have a substantial component of arbitrariness.

So what does all this mean for a first-trimester woman? Pregnancy sickness generally discourages first-trimester women from gaining much weight. In fact, women whose pregnancy sickness is so severe that they vomit tend to lose weight during the first trimester. Some of these women may worry that losing weight during the first trimester puts them too far behind their target weight gain. But although severe weight loss during the first trimester should be worrisome, as explained in Chapter 9, mild weight loss during the first trimester generally should not. (Weight loss during the second and third trimesters, however, is very worrisome.) The embryo is so small that its calorie requirements are scant. A woman's total weight gain during pregnancy does not seem to be much affected by whether she gains or loses weight during the first trimester. Weight lost during the first trimester generally is regained easily during the second trimester, when appetite returns.

Even if the mother is very thin, as long as she has adequate stores of vitamins and minerals the embryo usually can obtain adequate nourishment. In fact, even if the mother is subjected to famine during the first trimester but receives adequate nutrition during the second and third trimesters, her infant is likely to have normal weight at birth. For example, toward the end of World War II in occupied Netherlands, when the Nazis inflicted a six-month famine on the population, infants born during the famine had birthweights that were much lower than average; whereas infants conceived during the famine but born well after it had birth weights that were normal.

The infants conceived during the famine did have increased rates of neural tube defects and other nervous system disorders, and this fact is sometimes presented to emphasize the importance of good nutrition in early pregnancy. However, this increase in birth defects could have been caused by a number of war-related factors other than first-trimester food deprivation. At the start of the famine, the people were already undernourished because they had just been subjected to a couple of years of strict food rationing, which means that their stores of folate and other nutrients important for the health of embryos were probably abnormally low and easily depleted by the famine. In addition, the stress of being at war in a territory occupied by the enemy and nearly starved by them must have been tremendous, and great stress during the first trimester appears to be a risk factor for birth defects (as discussed in Chapter 11). Furthermore, an epidemic was occurring immediately after the famine, resulting in the deaths of many infants, and if the epidemic actually began toward the end of the famine, it may have caused malformations in the embryos of affected mothers, since maternal infections and fever are risk factors for birth defects.

In sum, the first trimester should not be the time to worry about weight gain (unless the woman is experiencing serious weight loss), but rather the time to worry about toxin avoidance and vitamin/mineral status.

Dietary Tips for Enhancing Nutrition During the First Trimester

Most people have a sense of what it means to eat a "well-balanced diet," even if they themselves don't do it. For a person *not* in the first trimester of pregnancy, a well-balanced diet generally consists of five servings of fruits or vegetables per day (preferably fresh); a diversity of grains in cereals, breads, and other starchy foods; and a variety of animal products, including meats, fish, poultry, eggs, and milk. A well-balanced diet is also low in sugar, fat, and salt.

For a woman in the first trimester, on the other hand, a well-balanced diet is one that heavily favors nutrients over toxins. For example, such a diet might consist of five or more servings of fresh fruit per day, preferably a variety of them; a diversity of grains (oats, wheat, corn, rice, etc.) in cereals, breads, pastas, and other bland starchy foods; and various easily tolerated animal products—such as boiled turkey, milk, yogurt, and eggs.

Diversifying the diet is a good strategy for obtaining the necessary variety of nutrients while avoiding high levels of any one toxin. Pregnancy sickness, however, makes diversifying the diet difficult, because it causes aversions to so many foods. But some diversity should be possible even within the shrunken set of tolerable foods.

"Sneaking" Nutrients into the Diet

If a woman wants to include more nutritious, low-toxin foods in her first-trimester diet but is hindered by an intolerance of these foods, there are ways to make the foods more tolerable. Women with severe pregnancy sickness may want to try some of the tips offered in the following chapter on extreme pregnancy sickness.

Ice-cold milk and plain yogurt are nutritious and generally very low in toxins, and they can be blended with fruit, fruit juice, or protein powder to make a nutritious, palatable shake. But many adults are intolerant of milk because their bodies don't produce enough of the enzyme "lactase," which is necessary for digesting the lactose in milk. (Ancestral hunter-gatherers had no dairy cows, did not drink milk after they were weaned, and thus had no need to produce lactase during adulthood.) A first-trimester woman who is unable to digest milk products because she's "lactose-intolerant" may want to buy lactose-free milk (available in many grocery and health-food stores) or consider taking lactase tablets (also available in many health-food stores), which will enable her to digest lactose. I have not found any studies about the use of lactase tablets in pregnancy, but I have no reason to suspect that they are unsafe in normal doses, since other women produce lactase naturally. However, a woman who is lactose-intolerant may want to consult her OB/GYN about appropriate doses of lactase.

Eggs are extremely nutritious, but their sulferous aroma may be aversive to many first-trimester women. Fresh eggs do not emit that aroma when they are included as components of homemade breads, waffles, and muffins. "Sneaking" eggs into such bland or sweet, starchy foods is one way for a first-trimester woman to enrich her diet palatably.

Vitamin and mineral pills and powders may be difficult to "stomach" during the first trimester—and may even cause the woman to vomit—especially if taken on an empty stomach. Although vitamins and minerals are nutrients and are not toxic in the doses found in standard multivitamin supplements, in nature vitamins and minerals come with food, and it's not natural to ingest a concentrated amount of them by themselves. Toxic overdoses of some vitamins and minerals can occur naturally—for example, from eating liver containing highly concentrated vitamin A. It's possible that the body guards against such overdoses by reacting aversely to concentrated doses of vitamins and minerals, such as occur in supplements not diluted by food. If a first-trimester woman finds that she can't stomach vitamin pills or powders by themselves, she may want to try blending vitamin powder with ice-cold milk and fruit or else sprinkling it on yogurt or cereal.

PREGNANCY SICKNESS

Trying to reconcile the two sometimes opposed goals of good nutrition and toxin avoidance can be tricky. Vitamin and mineral supplements can help to provide nutrients without the toxins. But it's important to discuss one's nutritional status and the pros and cons of vitamin and mineral supplementation with an OB/ GYN before conception or as early in pregnancy as possible. Women who are pregnant or planning to conceive should be aware that there currently is no consensus on whether all first-trimester women should take supplements or at what doses. In discussing the subject with any particular pregnancy expert, it's important to be aware that for some topics there is a substantial time lag between biomedical discoveries and widespread understanding of these discoveries among clinicians. Over the last few decades many millions of biomedical articles have been published in the thousands of different scientific and clinical journals. No one person can keep up with all this information or be an expert on every topic that is at least tangentially related to pregnancy. For example, although a growing number of biologists are aware that one of the body's defenses against pathogens is to deprive them of iron—by lowering the levels of iron in the bloodstream—most OB/GYNs and other health care providers have not yet come across this information. A woman who gathers pregnancy information from different sources is bound to get some conflicting information. Pregnant women should be encouraged to speak with different OB/GYNs and other pregnancy specialists (if that's an affordable option) and to read some of the scientific articles about nutrition during pregnancy in order to devise a good nutrition plan for each stage of her pregnancy.

Chapter Nine

$\sim\!\!\sim$

Too Much or Too Little Pregnancy Sickness and What to Do About It

ANY PART of the body can malfunction, any mechanism can go awry. Pregnancy sickness is no exception. A tiny percentage of women have so much pregnancy sickness that their own lives are in danger; while another tiny percentage have so little that their embryos' health is in danger. Understanding the function of pregnancy sickness and how it is triggered gives us some insight into how to intervene when it malfunctions.

Hyperemesis Gravidarum

In rare cases (about 3 per 1,000 pregnancies) a woman has such severe pregnancy sickness that she vomits excessively and is unable to keep down almost any food, necessitating at least a short stay in the hospital. This condition is called hyperemesis gravidarum (from "emesis" meaning "vomiting" and "gravid" meaning "pregnant"). The severity of pregnancy sickness among women represents a continuum—from none to unrelenting nausea and vomiting—but there isn't a precise, consistently defined point where severe pregnancy sickness becomes hyperemesis gravidarum. Most OB/GYNs would define hyperemesis gravidarum as pregnancy sickness that is severe enough for the woman to require intravenous fluids and nutrients (which usually means hospitalization).

Untreated, hyperemesis gravidarum can even cause death, because excessive vomiting leads to dehydration and an imbalance of electrolytes—the minerals (primarily sodium, potassium, and chloride) necessary for regulating fluid balance between the cells and the bloodstream. The main organs damaged by severe hyperemesis gravidarum are the liver, kidneys, and central nervous system. When fluid imbalance affects nerve cells, for example, the symptoms can include confusion, seizures, limb paralysis, and eventual coma. In industrialized countries, modern medicine has virtually eliminated the risk of death from pregnancy sickness, mainly through intravenous methods of rehydrating and feeding the woman. But for some women with unrelenting vomiting, the only way to save their lives is through getting an abortion.

The analogy of nausea to pain, mentioned in Chapter 2, can be extended to extreme manifestations of these mechanisms. Just as some pain syndromes are dysfunctional and debilitating, some nausea syndromes, such as hyperemesis gravidarum, are dysfunctional and debilitating. For example, in certain rare pain syndromes the pain that originates at the site of an injury spreads to parts of the body remote from the site of injury, such as to a noninjured limb; in other syndromes the pain amplifies intensely after the injured tissue has healed. Although nausea cannot spread throughout the body as pain can—that is, the sensation of nausea is localized to the gastrointestinal region and does not spread to the limbs—nausea can become dysfunctionally amplified. A woman suffering from hyperemesis gravidarum, for example, can feel extreme nausea even if she hasn't eaten or smelled food for hours, hasn't eaten pungent foods for weeks, or has completed her first trimester. Her nausea may become intractable, rendering her incapable of eating anything. If this happens, it is important that she realize that these symptoms are dysfunctional (but not her fault) and constitute a serious medical condition that requires immediate treatment.

Just because a particular woman's pregnancy sickness is dysfunctional does not mean that other aspects of her pregnancy are as well. It is not known why some women get hyperemesis gravidarum, but probably the CTZs of such women overreact to the estrogen produced by the ovaries and placenta. These women also tend to have higher-than-normal levels of estrogen circulating in their bloodstreams. Women are at greater risk for hyperemesis gravidarum if they are carrying twins, since twin placentas usually produce more total estrogen than does a single placenta, or if they are obese, since fat cells convert the steroid androstenedione to estrogen and release it into the bloodstream. Because the neurological and biochemical bases of nausea and vomiting are not fully understood, the various physiological factors that may contribute to hyperemesis gravidarum have not yet been pinpointed. Temporary thyroid anomalies, for example, have been implicated by some researchers as possible triggers of hyperemesis gravidarum, but further research is needed to determine whether a causal connection exists.

Hyperemesis gravidarum usually resolves by about week 20 after conception. When nausea lasts throughout pregnancy, it is usually much less severe during the second half. A woman who experiences hyperemesis gravidarum with her first pregnancy will not necessarily experience it with subsequent pregnancies, but she probably will experience at least severe pregnancy sickness again. Although most women with hyperemesis gravidarum

PREGNANCY SICKNESS

deliver healthy infants, a woman whose vomiting continues well into the second and especially third trimesters may fail to obtain adequate nourishment, which puts her fetus at risk for low birthweight. Some studies have shown that infants of women with severe hyperemesis gravidarum are at slightly greater risk for certain birth defects, but other studies have shown no increased risk. It would not be surprising if hyperemesis gravidarum turns out to increase the risk of birth defects slightly because it seriously disturbs a woman's nutritional status and fluid balance.

How to Recognize Excessive Pregnancy Sickness

Women whose pregnancy sickness is normal but includes regular vomiting tend to lose some weight during the first trimester. At what point should a woman become concerned that she has too much pregnancy sickness? If she loses more than 5 percent of her body weight (for example, if she weighed 120 pounds before pregnancy and drops below 114 pounds) she should alert her OB/GYN or midwife. If vomiting becomes unrelenting and prevents her from keeping down any food, she should alert her OB/GYN or other health care provider immediately, because she probably will need to receive fluids and electrolytes intravenously. Her OB/GYN or other health care provider also will need to perform tests to rule out the possibility that her vomiting is due to a medical condition unrelated to pregnancy sickness, such as appendicitis, hepatitis, infectious diarrhea, urinary tract infection, peptic ulcer disease, gall bladder disease, kidney insufficiency, liver disease, hyperthyroidism, inflammation of the pancreas, or diabetic ketoacidosis.

Ways to Keep Food Down and Avoid Odors

If a woman's pregnancy sickness is so severe that the smell of virtually every food sickens her, she should try to eat in ways that, as much as possible, bypass her sense of smell. For example, one thing she could try is the following: blend very fresh milk and fruit with ice (the cold helps suppress the odor); pour the mixture into a glass; cover the top of the glass tightly with plastic wrap; poke a straw through the plastic; then take small sips every few minutes. Juices can be diluted with water to make their odors less intense. Drinking diluted juice out of a baby bottle also can help to suppress the juice's odor.

A woman with hyperemesis gravidarum is likely to have more success keeping food down if she eats frequent meals consisting of small amounts of nonoily foods (oils are difficult to digest). If a woman is vomiting frequently, it is extremely important that she replenish lost fluids. Drinking liquids at meals, however, may make her stomach feel too bloated, which could exacerbate nausea. Most OB/GYNs and midwives therefore recommend drinking liquids between meals. But a pregnant woman who is losing a lot of weight may want to resort to liquid meals, such as clear broths or one of the high-calorie liquid nutritional supplements intended primarily for the elderly or for chemotherapy patients. Salting her foods to taste can help replace two of the important electrolytes—sodium and chloride—that her vomiting may have depleted.

A woman should try to eliminate excess and particularly offensive odors by following the guidelines in Chapter 6. If her pregnancy sickness is so severe that even the remaining odors repulse her, she can try to block them by wearing a surgical mask (available at pharmacies) at home, in the car, and wherever else it is feasible to wear one.

Diminishing Other Stimuli in Order to Diminish Nausea

When a person is very nauseated, almost any extra stimulus can exacerbate the nausea (perhaps because extra stimuli can cause

PREGNANCY SICKNESS

extra stress, which can contribute to nausea). A woman suffering from intense nausea should, whenever possible, dim the lights (unless she's reading), avoid looking at bright colors, turn off the TV and stereo, and block out other noises, unless these other stimuli do not worsen her nausea.

Treatments

Vitamin B-6. Vitamin B-6 (pyridoxine) appears to diminish nausea and vomiting in some women with severe pregnancy sickness (but not in women with mild or moderate pregnancy sickness). In one group of patients studied, the treatment consisted of taking a 25-milligram tablet of vitamin B-6 every eight hours for seventy-two hours (three days). A woman probably would need to repeat the treatment whenever severe pregnancy sickness returned. Although the U.S. RDA of vitamin B-6 for pregnant women is only 2.5 milligrams, the relatively high dose used to treat severe pregnancy sickness does not appear to pose a risk of toxicity to the mother or embryo.

It is not known why vitamin B-6 alleviates severe nausea in some women. The main functions of vitamin B-6 discovered so far involve helping to metabolize amino acids, fats, and carbohydrates. But it is also known that B-6 and estrogen interact, at least indirectly, and that high levels of estrogen—which apparently trigger nausea during the first trimester of pregnancy—cause certain changes in the body that mimic vitamin B-6 deficiency. Supplementing with high levels of vitamin B-6 apparently helps to counter some of these changes. If a woman with severe pregnancy sickness wants to try vitamin B-6 therapy, it's prudent for her first to consult with her OB/GYN or midwife about the latest information on it.

Intravenous Feeding. A woman with hyperemesis gravidarum can become dangerously dehydrated. The immediate treatment is an intravenous (IV) solution of water, sugar, vitamins, and minerals, usually given in the hospital initially. Many women with hyperemesis gravidarum need to repeat the IV treatment every few days over a period of a couple of weeks, and home intravenous services are available to facilitate this.

It is very important that a dehydrated woman receiving an intravenous sugar solution receive the vitamin thiamine as well. Otherwise, her thiamine levels—which her vomiting probably has severely depleted—can become dangerously low as her remaining thiamine is used to metabolize the sugar solution. The result can be a rare neurological disorder, known as Wernicke's encephalopathy, characterized by paralysis, coma, and sometimes death.

Gradual IV rehydration is sufficient to make many women feel well enough to start eating small amounts of food again. But for severe, long-lasting hyperemesis gravidarum, where the woman still cannot take anything by mouth without vomiting, more complete sustenance than is provided by a simple IV is needed. The options are enteral feeding—which entails inserting a feeding tube through the nose to the intestines to deliver protein, water, sugar, vitamins, and minerals—or parenteral feeding—which entails inserting a feeding tube into the subclavian vein (located where the chest joins the arm) to deliver amino acids, essential fatty acids, water, sugar, vitamins, and minerals. Such therapy can range from a few days to several weeks, depending on the severity and duration of hyperemesis gravidarum.

Medications. If basic IV treatment does not alleviate the woman's nausea and vomiting enough to enable her to regain weight—or at least to maintain her weight—then she will probably need to take antinausea medication. A number of anti nausea and antivomiting drugs have been developed, but none yet that are ideal for treating hyperemesis gravidarum. One of

PREGNANCY SICKNESS

the repercussions of the thalidomide tragedy is that manufacturers are extremely reluctant to develop drugs to treat severe pregnancy sickness. In fact, in the United States there are no such drugs currently on the market. The pregnancy sickness drug Bendectin was pulled from shelves in the early 1980s after a slew of lawsuits were filed against the manufacturers by parents claiming that Bendectin caused their babies' birth defects. The fact that extensive scientific studies found no causal connection between Bendectin and any birth defect did not dissuade them from pursuing costly litigation, which is why some investigators familiar with the science of teratogens branded Bendectin a litogen—that is, something that causes lawsuits, not birth defects.

However, some antinausea and antivomiting drugs that were originally developed to combat motion sickness and chemotherapy-induced nausea are also prescribed for hyperemesis gravidarum. These drugs act by inhibiting the particular chemical messengers of the nervous system (neurotransmitters) that are used in the CTZ (where food aversions, nausea, and vomiting are triggered). The main categories of such drugs are antihistamines, dopamine antagonists, and anticholinergics, which inhibit the actions of histamine, dopamine, and acetylcholine, respectively. These drugs have side effects because the neurotransmitters whose actions they inhibit are also used in other parts of the nervous system. Furthermore, these drugs have been effective in alleviating the nausea and vomiting of only some women with hyperemesis gravidarum.

Most drugs used to treat hyperemesis gravidarum have not been extensively tested for their capacities to cause birth defects, so if a woman can postpone taking medication until after the first trimester—or at least until after week 8, the end of the peak period of organ formation—so much the better. She should not

Too Much or Too Little Pregnancy Sickness

feel guilty, however, if she needs medication to combat hyper-emesis gravidarum: the health of her baby-to-be depends largely on her own health. Most drugs used to treat hyperemesis gravidarum can be obtained only by prescription, but some, such as Unisom, an antihistamine developed as a sleeping pill, can be obtained over the counter. Nevertheless, a pregnant woman should take such medication only after consulting with her OB/GYN.

Alternative Therapies. "Alternative" therapies, including acupressure, hypnosis, biofeedback, and relaxation therapy, lessen the severity of nausea for some women with severe pregnancy sickness. A woman may want to try one or more of these therapies in conjunction with intravenous feeding as a first step in trying to alleviate severe nausea. Women with severe pregnancy sickness that is not extreme enough to require IV treatment also may benefit from one of these therapies.

Hypnosis and biofeedback require the active assistance of professionals, but many relaxation techniques can be performed alone once they are learned. Acupressure is perhaps the simplest of the alternative therapies, but its effect on most women is unlikely to be dramatic. It entails wearing a special wristband on each arm three-fingers'-width up the arm from the main wrist crease (where the wrist joins the hand); each wristband has one spherical button that is supposed to be positioned in the middle of the inner surface of the forearm so that it makes a slight indentation in the skin. It's still a mystery why pressure at this particular point (known as the "Neiguan point") decreases nausea in some women.

A relatively new product based on the same principle is the Relief Band (MAVEN Labs, Citrus Heights, California; telephone 1-800-469-1518). This battery-operated device is worn like a wristwatch and emits low-voltage electrical pulses that modulate the sensations of nausea, apparently by interfering with the signals from the brain to the gastrointestinal tract that induce nausea. Like all products that are based on transcutaneous electrical nerve stimulation (TENS), in the United States it can only be obtained by prescription.

It is important to emphasize that just because psychological therapies, such as hypnosis or relaxation, may alleviate nausea in some women with hyperemesis gravidarum, this does not mean that their nausea was caused by psychological problems. Unfortunately, a lot of OB/GYNs and other health care professionals still cling to the belief that hyperemesis gravidarum has a strong psychological component. I believe that it is cruel and counterproductive to suggest to a woman suffering from hyperemesis gravidarum that she inflicted it on herself by getting stressed out about and failing to cope with her pregnancy or other aspects of her life. Even though stress undoubtedly exacerbates nausea in some cases, the primary cause of hyperemesis gravidarum is physiological, not psychological. At every large university thousands of students are stressed out during final exam week, and yet 3 out of every 1,000 students do not end up in the hospital because they vomited to the point of life-threatening dehydration. Many women with hyperemesis gravidarum are psychologically well-adjusted, happily married, and joyful about having a baby. They simply are having some temporary bad luck.

Beware of "Natural" Medicines Such as Ginger and Herbs

Many pregnancy books advocate eating ginger root or certain herb teas to alleviate pregnancy sickness. Their assumption

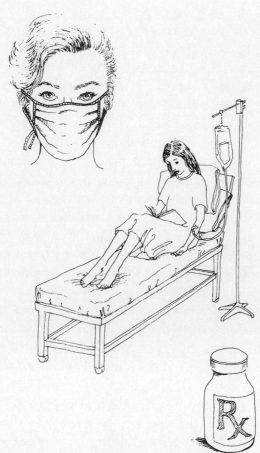

Certain remedies can help alleviate severe,
dysfunctional degrees of pregnancy sickness.

seems to be that medicine is safer if it comes directly from nature than from pharmaceutical companies. In stark contrast to
their advice, mine is to avoid "natural" medicines altogether during the first trimester, even if some of them do have antinausea
effects. The fact that ginger root and herbs are pungent indicates that their toxin levels are high, and the message of pregnancy sickness is precisely to stay away from such plants or plant
parts.

Since many medicines produced by pharmaceutical companies are really "natural," in the sense that they are of natural origin (derived from plants or molds), or are synthetic analogs of
natural plant compounds, I'll refer to medicines in the form of
herbs and roots as "herbal medicines" and medicines produced
by pharmaceutical companies as "pharmaceutical medicines."
Herbal medicines are potentially more dangerous to embryos
than pharmaceutical medicines for three reasons.

First, every plant root or herb contains a wide spectrum of
toxins, each of which is designed to disrupt one of the physiological systems of other organisms, such as animals that prey on
them. In a given plant, such as ginger, a particular toxin may happen to quell human nausea, but in order to consume this toxin a
woman has to consume all the other toxins in that part of the
plant. By contrast, the only toxic compounds in pharmaceutical
medicines are the ones desired for their medicinal effects.

Second, very few, if any, of the toxins in "natural" medicines
have been tested for their effects on embryos. In a study of one
small group of pregnant women who were taking ginger, no malformations were obvious in the newborns (although one woman
miscarried), but almost all of the women began their ginger
treatment after the peak period of organ formation—after the
period when major malformations would have occurred. We

simply don't know what kind of risks ginger may pose to embryos. Natural toxins that mutate DNA have been found in ginger and in many herbs; and most of the numerous toxins produced by these plants have not even been identified, much less analyzed for their effects on humans. We have far more information on the risks to embryos of various pharmaceutical medicines than of herbal medicines.

Third, a woman who consumes herbal medicines cannot know the dose of toxins she's consuming. Individual plants within a species vary in the levels of toxins they produce because of genetic variability, differences in soil conditions, ages of the plants, and the individual stresses that each has endured from attacks by insects and fungi. Thus, a gram of a given herb can contain ten times as much of a particular toxin as a gram of that same herb from a different plant. By contrast, a woman taking a pharmaceutical medicine usually knows exactly how much she's getting: it's written on the label. Because an herbal prescription, unlike a pharmaceutical one, cannot guarantee an exact dosage, a first-trimester woman who resorts to herbal medicines may end up unwittingly inflicting a high toxic load on her embryo.

If pregnancy sickness lasts longer than sixteen weeks, quelling it by eating ginger or drinking herb teas may be O.K., since the fetus is much less vulnerable to the toxins in herbal medicines than the embryo is. But pharmaceutical medicines still are generally safer than herbal ones. I would favor treating hyperemesis gravidarum with ginger toxins only if a pharmaceutical company isolated the antinausea compound in ginger, tested it on pregnant animals, conducted clinical trials, and, if it appeared to be safe, synthesized and mass-produced it. That way, a woman could benefit from ginger treatment without inflicting a whole spectrum of untested toxins on her embryo.

Pregnancy Sickness That Lasts
Well Beyond the First Trimester

Moderate or severe pregnancy sickness that lasts beyond about week 16 post-conception is dysfunctional. It is not a sign that the woman and her fetus need pregnancy sickness for a longer period of time than do other women and their fetuses; it is simply an aberration. If a woman who is several weeks into her second trimester still experiences substantial pregnancy sickness, she probably has not regained her appetite sufficiently, so she should consciously eat enough protein, fat, and calories to gain weight and nourish her fetus. Severe pregnancy sickness that lasts into the second half of pregnancy should be taken very seriously. If it prevents the woman from gaining weight and eating an ample amount of nutrients, she should get immediate help to resolve the situation through intravenous feedings, medication, and perhaps complementary alternative therapies such as biofeedback and acupressure.

An Absence of Pregnancy Sickness
in the First Trimester

A complete absence of pregnancy sickness during the first trimester also should be considered pathological (that is, a malfunction in her mechanisms to trigger pregnancy sickness). In fact, a first-trimester woman who experiences virtually no pregnancy sickness should try to protect her embryo by behaving as though she did have it. Unlike other first-trimester women, she can't simply listen to her body to know which foods and odors to avoid. How can a woman ascertain whether she really is deficient in pregnancy sickness? One thing she can do is to run through the checklist of "forbidden" foods in Chapter 7, asking herself questions of the sort, "If I imagine myself standing over a hot stove, could I tolerate frying, inhaling the odors of and eating onions, garlic, basil, oregano, cabbage, peppers, etc?" If the answer is "yes," then she isn't experiencing enough pregnancy sickness and should consciously avoid such foods.

Can Pregnancy Sickness Be Made Obsolete?

Since a first-trimester woman who doesn't suffer from pregnancy sickness can simply behave as though she does, is pregnancy sickness obsolete? In other words, if a first-trimester woman could squelch her pregnancy sickness through some trick of modern medicine, resolving instead to consciously avoid foods on the "bad list," should she? The answer is "no," because nature provides us with better deterrents than we can consciously provide ourselves. For one thing, many women begin having food aversions before they realize they are pregnant. For another, there are many cues of toxins that a woman without pregnancy sickness would not be able to detect. For example, signs of spoilage in meat—indicating bacterial toxins—are detected much more readily by a woman whose pregnancy sickness arms her with both a repulsion toward the odors of unfresh meat and a superacute sense of smell. Thus, an "enlightened" first-trimester woman without pregnancy sickness who tried to mimic the behavior of a woman with pregnancy sickness would not be able to protect her embryo as well as a woman who experienced the real thing. Pregnancy sickness is not obsolete in the modern world.

Chapter Ten

～∞～

Pregnancy Sickness Does Not Protect Against All Modern Toxins: Alcohol, Cigarettes, Medicines, and Pollutants

AN ANCIENT physiological mechanism transplanted into a modern industrial environment will not necessarily produce the same outcome as it did in the ancestral environment. Pregnancy sickness in women today is triggered by those substances that were likely to harm embryos during the course of human evolutionary history—substances whose toxins are detected by their bitter tastes or their pungent odors. (Although not all plant toxins are bitter or pungent, each plant produces dozens of different toxins, so that even those toxins that aren't bitter or pungent are likely to be associated with others that are.) On the other hand, toxic substances that are unique to modern environments— either in their chemical characteristics, in the quantities to which we are exposed, or in the ways in which we are exposed—can be especially dangerous to embryos, because such substances may not adequately trigger pregnancy sickness.

To begin this discussion, it's important to distinguish between toxins and toxic substances. A toxin is a natural poison, a chemical produced by a nonhuman organism for the purpose of harming another organism. Plant toxins, bacterial toxins, and snake venoms are all toxins. Many toxins come with what we perceive as warning labels—chemicals that we taste as bitter or smell as pungent, fangs and stingers we can see, or rattles we can hear. Substances that are toxic but not natural chemical weapons technically are not toxins, so I'll refer to them as toxic substances. Toxic metals and burnt material, such as charcoal and campfire smoke, are toxic substances that can be found in nature. Synthetic drugs are toxic substances that are not found in nature (even though many of them behave pharmacologically like natural toxins). This distinction between "toxin" and "toxic substance" is important because it highlights the fact that pregnancy sickness was designed to protect against natural chemical weapons in their natural forms and doses—that is, the toxins that were frequently encountered in ancestral environments—and not against substances that happen to be toxic in our current environment. (One exception is smoke, and burnt material in general, which are toxic substances that have probably been present on a regular basis in human environments for more than half a million years.)

There are at least four types of toxins/toxic substances that pregnancy sickness cannot be expected to protect against (which will be the focus of this chapter): (1) natural substances, such as alcohol and mercury, that are not toxic to adults or embryos in the small quantities that ancestral humans would have been exposed to; (2) toxins or toxic substances, such as drugs in the form of capsules or injections, that bypass our taste and smell detectors; (3) toxins or toxic substances, such as cigarette smoke, that are consumed in quantities large enough to damage the mechanisms that would otherwise protect against them; (4) toxins or toxic substances, such as the caffeine in colas and the active ingredients in syrupy medicines, whose bitterness is masked by sugar.

In addition, pregnancy sickness may be less effective against toxins and toxic substances that a woman is addicted to because her aversions must compete with her addictions. Recreational and potentially addictive drugs probably have been part of human life for hundreds of thousands of years; many contemporary hunter-gatherers use various plants to achieve "altered states." But it is very unlikely that our ancestors consumed enough of

Pregnancy sickness cannot protect against all modern toxic substances.

PREGNANCY SICKNESS

these drugs to become addicted. In other words, drug addiction probably is evolutionarily novel.

This chapter describes some of the toxins and toxic substances that are particularly relevant to first-trimester women living in modern industrialized societies.

Beware: Alcohol Consumption Isn't Greatly Discouraged by Pregnancy Sickness

Alcohol is a serious cause of birth defects, responsible each year in the United States for several thousand cases of fetal alcohol syndrome, which is characterized by mental retardation and facial anomalies. Alcohol is an extremely weak teratogen, yet it is one of the major causes of birth defects in the United States. It is a natural substance present in plant foods, yet pregnancy sickness does not greatly discourage its consumption. The reason for these apparent contradictions is as follows.

Pure alcohol is not a toxin produced by plants. Rather, it is a by-product of the fermentation of plant sugars by microorganisms. Although alcohol often is mixed with other plant extracts in beverages, pure alcohol is not bitter or pungent; in fact, the CTZ does not appear to respond to alcohol the way it responds to plant toxins. Alcohol exists naturally in many plants in tiny quantities. For example, if we eat an orange we consume a slight amount of alcohol. But the amount of alcohol that a pregnant woman could consume from her foods is much too small to cause birth defects. Ancestral hunter-gatherers could not have eaten or produced alcohol in teratogenic amounts. Thus, mechanisms to deter pregnant women from drinking alcohol did not evolve.

Women in modern agricultural societies have access to vastly larger amounts of alcohol than were obtainable in the ancestral environment. Heavy drinking during pregnancy—averaging five or more alcoholic drinks per day—is a very big risk factor for fetal alcohol syndrome, but light drinking—averaging one drink per day—does not seem to be. Nevertheless, a safe daily dose of alcohol during pregnancy has not been established. Some studies have detected mild mental impairment in a significant proportion of children whose mothers consumed moderate amounts of alcohol during pregnancy (more than one drink per day but less than four).

Another reason that pregnancy sickness does not prevent fetal alcohol syndrome is that pregnancy sickness is limited to the first trimester; whereas large quantities of alcohol can damage a fetus's brain during the second and third trimesters (the worst damage, however, occurs during the first trimester). Although the basic structures of the brain form during the first trimester, the brain continues to grow and develop throughout pregnancy and early childhood. Therefore, toxic substances that affect neurological development are dangerous not only for embryos but for fetuses and young children as well. To be on the safe side, a pregnant woman should refrain from drinking alcohol entirely, or limit her consumption to an occasional, single drink.

Pregnancy sickness does motivate many women to at least decrease their alcohol consumption during the first trimester, because almost all alcoholic beverages contain bitter plant toxins, which are aversive. Wine, for example, contains the grapes' natural tannins. (Vodka, however, is an exception, being composed only of pure ethanol and water.) Some women with pregnancy sickness may have aversions to alcohol for another reason: memories of the aftermath of "heavy partying." Most people who drink alcoholic beverages probably have at least once gotten drunk enough to experience severe nausea or vomiting.

PREGNANCY SICKNESS

Anything associated with a memory of nausea is likely to seem less palatable to a person suffering from nausea. Despite these deterrents, however, heavy alcohol consumption during pregnancy is a widespread problem with devastating consequences for embryos and fetuses. Women—especially alcoholics—need to be aware that pregnancy sickness is not an effective deterrent against overconsumption of alcohol.

To highlight the connection between pregnancy sickness and cues of natural toxins, we can contrast alcohol with coffee. Unlike pure alcohol, coffee contains a wide array of bitter and pungent toxins—precisely the sorts of substances that pregnancy sickness was designed to protect against—and almost all first-trimester women find that pregnancy sickness causes them to significantly decrease their coffee consumption. (As discussed in Chapter 7, coffee consumed in large daily doses during the first trimester appears to be a slight risk factor for birth defects; at moderate doses, coffee may also be a slight risk factor for miscarriage.)

Beware: Smoking Thwarts Pregnancy Sickness

A tobacco plant typically contains hundreds of different toxins—nicotine being only one of them. Burning tobacco produces still more toxic substances; one of the primary chemicals in the burnt material of cigarette smoke is "benzo[a]pyrene," which can mutate DNA. But not only does pregnancy sickness not deter most smokers from continuing to smoke; smokers tend to have less pregnancy sickness than nonsmokers. Although these findings may appear to invert the expected relationship between pregnancy sickness and toxins, they actually underscore how important pregnancy sickness is for detecting toxins: smoking disrupts the very mechanisms that trigger pregnancy sickness.

For one thing, smoking diminishes the senses of smell and taste—mechanisms critical for detecting toxins. It probably does this by destroying an excessive number of olfactory nerve cells. These types of cells normally can be regenerated well into adulthood, which may be why many smokers who quit suddenly rediscover the world of aromas. The thresholds for detecting pungent odors and bitter tastes are significantly higher in smokers, rendering smokers less sensitive to toxins.

Another way that smoking thwarts pregnancy sickness is by lowering the level of estradiol in the bloodstream. The type of enzymes that detoxify benzo[a]pyrene in smoke also metabolize estradiol (the two compounds have a similar chemical structure), so that when the body produces extra enzymes to detoxify the benzo[a]pyrene contaminating it, these extra enzymes are also available to metabolize estradiol, clearing it from the bloodstream at a faster rate. Thus, there is less circulating estradiol to stimulate the CTZ and (possibly) the growth of olfactory nerve cells.

In contrast to smokers, virtually all nonsmokers become repulsed (or more repulsed) by cigarette smoke during the first trimester. One study even found that nonsmoking women whose husbands smoke are more than twice as likely to have severe vomiting during pregnancy—presumably because the smoke nauseates them so much. Pregnancy sickness alerts women to noxious "burnt material" fumes, such as cigarette smoke, but long-term smoking thwarts this protective mechanism.

The toxins and toxic substances from tobacco smoke can circulate in the pregnant smoker's bloodstream and reach the placenta. Surprisingly, however, smoking during pregnancy does not appear to be associated with a marked overall increase in the risk of major birth defects. Although some large studies do show an increased risk of birth defects, most do not. However, cigarette smoking appears to be associated with a significantly higher risk of miscarriage (some, but not all, studies have found this association). It is possible that smokers produce more malformed embryos, but then spontaneously abort them. Furthermore, a number of studies show increased deficits in intellectual, behavioral, and physical development in the infants and school-age children of mothers who smoked during pregnancy (compared to infants and children of mothers of the same background who did not smoke). This suggests that smoking may damage embryos in subtle ways. There are at least three ways in which smoking may harm embryos: by inflicting a large spectrum of toxins on the placenta and embryo; by depleting the mother's bloodstream of vitamin C; and by decreasing the mother's degree of pregnancy sickness. Smoking also can harm a second- and third-trimester fetus, because it is a risk factor for premature birth, which can lead to infant death or lifelong medical problems.

A first-trimester woman who smokes should be aware that her smoking partially suppresses a mechanism designed to protect her embryo from birth defects. Since her smoking probably has impaired her ability to smell toxins, she should select foods cautiously, consciously avoiding a high level of dietary toxins. She should also consider taking vitamin C supplements (and, of course, consider stopping smoking).

Medicines and Other Drugs

Drugs are toxic by definition—that's why they have the effects on us that they do. Many drugs are toxins derived from plants, and many are synthetic mimics of such toxins. The drugs we buy in modern pharmacies are designed to circumvent our toxin-detection mechanisms; we need only swallow a capsule or inject a needle—methods of drug delivery that bypass the taste and smell receptors that normally would make us averse to consuming such toxic substances. Pregnancy sickness therefore does not prevent a first-trimester woman from taking drugs in these forms. (However, if her CTZ reacts to these drugs once they have been absorbed into her bloodstream, by causing nausea and vomiting, she may be averse to taking them again.)

Most legal drugs do not appear to pose major risks of birth defects when taken in normal therapeutic doses. Some drugs, however, are very dangerous to embryos, even if their effects on adults are fairly innocuous. The classic example is thalidomide, which was taken by many first-trimester women in the late 1950s and early 1960s to alleviate stress and nausea. The drug is highly teratogenic, causing severe limb defects—including missing limbs—in the babies of mothers who took the drug during the critical days of limb formation. A first-trimester woman could not have been warned of thalidomide's toxicity by smelling the nonaromatic capsule, even though she would have been very sensitive to odors if her pregnancy sickness was severe enough to cause her to seek medicinal relief. Thalidomide has made a partial comeback: it suppresses some aspects of the immune system, and so it is used to treat certain diseases in which the immune system responds too vigorously for optimal health, such as graft-versus-host disease in bone marrow transplant patients and inflammatory skin lesions in lupus and leprosy patients. Unfortunately, however, thalidomide is still causing birth defects in some countries, such as Brazil, apparently because some pregnant women are not properly warned about its hazards by their physicians and the drug's manufacturers.

In the three decades since thalidomide was acknowledged to be teratogenic, we still have not discovered *why* it is teratogenic. Since we can't always discover what makes even a known

PREGNANCY SICKNESS

teratogen teratogenic, we may never discover how to predict in advance which drugs will be human teratogens. We do not know what effects most drugs—even commonly prescribed ones—have on human embryos. We have extensive information on the effects of some drugs on animal embryos, but for other drugs we have none. Many commonly prescribed drugs cause birth defects in animals at high doses, but this does not necessarily mean that they can cause birth defects in humans at normal doses. We don't experiment on human embryos *in utero,* of course, so we don't find out whether a particular drug can cause birth defects in humans until we look for patterns of malformations and anomalies in the infants of mothers who have taken the drug during pregnancy. Thus far, we have excellent information about the risks to human embryos for only a few drugs; for the overwhelming majority of drugs, we have fair, poor, or no information.

When a first-trimester woman is deciding whether or not to take medication, she needs to analyze the trade-offs: the risks to her embryo of taking the medicine versus the risks to her own health of not taking it. As an extreme example, if a first-trimester woman is diagnosed with aggressive cancer and is advised to immediately begin taking lifesaving anticancer drugs, she will almost certainly want to follow this advice. But she should be aware that anticancer drugs can cause serious malformations in her embryo because they interfere directly or indirectly with the DNA of dividing cells—which is why they are so often effective against tumors. (As discussed in Chapter 12, a high-quality second-trimester ultrasound scan can help to ascertain whether major malformations have indeed occurred.)

The main categories of medications that are known to pose a significant risk of severe birth defects are the aminoglycoside antibiotics (such as streptomycin), androgenic hormones, anticancer drugs, anticonvulsants, antithyroid drugs, chemical antagonists, coumarin anticoagulants (such as warfarin), and vitamin A analogs. But this does not mean that all drugs in these categories are dangerous for embryos.

Many women taking chronic medication deliver healthy infants. In some cases, a woman can significantly reduce her embryo's risk of malformation simply by substituting one drug for another. For example, some epilepsy patients take the anticonvulsant trimethadione, which, if taken during the first trimester, causes serious birth defects in a large percentage of babies—possibly more than 80 percent; whereas the anticonvulsant phenytoin causes birth defects in about 10 percent of babies.

Drug substitutions also can be important for a first-trimester woman needing medication on a short-term basis. For example, a first-trimester woman who needs antibiotics to cure an infection may have a range to choose from, depending on the type of infection, and she should be aware that some antibiotics are riskier for her embryo than others. Streptomycin can disrupt her embryo's inner ear development so should be strictly avoided during the first trimester unless there is no effective alternative, but ampicillin and erythromycin are generally considered safe for embryos. It is important that a first-trimester woman feel confident that she is taking the antibiotic that is least risky to her embryo, yet still effective against her infection, so that she isn't tempted to skimp on the treatment. A person on antibiotics needs to take the full course prescribed (usually seven to ten days) in order to wipe out the infection completely.

A first-trimester woman may want to select one drug over another simply because more information about teratogenic risks is available for one than the other. A first-trimester woman who needs to take a pain reliever, for example, may want to choose acetaminophen (Tylenol) over ibuprofen (Advil) because many large studies have indicated that acetaminophen, taken in normal therapeutic doses, appears to be safe for embryos, but information on ibuprofen is relatively scant.

It is prudent to take only those drugs that are medically necessary during the first trimester of pregnancy. Anytime a pregnant woman is being prescribed medication, she needs to alert her physician that she is pregnant. In addition, she may want to double-check with her OB/GYN to find out what risks, if any, the medication has for her embryo or fetus. This includes topical medication (i.e., applied to the skin), because many of these can be absorbed into the bloodstream, particularly if they are in an oil base. As soon as a woman finds out that she's pregnant, she may want to collect all the medications in her medicine cabinet and store them in a closet where she won't have such easy access to them, so that she won't absent-mindedly take medicine for a familiar ailment before consulting with her OB/GYN. Exceptions are certain over-the-counter first-aid solutions for cuts, bites, and abrasions, such as rubbing alcohol.

Even though drugs taken after the first trimester don't cause major malformations, some drugs are more harmful during the second or third trimesters than the first. For example, taking aspirin during the third trimester—particularly near the time of delivery—greatly increases the baby's risk of intracranial hemorrhage during birth, whereas taking moderate doses during the first trimester appears to be relatively safe for the embryo. Taking the antibiotic tetracycline during the second and third trimesters often causes permanent staining of the fetus's teeth; whereas taking it during the first trimester is not believed to significantly increase the embryo's risk of any type of malformation.

Recreational drugs that are currently illegal in the United States should be avoided during pregnancy. Cocaine, for example, is teratogenic, causing an increased risk of malformations of the heart, eyes, kidneys, and urinary tract, and functional abnormalities of the nervous system. One of the problems with using illegal drugs during pregnancy is that the woman usually does not know exactly which chemicals and how much of each she's inflicting on her baby-to-be, since illegal drugs tend to be adulterated with other chemicals by the time they reach the consumer.

Every year new studies are performed on the teratogenic risks of various drugs. So rather than provide a soon-to-be-outdated list of the relative safety of the most commonly used drugs— most of which we still lack sufficient information on—I suggest that a first-trimester woman request from her OB/GYN an up-to-date list of over-the-counter drugs that are generally considered safe during early pregnancy (ideally the list should include dosages). If a hospital or agency in her state provides a Teratogen Information Service (see Appendix B) a pregnant woman can use it to obtain up-to-date information on the risks of specific medications to her baby-to-be.

"Invisible" Toxic Substances Produced by Industries

"Invisible" toxic substances are those that can't be detected by smell or taste. Toxic substances produced by industries either as products or as by-products of the manufacturing process (pollution) should not be expected to trigger aversions in a first-trimester woman unless they happen to have noxious odors or tastes. (Some manufacturers add a bittering agent to inedible but tasteless fluid products in order to discourage curious children from swallowing them.) An example of the problems that can arise when pregnant women are exposed to invisible industrial pollutants is the case of methylmercury, a natural substance that is teratogenic when pregnant women are exposed to it at unnaturally high levels. It is present in the natural environment in trace amounts because bacteria in the soil convert metallic mercury to methylmercury. However, some industries also use methylmercury. The industrial release of methylmercury into Japan's Minamata Bay in the 1950s and early 1960s caused severe neurological defects in the infants of mothers who consumed contaminated fish during pregnancy. These defects included mental retardation, cerebral palsy, blindness, and deafness. In Iraq in the early 1970s, the use of a methylmercury fungicide on grain caused the same defects in infants of mothers who ate bread made from contaminated grain.

One of the problems of pregnant women being exposed to high levels of substances that are toxic to the nervous system is that the second- and third-trimester fetus also can be affected. In fact, in the case of methylmercury, it is believed that exposure during the second trimester causes greater damage than exposure during the first. The reason that humans did not evolve a physiological mechanism to protect second- and third-trimester fetuses from chronic high-level exposure to neurological toxins is that the problem didn't exist (or was extremely rare) in ancestral environments.

Although it's very unlikely that a first-trimester woman living in a modern industrialized society would be exposed to high levels of methylmercury (because of strict regulation of this pollutant), she could be chronically exposed to other industrial toxins in her workplace. Most pollutants that people in modern

Pregnancy Sickness Does Not Protect Against All Modern Toxins

industrialized societies come into contact with outside the work-place are at such low levels that they probably do not present a significant risk of birth defects (although we don't know for sure, since most of them have not yet been tested for their effects on embryos). Workplace exposures to toxic substances, however, tend to be chronic and sometimes are at relatively high levels. Therefore, a woman who is pregnant or trying to conceive and who works with solvents, cleaning fluids, resins, toxic metals, or other potentially hazardous fluids, gasses, or solids should be especially careful to wear appropriate protective gear, such as gloves, mask, and goggles, and to ventilate her workspace to prevent large amounts of these substances from being absorbed through her skin or lungs.

In sum, since a first-trimester woman in a modern industrial-ized society will not necessarily be deterred by pregnancy sick-ness from exposing her embryo to high levels of many modern toxic substances, she needs to consciously avoid such exposures.

Chapter Eleven

Other First-Trimester Hazards to Embryos

EACH EMBRYO faces an array of potential dangers in addition to those relating to diet, nutrition, and drugs, which have already been discussed. This chapter describes some of these first-trimester dangers, including certain microorganisms, certain physical activities, and various other bodily stresses. (There are undoubtedly some minor dangers to embryos that currently are not even recognized as such.) Whenever a pregnant woman hears that something pertaining to her first-trimester experience is a risk factor for birth defects, it's very important that she understand the magnitude of that risk before becoming anxious. For example, exposing the embryo to a given teratogen may increase its risk of birth defects 1 percent above the 2–3 percent background rate (1 percent is still a significant increase, considering the devastation that birth defects can cause), whereas exposing it to a different teratogen may increase its risk to 50 percent. (Chapter 12 discusses how prenatal testing can give the pregnant woman information about whether a teratogen she was exposed to during the first trimester has actually harmed her embryo/fetus.)

This chapter also discusses some things that many pregnant women have suspected to be teratogens but that actually entail undetectable or minuscule risks. If one were to perform a large epidemiological study of mothers of infants with birth defects, any randomly chosen activity—for example, watching a particular soap opera, using a particular brand of shampoo, or having blue as a favorite color—would be likely to correlate mildly with at least one of the hundreds of birth defects simply by chance. But correlation does not necessarily imply cause and effect. To drive home this point, in the 1980s the epidemiologist Helmut Sies tabulated and graphed the numbers of breeding pairs of storks and the numbers of newborn babies in Germany over the preceding fifty years. The declines in both were highly correlated; in fact, they tracked each other very closely. But that doesn't mean that babies come from storks! Sometimes chance correlations make headlines in the press before rigorous scientific studies refute the presumed cause-and-effect relationship. In this chapter I've tried to disentangle real from fictional risks to provide the reader with a more accurate picture of the science of the causes of birth defects than is available in the mass media.

Microorganisms and Immunizations

Several viruses and other microorganisms cause birth defects in humans. Viruses (which are essentially packets of foreign genetic material that exploit the machinery of our cells to make copies of themselves and to have their own genetic instructions carried out) seem to be able to traverse the placenta more readily than most bacteria and other parasites can. Microorganisms that infect the placenta often proceed to infect the embryo. Some of them are teratogenic because they directly interfere with organ formation—for example, by preventing the embryo's cells from differentiating, proliferating, and functioning properly. Microorganisms also can be teratogenic by infecting the placenta extensively enough to prevent it from properly nourishing the embryo or by altering the mother's physiology sufficiently to disrupt the embryo's environment. The type of birth defects that result from a given infection depend in part on the embryo's stage of development at the time of infection. Organs develop in stages, and different organs develop at different times. Not all organs in all stages of development are susceptible to a given microorganism.

Second- and third-trimester fetuses also can suffer permanent damage, such as mental retardation or blindness, when microorganisms destroy too many of their cells, but embryos are more likely than fetuses to suffer permanent damage. Not only are embryos vulnerable because their organ formation can be disrupted; they also lack functioning immune systems (although some of the mother's antibodies—molecules of the immune system that circulate throughout the body and inactivate foreign particles like viruses—cross the placenta to help the embryo fight infections). Women whose immune systems are partly suppressed—for example, from taking immunosuppressive drugs after an organ transplant—need to be especially careful not to contract teratogenic microorganisms during pregnancy.

Viruses, bacteria, and other disease-causing microorganisms have always been part of human life, but mass epidemics are relatively recent phenomena—the result of high population densities, where tens of thousands, hundreds of thousands, or even millions of people trade germs by living in close contact, sharing the same water supplies, and transporting themselves and their germs across many regions. Some epidemic diseases are particularly dangerous for embryos. Several of these are discussed below, along with information about how to avoid them. A

PREGNANCY SICKNESS

number of microorganisms can be transmitted to fetuses later in pregnancy or during the birth process and can cause serious illness or even death in infants, but this chapter will focus on those microorganisms that can cause first-trimester birth defects.

Viruses

Rubella (German Measles). The rubella virus infects about 80 percent of the embryos of infected first-trimester women, causing many of these embryos to have severe birth defects, including cataracts, deafness, mental retardation, bone malformations, and other abnormalities. A second-trimester fetus also can suffer permanent damage if its mother contracts rubella, because the virus can infect its brain and eyes, whereas a third-trimester fetus usually emerges relatively unscathed, even if it becomes infected. A person can contract rubella only once (as far as is known), but many women who contract it are unaware they have it because the distinctive rubella rash accompanies the infection in only about two-thirds of the cases. Women of child-bearing age who are not absolutely certain that they have had rubella (confirmed by blood test) should be immunized with the measles-mumps-rubella vaccine at least three months before becoming pregnant. However, it is recommended that women not get this vaccine during pregnancy (for reasons described below) unless there is a serious rubella outbreak in their region.

Herpes Simplex Virus (HSV). Primary genital herpes infections (which almost always are herpes type 2 infections, in contrast to "cold sores," which usually are type 1 infections) during pregnancy are very dangerous for both embryos and fetuses. (A primary infection is a first-time outbreak in a woman previously uninfected with the virus—that is, in a woman who has not already built up antibodies against the virus.) Herpes infections

Other First-Trimester Hazards to Embryos

often recur throughout life, but recurrent infections are rarely dangerous to the embryo or fetus, so women with genital herpes need not feel anxious about conceiving. Roughly 40 percent of pregnant women with a *primary* genital herpes infection transmit it to their embryo/fetus, which often leads to miscarriage, premature birth, or a suite of defects, including mental retardation, eye damage (often blindness), central nervous system abnormalities, scarring of the skin, and other problems. Although embryos appear to be less susceptible than third-trimester fetuses to acquiring herpes from their mothers, infected embryos usually undergo more extensive damage.

Currently there is no effective vaccine against herpes. The antiviral drug acyclovir is effective in lessening the severity of primary herpes infections in adults and in reducing the number of recurrences, but its use during pregnancy has not yet been approved. Since infants of women who took the drug inadvertently during pregnancy have not shown an increased rate of malformations, a pregnant woman with a primary genital herpes infection may want to ask her OB/GYN about immediate treatment with acyclovir.

Above all, it's very important to prevent a primary infection from occurring during pregnancy, especially during the first trimester. If a pregnant woman who has never been infected with genital herpes has a partner who has been infected, she should insist that he use condoms during her pregnancy. Even if he takes acyclovir to inhibit recurrences, he may shed the herpes virus asymptomatically in his genital secretions, and studies indicate that acyclovir does not necessarily prevent the transmission of herpes to a sexual partner.

During the birth process, an active herpes infection in the woman's birth canal can infect her baby and cause permanent neurological damage or even death. Although this happens only rarely (especially considering the number of pregnant women with genital herpes), many women with active herpes lesions at the time of labor opt for cesarean section in order to avoid transmitting herpes to the vulnerable newborn.

Cytomegalovirus (CMV). A woman infected with CMV during pregnancy can transmit the infection to her embryo or fetus, which may consequently suffer a variety of neurological defects, such as mental retardation, hearing loss, and visual disturbances, among other problems. Fetuses appear to be more likely than embryos to get CMV infection, but embryos usually suffer worse effects. An adult infected with CMV often has no overt symptoms but may have symptoms resembling mononucleosis. CMV infection is common: more than 50 percent of the U.S. population has it or has had it. It is transmitted through bodily secretions, including saliva, semen, cervical secretions, breast milk, and urine. CMV belongs to the herpes family of viruses, and, like herpes simplex virus, no effective vaccine for it yet exists. A person can become reinfected with CMV, but a primary infection is much riskier for the embryo or fetus than reinfection is.

Roughly 1 percent of newborns have congenital CMV infection, and, of these, about 10 percent show signs of impairment from birth, including mental retardation and hearing problems; severely infected infants often die. About 10 percent of the infected newborns who are asymptomatic at birth develop permanent neurological and other problems, but the rest develop normally.

Although CMV is common and is spread by casual contact, careful hygiene can help prevent infection. For example, CMV is common in children who attend day-care centers, so pregnant women should wash their hands thoroughly after exposure to children's urine or other secretions. The only way for a woman to find out whether she has CMV or has had it previously is to get a blood test.

Varicella (Chicken Pox). Fetal varicella syndrome is characterized by malformations or scarring of the eyes, brain, limbs, and skin. It occurs in about 1–5 percent of the embryos whose mothers contract chicken pox during the first half of pregnancy. Fetuses infected in the last half of pregnancy are much less likely to have permanent damage. Most women in the United States have already had chicken pox in childhood and therefore are immune to it. A pregnant woman who has never had chicken pox, however, should take care to avoid being exposed to it during pregnancy, since it's very contagious. This may mean avoiding day-care centers and preschools, places of frequent outbreaks of chicken pox. If a pregnant woman who has not had chicken pox is exposed to the virus during the first trimester, she may be given an injection of antibodies (pooled from the blood of former chicken-pox patients) to help her and her embryo/fetus ward off the infection. A chicken-pox vaccine has recently been developed but is not currently used in mass immunization programs.

Miscellaneous Viruses That May Harm Embryos. The common cold (with or without fever) during the first trimester has been associated in preliminary studies with about a fourfold increase in the rate of neural tube defects (which normally occur in about 1 out of every 1,000 infants) and an increased rate of various other birth defects, including cleft palate. Influenza and other "flus" have also been associated in many (but not all) studies with increased rates of various birth defects, including neural tube defects, cleft palate, and limb defects. Since no specific pattern of defects analogous to that characterized by rubella syndrome has yet emerged from studies of malformed infants of women who had colds and flus during the first trimester, cold and flu viruses are not widely regarded as teratogens. It is prudent, however, for a first-trimester woman to actively try to avoid catching colds and flus by, for example, avoiding crowds (when possible), leaving the room when someone with a cold or flu enters it, and washing her hands often.

An assortment of other viruses apparently can harm human embryos. The measles (rubeola) virus does not appear to cause birth defects, but it can cause miscarriage. A woman planning to conceive should first get a measles vaccine (usually given in conjunction with rubella and mumps vaccines). Less familiar viruses known as the coxsackie viruses, which are spread by personal contact and tend to cause brief mild illnesses in adults, are associated with a slightly higher rate of birth defects when contracted by first-trimester women.

Bacterial Infections

Syphilis. Congenital syphilis can cause abnormalities in multiple organ systems, including mental retardation, blindness, and deafness. When a pregnant woman has syphilis, there is more than a 50 percent chance that her embryo or fetus will contract it. Pregnant women can be treated for syphilis (penicillin is commonly given), and the treatment usually cures syphilis in their embryos and fetuses as well. A woman who has been cured of syphilis can still become reinfected, so any pregnant woman whose sexual partner may have syphilis (or any other sexually transmitted disease) should not have unprotected sexual intercourse during pregnancy.

Miscellaneous Bacteria in the Uterus Before Conception. Before a woman tries to conceive, it's important that she have a healthy uterus. If she experiences a sudden onset of heavy and frequent uterine bleeding—for example, if her menstrual periods suddenly have triple the usual amount of blood or if she starts bleeding between periods—she should alert her OB/GYN and request that the possibility of uterine infection be investigated. If her uterus is infected, she should postpone trying to conceive until the infection is eradicated. Otherwise, if she does conceive, the placenta could become badly infected, resulting in miscarriage or infection of the embryo.

The relationship between uterine bleeding and infection is as follows. Bacteria colonize whatever tissues they can, and mucous membranes and skin are accessible targets. Consequently, numerous bacteria normally reside in a woman's vagina and cervix and on a man's penis. When a man ejaculates, his sperm have to travel through a reservoir of bacteria in the vagina and cervix to reach the uterus and Fallopian tubes. Some of these bacteria cling to sperm and "hitch a ride" to the uterus, where they try to colonize the uterine lining, the tissue that is supposed to nourish a future embryo. Menstrual bleeding helps to eradicate these bacteria, and "wipe the slate clean" for the implantation of an embryo, by killing and tearing off a large chunk of potentially infected uterine tissue and by conveying large numbers of immune cells from the blood to the potentially infected area. Sometimes, however, bacteria and other microorganisms are so tenacious that the uterus has to enhance its defenses, which it does by causing unusually heavy and frequent bleeding. Some microorganisms, however, are so successful at outmaneuvering our defenses against them that the only way to eradicate them is to take antibiotics.

In cases of sudden, atypical uterine bleeding, the initial strategy of many OB/GYNs is to try to curtail the bleeding with

PREGNANCY SICKNESS

hormones instead of first investigating the possibility of uterine infection. But if one of our defenses against invading microorganisms is increased uterine bleeding, it may be dangerous to curtail bleeding artificially unless infection has been ruled out. Although uterine bleeding can be caused by other problems, such as certain kinds of tumors and hormone abnormalities, the possibility of infection should be investigated promptly because infection can lead to infertility. (Uterine bleeding during pregnancy is discussed in the next chapter.)

Other Parasitic Infections

Toxoplasmosis and Cats. Congenital toxoplasmosis occurs in about 1 to 8 infants per 1,000 worldwide (about 1 to 2 per 1,000 in North America). Although the affected newborn may appear normal at birth, the infection often leads to mental retardation, blindness, hearing impairment, other neurological impairment, and sometimes death. In adults, toxoplasmosis often is asymptomatic, but it sometimes resembles mononucleosis, with vague symptoms that can last for weeks or months. Having toxoplasmosis once does not protect a person from contracting it again, but a first-time infection in a woman is much more likely than a reinfection to be transmitted to an embryo or fetus. About half the women who contract toxoplasmosis for the first time during pregnancy give birth to a congenitally infected baby. Transmission of toxoplasmosis occurs more readily in fetuses than in embryos, but the effects are generally much worse in embryos. If a pregnant woman contracts toxoplasmosis, treatment will decrease the chance of it being transmitted to her embryo or fetus.

Prevention of toxoplasmosis is fairly straightforward, once a person is familiar with the sources of infection. Toxoplasmosis is

Other First-Trimester Hazards to Embryos

common in domestic cats, who transmit the disease to humans by shedding parasitic cysts in their feces. A woman cleaning a litter box, petting a cat near its rear end, or gardening where a cat defecates can pick up the parasite on her hands or under her fingernails; if she then touches her food, eating utensils, or mouth she is likely to ingest the parasite. Most women who have grown up around cats have had toxoplasmosis at least once. The other major source of toxoplasmosis is undercooked meat and poultry; farm animals can acquire the parasite from soil contaminated by cat feces, and they can then harbor the parasite in their tissues.

To avoid getting toxoplasmosis, it is extremely important that a pregnant woman with a cat not touch its feces. This means that she should wear gloves when handling the litter box (or else delegate litter box responsibilities to someone else) and when gardening in soil where a cat may have defecated. Also, she should wash her hands and fingernails thoroughly after handling the litter box or petting a cat. A pregnant woman should cook her meat thoroughly before eating it, and she should be careful to wash her hands after handling raw meat and after handling raw fruits or vegetables that harbor soil residues. If a woman has a cat at the time she is planning to conceive she may want to get a blood test to determine if she has toxoplasmosis. (The blood test usually can distinguish a present from a past infection.) A toxoplasmosis vaccine for humans does not yet exist, but an experimental vaccine for cats has been developed.

Immunizations During the First Trimester

Many viruses can be contracted only once in a lifetime because the infected individual subsequently becomes immune to them—that is, the individual's immune system develops strong enough defenses against those specific viruses to prevent rein-fection in the future. The purpose of vaccines, of course, is to make people immune to specific diseases without their actually having to contract the diseases. ("Vaccine" comes from the Latin "vacca," meaning "cow," because in the 1700s the British physi-cian Edward Jenner noticed that farmers and milkmaids who were exposed to cows infected with cowpox did not come down with the dreaded disease smallpox, so he deliberately infected people with cowpox pus, thus creating the first vaccine.) Vac-cines come in three main forms: killed viruses or bacteria; live but attenuated (weak) strains of the virus or bacterium; and tox-oids, which are inactivated forms of bacterial toxins, such as tetanus toxin. Vaccines are not 100 percent effective, and some, such as tetanus vaccine, are routinely readministered after an interval of time has passed.

Although it is important for women to be immunized against certain diseases before pregnancy, some vaccines are themselves potentially harmful to embryos and should be avoided during pregnancy and for a couple of months preceding conception. Many vaccines, for example, induce fever because the immune system recognizes them as foreign, and fever is a risk factor for birth defects (fever is discussed in the next section). Vaccines consisting of live viruses can potentially infect the mother and her vulnerable embryo. Fever and mild rash can follow live-virus vaccinations by some weeks, which is why a buffer period be-tween immunization and conception is recommended.

Measles-Mumps-Rubella Vaccine. The measles-mumps-rubella vaccine is strongly recommended for women of child-bearing age. Since it is a live-virus vaccine, however, it is not generally given to first-trimester women, although women who have been immunized inadvertently during the first trimester have not, as far as is known, given birth to infants with congenital rubella syndrome.

Polio Vaccine. Live oral polio vaccines are not usually given during pregnancy, unless there is a polio epidemic, because they can induce fever. In one recent large-scale immunization program in Finland, however, pregnant women (including first-trimester women) who had already been vaccinated during childhood were revaccinated and did not have an increased risk of bearing infants with malformations.

Tetanus Vaccine. Tetanus booster vaccine is commonly given during pregnancy if the woman has not received a booster in ten years.

Travel Vaccines. Vaccines that are necessary or recommended for people traveling to regions of the world where virulent diseases are endemic are discussed later in this chapter.

Elevated Body Temperature

Significant elevations in body temperature (hyperthermia) during the first trimester increase the embryo's risk of birth defects—particularly neural tube defects—according to many experimental animal studies and epidemiological human studies. Although the developing nervous system appears to be particularly heat-sensitive, other organ systems may also be affected. Getting a high fever (101 degrees or more) and soaking in a hot tub are the main ways that first-trimester women undergo significant, prolonged increases in body temperature, as discussed below. Vigorous exercise, which can induce a short-term increase in body temperature, also is discussed.

The effect on human embryos of lowering the body temperature (hypothermia), as occurs during prolonged exposure to

PREGNANCY SICKNESS

cold, is unknown. Although some studies have found marked hypothermia to be teratogenic in animals, mild hypothermia is not thought to be harmful to human embryos.

Fever

When the body senses that it is being invaded by microorganisms, it induces fever in order to raise the temperature of the infecting organism's environment. This helps to kill many infecting microorganisms, while generally taking only a minor toll on the infected person. During early pregnancy, however, fever entails a bigger trade-off than usual: various studies have shown that it increases the risk of neurological defects in the embryo. The more severe and prolonged the fever, the bigger the risk is thought to be. A fever that rises to 101 degrees appears to roughly double the risk of neurological birth defects.

Does this mean that first-trimester women should lower fever with medication, such as acetaminophen, aspirin, or ibuprofen? (Neither acetaminophen nor aspirin appear to be teratogenic in humans; little information is yet available on ibuprofen's effects on embryos.) If a woman is not pregnant, it is usually better for her health not to artificially lower moderate fevers with aspirin or other fever-reducing medications. Fever occurs for a purpose, and people who lower their fevers with medication tend to prolong their illnesses. It's possible that when a first-trimester woman suppresses her fever she increases the likelihood of transmitting her infection to her embryo. So if the particular microorganism infecting her is a likely or possible teratogen—including cold and flu viruses—she probably should not lower her fever unless it becomes very high (for example, above 102 degrees). For fevers caused by microorganisms that do not appear to be ter-

Other First-Trimester Hazards to Embryos

atogenic, one solution may be to let the fever do its job unless the temperature climbs above 100 degrees, and then to take just enough fever-reducing medication (or to reduce fever by other means, such as cold baths) to keep the temperature from exceeding that threshold. In any case, a first-trimester woman whose temperature reaches 100 degrees should contact her OB/GYN and discuss the trade-offs of taking fever-reducing medication.

Ideally, a first-trimester woman should try to prevent fever by preventing illness, particularly around the time that the neural tube closes—from week 3 to week 4 after conception. This may be difficult for a woman with preschool children, especially if they attend day care, because she is likely to be exposed to the assortment of cold and flu viruses that children bring home.

Hot Tubs and Saunas

Soaking in a hot tub can raise body temperature considerably. "Hot tubbing" during the first trimester has been associated in several studies with an increased risk of birth defects—particularly neural tube defects—and some studies even report that hot tub use is a bigger risk factor for neural tube defects than fever is. The hotter the tub and the longer the woman soaks, the greater the increase in her body temperature and, presumably, the greater the risk to her embryo. Basking in a sauna for brief periods of time does not seem to pose clear-cut risks to the embryo (the evidence is ambiguous); but, to err on the side of caution, a woman in early pregnancy may want to refrain from visiting the sauna, at least until after her embryo's neural tube has closed. The window of risk from elevated body temperature has not yet been precisely determined. For example, it is not known whether fever, hot tub use, or sauna around the time of con-

PREGNANCY SICKNESS

ception or during the two weeks following it can be risky to the future embryo. (In men, however, significantly elevated body temperature, resulting from fever or hot tub use, may render them temporarily less fertile, since sperm are very heat-sensitive.) Although hot tubbing may provide a pleasurable, romantic prelude for making babies, it may not be ideal for the task.

Vigorous Exercise

Vigorous exercise can temporarily raise a person's body temperature, which is why many OB/GYNs and midwives advise first-trimester women who want to exercise to do so below their peak level of exertion and endurance. Some OB/GYNs even recommend the "talk test" to avoid overexertion: if the woman can't comfortably carry on a conversation while exercising she should reduce her exercise rate. The infants of athletic women who continue to exercise vigorously throughout the first trimester do not appear to have an increased rate of birth defects (runners who continue to race during early pregnancy, for example, have not been found to deliver a higher rate of malformed infants or to have a higher rate of miscarriage). However, since certain other forms of elevating the body temperature are proven risk factors for birth defects, vigorous exercise is considered a potential risk factor. Some OB/GYNs recommend that women who do not regularly exercise refrain from starting an exercise program until the second trimester, because for these women any such program would constitute vigorous exercise, although other OB/GYNs believe that a woman should be encouraged to improve her physical fitness anytime during pregnancy.

Considering the lives of our hunter-gatherer ancestors may help to shed light on the question of exercise during pregnancy. It is only relatively recently that any pregnant women have had the option of not exercising during pregnancy. Virtually all of our hunter-gatherer ancestors had to exercise throughout pregnancy in order to locate food and water, carry it back to camp, and travel with their nomadic group. However, from what we can infer about hunter-gatherer life, it is unlikely that hunter-gatherer women often engaged in sustained vigorous exercise—comparable, say, to running a 10km race. They were more likely to engage in slower-paced exercise, as would be required for hauling plant foods miles back to camp, or in short bursts of fast-paced exercise, as would be required for fleeing from an angry animal. Furthermore, first-trimester fatigue probably tended to prevent women from exercising at peak levels (it's even possible that this is one of the benefits of first-trimester fatigue). What this means for a pregnant woman in a modern industrialized society who is usually sedentary but wants to start an exercise program isn't clear. For a healthy, physically active first-trimester woman it probably means that *moderate* exercise is unlikely to harm embryos, but that vigorous exercise should be regarded with caution.

There are some precautions that a first-trimester woman can take to avoid overheating during exercise. If she swims, she can avoid swimming in very warm water. She can drink ample water before and during exercise to avoid dehydration and promote sweating, which functions to cool the body. She can wear clothing that is sufficiently lightweight that heat can be dissipated. She can avoid exercising in the sun on hot days. (Seasonal increases in outdoor temperature are not generally believed to influence the rate of birth defects.) If pregnancy complications arise—such as pain or vaginal bleeding—the woman should refrain from exercising until she discusses the problem with her OB/GYN.

Pressure Changes

Commercial Flying. The moderate decreases in air pressure experienced while flying in commercial aircraft—whose cabins are pressurized at levels simulating 5,000 to 8,000 feet above sea level—do not appear to be harmful to embryos. Flying at high altitudes in unpressurized cabins, however, may be risky.

High-Altitude Trekking. Dramatic decreases in air pressure are presumed to be risky to embryos, because they sharply decrease the supply of oxygen to embryonic tissues, but data are too sparse to be conclusive. The current consensus seems to be that first-trimester women should not trek to high altitudes—for example, above 14,000 feet elevation—and the cautious first-trimester woman may want to avoid overnight stays above 10,000 feet if she's not acclimated to such elevations.

Scuba Diving. Dramatic increases in external pressure, such as those experienced during scuba diving, are believed to be dangerous to embryos. The pressure during diving, which results from the weight of water, increases with depth. Inside the body, the various gasses in the lungs, airways, and arteries become compressed. Just how this compression affects the developing tissues of an embryo is not known, but one preliminary study showed that women divers who dove during the first trimester had a much higher rate of infants with malformations than did divers who refrained from diving during the first trimester. The position currently taken by the Undersea Medical Society is that pregnant women—especially first-trimester women—should not dive. If a woman diver is trying to conceive, she should try to ascertain whether she's pregnant before deciding whether or not to go on a dive. If she feels that she must dive during pregnancy (for professional or other reasons), she should limit, as much as possible, the depth, duration, and frequency of her dives.

Stress

Stress comes in many forms, names, and descriptions, including anxiety, emotional disequilibrium, fear, resentment, anger, obsession, worry, experiencing a major life event or crisis, feeling "trapped," feeling bombarded by noise, light, or other stimuli, feeling that events are out of one's control, feeling isolated or alienated, feeling a sense of loss, and feeling a lack of social support. Some stress is part of everyone's life; but inordinate amounts of stress take a toll on a person's health—and apparently on the embryo's health as well. The body is adapted to respond to different types of acute (i.e., short-term) stress in specific ways, such as by releasing stress hormones, which have specific effects on different physiological systems. Like other adaptive responses, stress responses entail costs, which is why chronic or severe stress can have detrimental effects on the body, including increasing susceptibility to certain diseases. High levels of stress also take a toll on reproduction: they are associated with increased rates of infertility, miscarriage, premature birth (which in many cases really is late miscarriage), and birth defects.

The link between stress and birth defects is still obscure, in part because stress has so many different sources, encompasses so many different states of mind, characterizes so many different life events, and tends to be vaguely defined. Most of the studies investigating stress and reproduction have focused on birthweight and premature birth rather than on birth defects, but several studies in humans have shown what appears to be a causal connection between birth defects and high levels of stress

PREGNANCY SICKNESS

that occur near the time of conception or during early pregnancy, and many studies in animals have shown that high levels of stress—such as excessive noise, lights, restraints, or handling— increase the rate of malformation. The reason for this connection isn't known, but it's possible that high levels of stress hormones harm embryos directly, or else harm them indirectly by interfering with other hormones or nutrients essential for proper development. One of the main types of stress that appears to be detrimental to the health of embryos is social stress—that is, stress that occurs when the woman senses conflict with, or inadequate support from, her partner, parents, siblings, close friends, or in-laws. It's possible that her body interprets high levels of social stress as a cue that her current situation is unfavorable for having a baby, and it therefore does not invest the optimal level of nutrients in that particular embryo, instead risking birth defects.

What can a first-trimester woman or a woman planning to conceive do about stress? Her life may be filled with stresses that she can't feasibly eliminate. For example, she may have a high-powered job that she finds fulfilling and that enables her family to have a high standard of living but that is also stressful. Or she may be experiencing a family trauma over which she has no control. Although a woman may not be able to eliminate the sources of stress in her life, she may be able to change—at least slightly— the way that she reacts to some stressful events. Self-help books or counselors can provide stress-reducing techniques that a pregnant woman may find useful. For example, there are techniques for learning how to stop obsessing about relatively inconsequential things, such as by yelling "stop!" out loud when one catches oneself obsessing. There are also various techniques for decreasing anxiety, some of which employ music, meditation, or massage. Some people relieve stress by actively focusing on the beautiful details in life, such as the patterns of light and color on a lake or ocean at sunset. Some people come to realize that certain stresses are extraneous and can be reduced or eliminated—for example, by their learning to say no more often. And some people counter stress simply by doing more things that make them feel joyful.

Traveling

Traveling to regions of the world where "exotic" diseases are endemic, such as to many parts of Africa and South America, is especially risky to embryos. Some of these diseases are life-threatening to the embryo or fetus, some are suspected of being teratogenic, and some induce high fevers, a risk factor for birth defects. Being stranded in a country without good medical care is in itself risky for a first-trimester woman and her embryo.

Travel Shots. Some countries strongly recommend or even require proof of immunizations against cholera, yellow fever, typhoid, and hepatitis. But these immunizations may be risky for embryos because they can induce fever; in addition, yellow fever vaccine is a live-virus vaccine. A first-trimester woman traveling to such countries needs to analyze the trade-offs between risking getting the immunizations and risking getting the diseases: for example, does her trip entail merely a brief stay indoors in an urban area or long-term fieldwork in remote areas dense with mosquitoes?

Booster vaccines for tetanus appear to be safe during pregnancy, so if a pregnant woman who is planning to travel to developing countries is due for a booster she should discuss getting one with her OB/GYN.

PREGNANCY SICKNESS

Malaria prophylaxis is very important when traveling to certain regions of the world, but the drugs taken to prevent malaria are not necessarily safe during early pregnancy. Chloroquine is generally thought to be the safest antimalarial drug during pregnancy, but the malarial parasites in many regions of the world are resistant to it, and it may carry a small risk of birth defects.

Severe Diarrhea. Traveler's diarrhea is a common ailment. The function of diarrhea is to rapidly expel harmful levels of

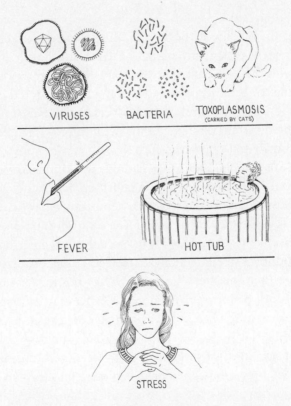

VIRUSES BACTERIA TOXOPLASMOSIS
(CARRIED BY CATS)

FEVER HOT TUB

STRESS

There are also nondietary risks to the embryo.

dietary toxins, bacterial toxins, and parasites from the gastrointestinal tract. But if diarrhea becomes severe, it can itself be dangerous, because it leads to dehydration and an imbalance of electrolytes. A first-trimester traveler should ask her OB/GYN about the safest effective antidiarrheal agent to pack in case of severe diarrhea. If the woman will be spending considerable time in remote areas, she may want to bring along hydration packets (solutions of water, glucose, and electrolytes) to counter a potential bout of severe diarrhea.

Drinking Water. Precautions for traveling in certain foreign countries include not drinking water fresh from the tap. The "drinking" water in some developing countries can transmit serious diseases. This situation exists when the source of drinking water is not sufficiently separate from the sewage, and microorganisms from feces contaminate the drinking water, or when the drinking water is not properly treated with chemicals to kill the microorganisms that normally inhabit it at its source. The options for the traveler are boiling the water, chemically treating it, drinking only bottled water, or using a good antimicrobial water purifier (one that has a microfilter to remove parasitic cysts and that releases iodine to kill bacteria and viruses). Other measures to avoid consuming contaminated water include peeling or cooking fruits and vegetables (since they may have been washed in contaminated water), not putting ice in drinks, not using eating utensils and glasses washed with contaminated water (paper utensils are a safe option), and washing one's hands in chemically treated water before using them to eat with or to prepare food. Careful hygiene is extremely important for protecting the embryo from infectious diseases.

Mosquito/Insect Repellent. Mosquitos (as well as tse-tse flies and certain other insects) are vectors of some of the worst diseases that plague humans, particularly in many developing countries. Some mosquito-borne diseases, such as malaria, tend to be more severe in pregnant women than in nonpregnant people. Therefore, a pregnant woman traveling to mosquito-infested areas needs to take special precautions against being bitten. Some mosquito repellents that are rubbed on the skin may be absorbed through the skin, and it's not known whether the chemicals in these repellents are harmful to embryos. (There's no evidence that they are harmful in moderate doses, but the relevant studies to detect an effect have not been done.) A first-trimester woman can employ other means to avoid getting bitten, however, such as wearing long-sleeved shirts, pants, high socks, and covered shoes and using mosquito netting. If the mosquito infestation is high and these methods are unlikely to be completely effective, the woman may want to risk using repellent rather than risk getting a mosquito-borne disease. She can spray the repellent on the outside of her clothing rather than on her skin; if she puts repellent on her skin she should probably use a low-dose preparation and apply it sparingly.

Flying. Flying in commercial aircraft probably increases the risk of acquiring colds and other infectious respiratory diseases, since air is recirculated throughout the cabin, and some passengers may be sneezing and exhaling cold, flu, or other viruses. Otherwise, flying does not appear to be harmful to embryos, as discussed earlier.

Venom and Systemic Allergic Reactions to Them. One of the risks of traveling in wilderness areas is getting a venomous bite or sting. It is not known if venoms or the antidotes to venoms are teratogenic in humans. But if the venomous bite or sting causes the pregnant woman to go into anaphylactic shock, her embryo or fetus may be irreparably harmed, even if the woman recovers fully through an injection of epinephrine or other drug. Information on the effects of transitory anaphylactic shock on embryos and fetuses is sparse, but it appears that shock abruptly deprives the placenta of an adequate supply of oxygen.

Sunburn and Sunscreens. Many vacation destinations and activities can bring sunburn. Although it's extremely unlikely that a mild sunburn on a first-trimester woman would harm her embryo, it's possible that a severe sunburn could, by inducing fever. Sunscreens have not been widely investigated for their effects on embryos, but they appear to be poorly absorbed through the mother's skin, and they are unlikely to pose much risk to embryos. Since it is not known for sure whether sunscreens are safe for embryos, a first-trimester woman may want to avoid lengthy sun exposure rather than use a lot of sunscreen. If she uses sunscreen, she may want to choose one with a low rather than a high SPF factor—that is, one with a low concentration of the active chemical—and to apply it sparingly.

Sexual Intercourse and Spermicides

Sexual Intercourse. Sexual intercourse during the first trimester does not appear to harm embryos unless the woman's partner has a sexually transmitted disease that he transmits to her and the embryo. If the partner has a sexually transmitted disease that she does not, she should postpone having sex with him until his infection is completely cured; in the case of a partner with genital herpes, which is permanent, condoms should be used throughout the pregnancy.

During the third trimester, however, sexual intercourse without condoms appears to be risky even when the partner does not have a sexually transmitted disease. During most of pregnancy, sperm and the bacteria that attach to them do not reach the uterus because mucus in the cervix forms a dense barrier. During the third trimester, however, this cervical mucous "plug" thins in some women, enabling sperm-borne bacteria to reach the uterus and infect the placenta, which can lead to an infected fetus and premature birth.

Spermicides. If a woman finds out that she is pregnant after having used vaginal spermicides around the time of conception or during early pregnancy, should she worry? The answer is no. Altogether, the many studies on the effects of spermicides on embryos indicate that spermicides (the main one currently in use in the United States is nonoxynol) do not measurably increase the risk of birth defects or miscarriage, even if a woman uses spermicide when she's already pregnant. To err on the side of caution, however, a pregnant woman may want to avoid using lubricants that contain spermicide or other active chemicals.

Birth Control Pills. Recent studies indicate that the embryos of women who get pregnant while on "the pill" do not appear to be at increased risk for birth defects. Earlier studies had indicated slight risks for a variety of birth defects. To be cautious, a woman taking birth control pills who discovers that she's pregnant should immediately stop taking the pills.

Personal Care Products

Personal care products, such as cosmetics, hair spray, and hair dye, are not known to cause human birth defects, but information is sparse regarding the effects of these types of products on human embryos. Some of these products are likely to be absorbed through the skin, which means that at least trace amounts of their chemicals could circulate to the placenta. There have been almost no studies on the effects of personal care products on human or animal embryos. In erring on the side of caution during the first trimester, therefore, it is prudent to minimize use of products, such as hair dyes, that may contain particularly strong chemicals. Personal care products that are scented, such as perfumes and most hair sprays, should be avoided, for reasons discussed in Chapter 6.

Radiation

Diagnostic Radiation

The malformation risk to the embryo or fetus from a single exposure to diagnostic radiation, such as a chest or dental X ray, is extremely small (as is the later risk of childhood leukemia). To err on the side of caution, however, diagnostic radiation should be minimized during pregnancy, particularly during the first sixteen weeks. In other words, it should be postponed until the third trimester or after pregnancy unless doing so would compromise the woman's health. Almost all diagnostic radiation procedures involve low doses of radiation—usually well under 5 "rads," and the dose of radiation absorbed by the embryo or fetus generally is much lower than that absorbed by its mother, depending on what part of her body was irradiated and whether her uterus was shielded. Researchers in the field of radiation teratogenesis have found that human embryos and fetuses can absorb up to 5 rads total without showing a detectable increase in risk of malformations. Above 20 rads, however, the embryo or fetus has a measurable risk of being harmed.

High doses of radiation, such as are given in many cancer treatments, are very dangerous for embryos and fetuses. Much of what we know about the effects of massive doses of radiation come from studies of the infants of survivors of the World War II atomic bomb explosions in Hiroshima and Nagasaki who were pregnant at the time. Fetuses that absorbed more than an estimated 50 rads had a greatly increased risk of mental retardation and microcephaly (small brains) if they were between weeks eight and sixteen of development (the younger embryos that survived did not appear to be affected). At this stage of fetal development the brain can be greatly harmed by high doses of radiation, apparently because neurons that are proliferating rapidly to form the cerebral cortex are killed. Mental retardation and microcephaly are the primary malformations suffered by human fetuses that are exposed to high doses of radiation.

Misguided hysteria over radiation exposures, however, has led to thousands of unnecessary abortions. The gap between the perception of risk and the actual risk of radiation is sometimes huge—both among many pregnant women and some of the people who counsel them. It is estimated that in Greece anxiety over the possible teratogenic effects of the Chernobyl nuclear fallout led about 2,500 pregnant women (who wanted to be pregnant) to abort their fetuses, even though the increased risk of malformation there is thought to have been virtually nil. This pattern of fear and abortion immediately following the Chernobyl disaster was prevalent throughout Western Europe. Studies of infants in Norway who were embryos or fetuses at the time of the disaster did not show any increase in the overall rate of malformations.

Everyone is exposed to low levels of natural radiation all the time—the main source being the sun. Our cells have adaptations to cope with the damage induced by low levels of radiation: when radiation rips our DNA, for example, our DNA-repair enzymes go to work to repair the damage. But cells can take only so much damage before irreparable harm (such as cell death) is inflicted.

If a woman who is advised to get X rays or other forms of diagnostic radiation is pregnant or may be pregnant, she needs to inform her physician and the radiation technician. If, for health reasons, diagnostic radiation should not be postponed, she should make sure that her uterus receives as much shielding as the procedure allows. She should also ask what the dose of radiation is to her and to her embryo or fetus. If she is told that the radiation exposure she receives will probably harm her embryo or fetus and that she should consider an abortion, she should call a teratogen information service (see Appendix B) or someone very knowledgeable about radiation teratogenesis to find out what risk, if any, the exposure actually entails.

Other Forms of Radiation

Video Display Terminals (VDTs). Working with VDTs (computer screens) on a regular basis (twenty or more hours per week) does not appear to increase the risk of birth defects. (Information on the risk of miscarriage, however, among women exposed for more than twenty hours per week is ambiguous.)

Power Lines. Women living near power lines may be worried about the effect of electromagnetic radiation on their embryos. If there is a risk to embryos, it has yet to be detected, and it probably is very small.

Airport Magnetometers. The magnetometers at airport security stations are extremely unlikely to harm embryos.

Occupational Sources of Radiation. Women who work with sources of radiation should take precautions to avoid excess exposures and should follow the occupational health guidelines for pregnant women.

Miscellaneous Medical Procedures

Surgery. According to preliminary studies, having surgery—even in a region of the body remote from the uterus—may increase the risk of neural tube defects if it occurs during the week that the neural tube closes. It is not known whether this apparent association is causal or coincidental, or, if causal, whether the factor responsible is simply the stress of having surgery. Minor dental surgery (such as getting a tooth filled) was not included in these studies and is extremely unlikely to be a risk factor for birth defects (unless, perhaps, the woman is hysterical about visits to the dentist).

Allergy Shots. Immunotherapy (allergy shots) in pregnant women appears to be safe for embryos, as long as the doses administered are low enough that they do not precipitate anaphylactic shock.

Chapter Twelve

Beyond the First Trimester

BY THE END of the first trimester, a woman who has been experiencing weeks of nausea and aversions and is greatly anticipating the end of it may feel a bit like the kid in the car who keeps asking, "Are we there yet?" Although a tiny percentage of women are unfortunate enough to experience pregnancy sickness throughout their entire pregnancies, for the vast majority of women pregnancy sickness resolves within the first few weeks of the second trimester. Nausea and aversions wane, and foods begin to smell and taste good again. Things that could endanger the baby-to-be are no longer lurking everywhere.

The disappearance of pregnancy sickness, however, does not mean that the fetus is completely out of danger. As discussed in Chapter 10, during the second and third trimesters exposure to toxic substances won't cause major malformations, such as missing limbs, but certain substances can cause minor defects (for example, tetracycline can cause severe staining of the teeth), brain damage (high doses of mercury, radiation, or alcohol can lead to mental retardation), or problems during delivery (aspirin increases the fetus's risk of cerebral hemorrhage during birth). As discussed in Chapter 11, certain microorganisms also can wreak havoc during the second and third trimesters. In addition, abnormalities of the amniotic sac can deform the fetus. Furthermore, serious complications can arise during delivery: disease microorganisms in the mother's birth canal can be transmitted to the baby, and certain types of birth trauma (such as the cord wrapped around the baby's neck) can cause permanent damage. In general, however, the fetus is relatively safe if it emerges from the first trimester in good health.

Pregnancy Sickness Isn't Fail-Safe

Pregnancy sickness is protective but not fail-safe. A woman who obeys all the warnings of pregnancy sickness and abstains from alcohol, cigarettes, and drugs can still give birth to an infant with a major defect. Many types of chromosomal or other genetic defects in the egg or sperm doom the embryo to malformations. Embryos with genetic defects frequently are aborted spontaneously—often before the woman is even aware that she's pregnant. In fact, at least half of all fertilized eggs and early-stage embryos never make it to the fetal stage because they are aborted, and most of the spontaneously aborted embryos that have been analyzed have detectable chromosomal abnormalities.

"Advanced" age of the mother is a risk factor for various chromosomal abnormalities, such as Down syndrome (which is characterized by an extra twenty-first chromosome). The risk to a pregnant woman that her infant will have Down syndrome is, at age 20, about 1 in 1,400; at age 30, about 1 in 700; at age 35, about 1 in 350; at age 40, about 1 in 100; and at age 45, about 1 in 25. There probably are several reasons why the risk of chromosomal abnormalities in embryos increases as a woman's age increases. One appears to be that a woman's reproductive system becomes less discriminating with age. Although older women are more prone than younger women to miscarry, younger women spontaneously abort a higher percentage of their genetically flawed embryos. It has been suggested that a woman's reproductive system becomes less selective with age because it senses that "time is running out." With fewer reproductive years left, it relaxes its "quality control" mechanisms, which detect defective embryos, rather than risk aborting a possibly viable, though less than "perfect," embryo. Thus, more embryos with very serious genetic disorders (that is, disorders that would be incompatible with life outside the womb in a natural environment) escape detection and are carried to term.

Prenatal Testing

Many women go through pregnancy with an undercurrent of anxiety about birth defects. This anxiety can be partly allayed in the first trimester by following the warnings of pregnancy sickness to help prevent birth defects from occurring, and in the second trimester by using modern technology to help detect birth defects that may have occurred. The purpose of diagnosing defects in the fetus is twofold: (1) to enable the woman to decide whether she wants to continue a pregnancy involving a fetus with a particular type of defect; and (2) to prepare the woman and her OB/GYN to have her baby operated on or otherwise treated for a defect immediately after birth (for some defects, fetuses even can be operated on in utero).

Some pregnant women try to shrug off the possibility of birth defects by convincing themselves that nothing bad could happen to their embryos. But it could. No woman is invincible and no embryo is invincible. I think that it's important for a pregnant woman to be realistic about the possibility of birth defects so that she is sufficiently well informed to make the best possible decisions. Even if a pregnant woman is only in her twenties, the risk that her infant will have a major birth defect is about 2 percent, and the risk that it will have a minor birth defect is another several percent. If a woman is willing to accept her baby no matter what birth defects it may turn out to have, however, then the methods of prenatal testing that are risky to her fetus (some methods are risky; others are not) probably are not options that she will want to choose.

There are several methods of prenatal testing/screening/diagnosis. The four main ones are ultrasound, maternal serum screening, chorionic villus sampling, and amniocentesis. Some types of defects can be detected prenatally only by analyzing the genes, via chorionic villus sampling or amniocentesis. Most defects, however, cannot be detected via genetic testing, either because they are not of genetic origin or because current technologies are not advanced enough to detect them, but some of the other defects can be visualized by looking at an image of the fetus, via ultrasound. Ultrasound can reveal many defects that arise during development as well as some defects of genetic origin. Women who do not opt for amniocentesis often get a type of blood test—maternal serum screening—that screens for neural tube defects and that can detect some cases of Down syndrome (see below). Prenatal testing isn't fail-safe, but when both a thorough ultrasound examination and genetic testing are performed such screening can ensure that most major defects are detected.

Ultrasound Scanning/Imaging

Ultrasound scanning of the pregnant uterus produces an image (a sonogram) of the embryo or fetus, enabling the OB/GYN or other ultrasound diagnostician to assess the health of the

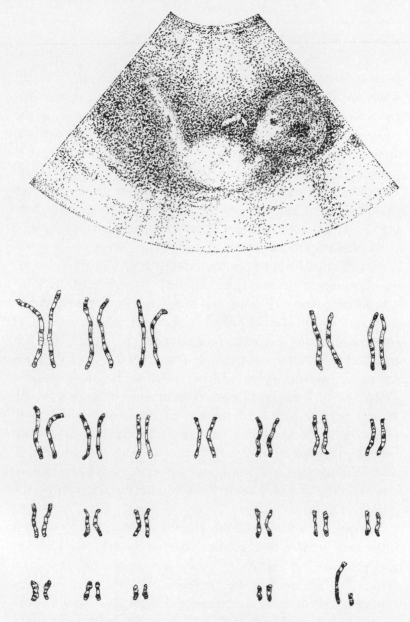

Prenatal testing enables one to visualize fetal structures and chromosomes and thereby to detect many developmental and genetic defects.

fetus and to detect various abnormalities. High-frequency sound waves are directed at the part of the fetus to be imaged, and then the returning echoes, which vary according to the density of the tissues and their distance from the source of the sound waves, are analyzed. The echoes are translated on a computer screen into images of light and dark, to be interpreted by the diagnostician. Ultrasound performed during early pregnancy usually involves inserting a transducer mounted on a probe into the vagina; during the second and third trimesters it usually involves moving a transducer over the abdomen.

An ultrasound may be performed early in pregnancy for a variety of reasons: to make sure that the embryo is alive; to check for ectopic pregnancy; to count the number of embryos; to determine the cause of bleeding or pain; or to precisely locate an IUD (if the woman has become pregnant while using one). Second-trimester ultrasounds are performed in order to survey the fetus for major malformations, evaluate placental health, assess the growth of the fetus, and measure the amount of amniotic fluid. Most types of malformations are visualized with ultrasound more readily during the second than the first trimester, both because the fetus is much larger than the embryo and because any malformations it is destined to have are more likely to have developed by the middle of the second trimester than by the middle of the first.

Ultrasound cannot explicitly test for genetic disorders, but it often detects them by recording some of the structural defects they produce. Defects are detected in sonograms of embryos and fetuses by looking for: the presence of abnormal structures; the absence of normal structures; abnormal sizes, shapes, contours, or proportions of normal structures; abnormal locations of normal structures; and abnormal motions of the fetus. Well over a hundred different defects can be identified by ultrasound; however, the detection of these defects is not guaranteed. Sonograms are not like crisp, clear photographs, and many subtle structural abnormalities—such as those associated with Down syndrome—are not always easily visualized with ultrasound, even by a person skilled in interpreting sonograms. Furthermore, ultrasound cannot detect defects like deafness or mental retardation, which in some cases are caused by genetic abnormalities that can be detected by amniocentesis.

Ultrasound is an extremely valuable tool for diagnosing defects, but a person inexperienced in interpreting sonograms can fail to notice defects that are obvious to a trained eye, or can mistake a normal part of the fetal anatomy for an abnormal part. Obtaining a useful sonogram requires, for starters, a good ultrasound scanner. Some OB/GYNs apparently use scanners so rudimentary that the resulting sonogram barely reveals the number of limbs, much less defects of the spine, heart, or face. Interpreting a sonogram of a fetus requires considerable skill, knowledge, and experience; it entails deciding what to image and how to image it, as well as knowing what to look for.

Certain women undergoing ultrasound may want to have their sonograms analyzed by a dysmorphologist, a person specially trained to detect defects in fetuses. Such women include those who have already had one fetus or infant with birth defects, those with a family history of birth defects, and those exposed during pregnancy to teratogenic drugs or microorganisms.

Many women who opt for invasive genetic testing (described below) also opt for a thorough ultrasound examination. (The ultrasound that is performed just prior to and during amniocentesis and chorionic villus sampling is not thorough enough to detect most defects; its purpose is to locate the fetus and placenta, make sure the fetus is alive, and guide the needle safely to the placental tissue or the amniotic fluid.) One of the main advantages of ultrasound over the current methods of genetic testing is that it's noninvasive. Ultrasound does not place the fetus at risk for miscarriage, and follow-up studies on tens of thousands of infants and children exposed in utero to ultrasound have found no adverse effects. Another advantage of ultrasound is that the fetus can be imaged directly, which means that many defects that arise during development rather than from abnormal genes can be visualized.

Many OB/GYNs recommend routine ultrasound for all pregnant women, and I think that this is a very good idea, as long as the sonogram is interpreted by someone proficient in detecting fetal abnormalities. Some OB/GYNs recommend that women get their first ultrasound as early as week 6 or 7 after conception in order to rule out ectopic pregnancies and to assess placental health, but others recommend delaying ultrasound in apparently uncomplicated pregnancies until after the embryonic period because of the theoretical risk to the embryo from the heat generated by high-frequency sound waves. There is not universal agreement among OB/GYNs on whether or not to perform ultrasound scans on all pregnant women, or even on what a routine ultrasound examination should include. For example, some OB/GYNs, but not others, advocate a detailed scan of the heart in all fetuses, because heart defects are among the most common types of birth defects, are often associated with other malformations, and carry a high risk of infant death. A pregnant woman anticipating an ultrasound exam should find out in advance what her particular exam will and will not be able to reveal in order to determine if that type of exam is thorough enough for her needs.

Maternal Serum Screening or AFP Test

Women who do not want to have a procedure as invasive to the fetus as genetic testing are often advised to get a blood test (often known as maternal serum screening) that measures their levels of alpha-fetoprotein (AFP), a protein produced by the fetus and present at low levels in the pregnant woman's blood. Unusually high levels of AFP indicate that the fetus may have neural tube defects, because the proteins leak out of the open neural tube into the amniotic fluid and then across the placenta into the woman's bloodstream. Maternal serum screening sometimes also includes a measurement of the woman's levels of the hormones human chorionic gonadotropin (HCG) and estriol, which the placenta produces. Unusually low levels of AFP, high levels of HCG, and low levels of estriol indicate that the fetus may have Down syndrome. Abnormal values for these three substances sometimes indicate other chromosomal abnormalities as well.

A major drawback of maternal serum screening is that it produces a huge number of "false-positives"—that is, test results indicating that the fetus may have a defect when in fact it doesn't. For every real case of spina bifida or other neural tube defect, there are between ten and fifty false-positives. There is also a high rate of false-positives for each actual case of Down syndrome. If the maternal serum screening test is positive, indicating the possibility of a defect, the woman is usually advised to get a follow-up amniocentesis or, at least, a detailed ultrasound. (Detailed ultrasound exams now are highly accurate in visualizing neural tube defects, so a woman whose serum tests indicate the possibility of a neural tube defect and who does not want to risk amniocentesis can feel fairly confident in a subsequent evaluation by detailed ultrasound.) Women whose serum screening tests come back positive often are extremely upset and anxious, and even if a subsequent amniocentesis or ultrasound indicates that the fetus is normal, a shadow may be cast over the rest of the pregnancy.

Another major drawback of maternal serum screening is its late date. For maximal accuracy, the test usually is performed between weeks 15 and 18. But if the results indicate a possible defect, and the woman has to wait for confirmation from a follow-up amniocentesis, she could be well into her second trimester before she is confronted with the decision of whether or not to continue the pregnancy.

A third major drawback of maternal serum screening is that it fails to detect about 10 percent of the cases of neural tube defects and a sizable percentage of the cases of Down syndrome (if only AFP is measured, most cases of Down syndrome are not detected; whereas if HCG and estriol are measured as well, more than half of the cases of Down syndrome are detected). Thus, a woman should not view maternal serum screening as a very reliable method of detecting defects.

Genetic Testing: Amniocentesis and Chorionic Villus Sampling

Current methods of genetic testing of the fetus are invasive, because they entail obtaining fetal cells from the placenta (in chorionic villus sampling) or the amniotic fluid (in amniocentesis). Noninvasive ways to obtain fetal cells for genetic analysis are being investigated. Some fetal blood cells and placental cells break off and enter the woman's bloodstream, but methods to extract and isolate sufficient numbers of them to make genetic analysis from a standard blood sample possible have not yet been developed.

It is standard practice in the United States for OB/GYNs to offer genetic testing to all pregnant women over the age of thirty-five, although younger women can request testing as well (but insurance companies often do not cover the cost for younger women). Thirty-five was chosen as the cutoff because at this age the risk of chromosomal abnormalities approximately equals the minimal risk of miscarriage due to genetic testing—about 1 in 200. There is no sudden, precipitous increase in the risk of having a fetus with defects at age thirty-five; a thirty-four-year-old woman has almost the same risk as a thirty-six-year-old.

Twin fetuses also can be genetically tested via amniocentesis or chorionic villus sampling. (Some studies have indicated that twin fetuses are at above-average risk for chromosomal abnormalities.)

Amniocentesis. Standard amniocentesis usually is performed between fifteen and eighteen weeks after conception. Early amniocentesis, a relatively new alternative, is performed between eleven and fourteen weeks after conception. Amniocentesis entails inserting a slender hollow needle (guided by ultrasound) through the woman's abdomen and into the amniotic fluid, attaching a syringe to the needle, and drawing out some amniotic fluid. Cells from the fluid are then cultured in the laboratory and analyzed for chromosomal abnormalities as well as for specific genetic defects that run in the woman's family or that are common in her ethnic group. In addition, the amniotic fluid is analyzed for levels of AFP, because an abnormally high level indicates a neural tube defect. In some cases in which a woman acquired an infection during pregnancy that is harmful to fetuses, the amniotic fluid also is checked for evidence of the infection to help ascertain whether or not it was transmitted to the fetus.

In a given woman, only a small subset of the hundreds of different genetic disorders that amniocentesis is able to test for actually is tested, because of the time and expense that would be required to test for each genetic disorder and because of the limited number of viable fetal cells in the amniotic fluid sample. For example, a fetus whose parents have ethnic backgrounds that render them extremely unlikely to be carriers of Tay-Sachs will not be genetically tested for the disease, but occasionally Tay-Sachs infants are born to very low-risk parents.

The main advantage of amniocentesis over a routine ultrasound in detecting genetic defects is the extremely high degree of accuracy of the results. But in very rare instances, the amniotic fluid sample is contaminated by so many of the mother's cells that her cells, rather than the fetus's, end up being genetically analyzed. Early amniocentesis is considered to be almost as accurate as standard amniocentesis; limitations in its accuracy are usually due to the paucity of fetal cells available for testing in the sample of amniotic fluid that can be safely withdrawn at an early stage of gestation. Very early amniocentesis (before the end of week 11), however, cannot be depended upon to detect neural tube defects because at that stage of development the AFP levels in amniotic fluid appear to be too variable.

One of the main drawbacks of amniocentesis is its risk to the fetus. Roughly 0.5–1.0 percent of fetuses miscarry because of the procedure (after taking into account the normal background rate of miscarriage for that stage of pregnancy). Occasionally, amniocentesis inflicts other types of harm to the fetus: it can introduce an infection; the needle can prick the fetus's brain, eye, or other

Beyond the First Trimester

bodily part (with continuous ultrasound guidance of the needle, this hazard has become increasingly rare); or it can rupture the fetal membranes, leading to leakage of amniotic fluid and a greater chance of infection.

The other main drawback of amniocentesis is the lateness of its results. Since standard amniocentesis usually is not performed until at least fourteen weeks after conception, and it takes about two weeks to get the results, a woman who learns that her fetus has defects is well into her second trimester when she has to decide whether or not to continue the pregnancy. A second-trimester abortion is medically much riskier than a first-trimester one because of the size of the fetus. For many women it is emotionally more traumatic as well, because fetal movements can often be felt by this time. And for some women, it may be less acceptable morally, because of the more advanced development of the fetus. Furthermore, even if test results indicate a healthy fetus, the woman is likely to have experienced months of anxiety, and she may have been wary of bonding with her baby-to-be until she received the assurance of "good" test results.

Chorionic Villus Sampling (CVS). CVS usually is performed between weeks 10 and 12. It entails directing a slender needle (guided by ultrasound) to the placenta through the cervix (in the case of "transcervical CVS") or through the abdomen (in the case of "transabdominal CVS"), and then, with a syringe, suctioning out pieces of the chorionic villi, which are little sprout-like protrusions of the placenta that attach to the uterus. The placental cells are then genetically analyzed.

The main advantage of CVS over amniocentesis is that the results—which are available about one week after the procedure—are obtained in the first trimester rather than the second, making possible a first-trimester abortion.

PREGNANCY SICKNESS

The main drawback of CVS is its risk to the fetus. Roughly 1.5–2.0 percent of fetuses miscarry because of the procedure (after taking into account the normal background rate of miscarriage for that stage of pregnancy), a rate 1 percent higher than that for amniocentesis. Some, but not all, studies show a much higher risk of miscarriage after transcervical than transabdominal CVS. (Bleeding and spotting are much more common following transcervical than transabdominal CVS, but cramping is much more common following transabdominal CVS.) Some studies also have reported that CVS—particularly if performed before the end of week 10 after conception—is associated with an increased risk of certain otherwise rare birth defects; it has been suggested that such defects may occur when the CVS technique is so vigorous that the vascular system supplying the fetal circulation is badly disturbed. Most studies, however, indicate that CVS performed after ten weeks is very unlikely to cause birth defects, and CVS has become much safer in recent years as health care professionals gained experience in performing it.

Another drawback of CVS is that it cannot detect neural tube defects, as amniocentesis can. Therefore, women who have CVS performed need to have their AFP levels measured via maternal serum screening at about week 16 if they want to screen for neural tube defects; if that test indicates a possible defect, they then need a follow-up amniocentesis or detailed ultrasound.

Yet another drawback of CVS is the relatively high rate (1 percent) of false-positives for "mosaicism." When embryonic cells divide and the chromosome pairs don't disassociate correctly—resulting in chromosomally different cell lines in the same embryo—the defect is known as mosaicism. Mosaicism is much more common in placental cells, where it is not particularly harmful, than in cells of the embryo itself, where it is harmful. Therefore, when placental cells are genetically analyzed by CVS and found to be mosaic, a follow-up amniocentesis is needed to determine whether the embryo is mosaic as well.

Other Invasive Tests. Various tests that are more invasive than amniocentesis and CVS sometimes are performed to screen for certain rare hereditary diseases that amniocentesis and CVS cannot diagnose accurately. These tests include fetal blood sampling, fetal skin sampling, fetal liver biopsy, and fetal muscle biopsy. The rates of miscarriage and fetal infection from these tests are assumed to be much higher than those for amniocentesis or CVS.

Summary of Considerations in Prenatal Testing

A woman deciding whether to get prenatal testing or which types to get should consider the following things: (1) The risk that her baby will have birth defects, based on her family (genetic) history, her age, her ethnic background, and her exposure during pregnancy to known teratogens, such as certain medications or viruses; (2) the risk of miscarriage that a given test entails; (3) the ease with which she gets pregnant and the number of reproductive years she has left (that is, if she risks miscarriage because of invasive prenatal testing, how good is her chance of getting pregnant again soon); (4) how she feels about giving birth to a baby with defects; (5) how she feels about aborting a fetus with particular types of defects—that is, for which type(s) of defects, if any, would she abort a fetus (women who would not abort a fetus no matter how serious its defects probably would not want to risk invasive testing), and at which stage of pregnancy would she be willing to abort (for example, some religions permit first-trimester, but not second-trimester, abortions).

Dating the Pregnancy

It is important for a pregnant woman and her OB/GYN to know precisely when her pregnancy began (give or take a few days) in order to know the stage of development of the embryo or fetus. This way, the woman knows when to plan for prenatal testing and also how vulnerable her embryo or fetus is to teratogens at any given time. If an OB/GYN or other pregnancy consultant specifies the age of the embryo as, say, "six weeks gestation," it's important to ask whether that age was measured from the first day of the last menstrual period or from the approximate day of conception. Six weeks "menstrual age" is really only a four-week-old embryo. As discussed in Chapter 1, this book dates pregnancy from conception.

Many women who have just become pregnant are fooled by "implantation bleeding" into thinking that they're menstruating rather than pregnant. When an embryo implants in the uterus—beginning roughly a week after conception—the uterus bleeds from the site of implantation for several days (this occurs in monkeys and apes as well). Sometimes this bleeding is overt—that is, there is a sufficient quantity of blood that some reaches the vagina instead of being resorbed by the uterus or cervix. (Implantation bleeding and menstrual bleeding probably have similar functions: to clear the uterus for an embryo by eradicating bacteria that have been transported there by sperm since the end of the last menstrual period.) Many women who are one to three weeks pregnant simply assume they're having a menstrual period, and, therefore, when they later find out they're pregnant, their estimate of the date of conception is at least three weeks off. In order to date the pregnancy accurately, it's important to distinguish between menstrual and implantation bleeding; if a woman doesn't know when she got pregnant, an ultrasound scan usually can date the pregnancy accurately.

Uterine bleeding (usually referred to as "vaginal bleeding") any other time during the first trimester, however, is not regarded as normal, although it occurs in about 15 percent of first-trimester women. The causes of most cases of bleeding (other than implantation bleeding) are not known, but can include impending miscarriage and complications of the placenta. First-trimester bleeding that does not portend miscarriage is associated with a roughly twofold increase in the risk of premature delivery and neonatal death. Second-trimester bleeding is associated with a roughly threefold increase in the risk of miscarriage, premature delivery, growth retardation, stillbirth, and birth defects. Heavy bleeding is more worrisome than light bleeding. If bleeding other than implantation bleeding occurs during pregnancy, the woman should alert her OB/GYN immediately.

If Defects Occur

If the results of genetic testing indicate that the fetus is fine, but then malformations are discovered with ultrasound or at birth, this does not necessarily mean that the malformations were caused by anything tangible—that is, anything that can be pinpointed or that the mother had any control over. Malformations are bound to occur by chance in the development of some embryos because there are thousands of things that can go wrong during the formation of a fetus from a fertilized egg; one tiny

PREGNANCY SICKNESS

perturbation in the developmental pattern may result in a serious defect. If a woman who learns that her fetus or infant is malformed reviews her entire first trimester, she probably will be able to ferret out all kinds of possible culprits: the potatoes she ate at Christmas dinner; the antihistamine she took for hives after a hike; the long hot bath she took one evening; the X ray she got when she sprained her ankle; the four glasses of wine she drank at the New Year's party before she realized she was pregnant; the fumes she accidentally inhaled while pumping gas one day; the make-up she wore to conceal the fact that she didn't feel well. But the real culprit may simply be fate.

If a pregnant woman realizes that during the first trimester she ate some of the foods on the "sin" list, inadvertently took some medicine, came down with a cold, or was exposed to something else "bad," she shouldn't panic. Most babies are born healthy, even though almost all first-trimester women are exposed to substances that, at some dose, are teratogens. It's the dose that makes the poison, and even at relatively large doses, most teratogens increase the risk of birth defects only slightly. A pregnant woman who has been exposed to a teratogen at a dose that measurably increases the risk of birth defects—such as chronic anti-epilepsy medication—may want to schedule an ultrasound with a dysmorphologist to screen specifically for the type of defects associated with that teratogen. If a woman is uncertain whether the substance she was exposed to poses a realistic risk of harming her embryo or fetus, she may want to consult a teratogen information service (see Appendix B).

This book isn't meant to frighten people. Sometimes when I tell nonpregnant people about natural toxins in plant foods they say, "Oh no, does this mean that it's bad to eat vegetables? What about broccoli? What about tomatoes? What about . . ." If a woman is not experiencing her first trimester of pregnancy, it's usually good for her to eat a lot of vegetables—especially if she's eating a diversity of them. Plant toxins have been around for hundreds of millions of years, and humans have never *not* been exposed to them. We're adapted to handle toxins in certain doses. The goal of this book isn't to scare people about plants, but one of its goals *is* to warn first-trimester women about the particular dangers that plants pose during a temporary period in the life of her baby-to-be.

In Tandem: Natural World and Technological World

Pregnant women living in modern industrialized societies can have the best of both worlds—the protective mechanism of the natural one and the technological benefits of the modern one. In addition to having the natural protection of pregnancy sickness, a pregnant woman can get up-to-date information about which natural substances, synthetic substances, microorganisms, and activities may be teratogenic, enabling her to avoid these dangers during vulnerable stages in the development of her baby-to-be. In addition, she can take vitamin and mineral supplements to ensure an adequate supply of nutrients without having to eat large amounts of toxins normally associated with vegetable sources of nutrients. Furthermore, she can have prenatal imaging and genetic testing performed to help detect whether the fetus is malformed. Finally, she can have the psychological benefits of understanding the function of pregnancy sickness. One of the hopes of this book is that if a first-trimester woman understands that pregnancy sickness is a way to protect her baby-to-be, and not an arbitrary affliction, she will come to a fuller acceptance of pregnancy sickness and experience greater joy during pregnancy.

Appendix A

Pre-Conception Checklist to Help Prevent Birth Defects

THIS APPENDIX summarizes the things that were mentioned in this book that women (and, in some cases, men) can do in the three to six months prior to conception to help decrease the chance that their future embryos will be malformed.

Women Planning to Conceive

What to Discuss with the Physician

Women planning to conceive should consider getting a full medical (and dental) checkup to prevent, detect, or treat any medical conditions that might interfere with the health of the baby-to-be. Topics that a woman may want to bring up with her physician include the following:

Immunizations. As discussed in Chapter 11, a woman planning to conceive should make sure that she is immunized against rubella and tetanus. Since the measles-mumps-rubella vaccine contains live viruses, the general recommendation is that women receive it at least three months before conception.

Medical Diagnostic Procedures and Treatments. If a woman needs diagnostic radiation, radiation therapy, surgery, or other

PREGNANCY SICKNESS

medical treatment, it should be performed before she tries to conceive. A woman whose medical treatment requires high doses of radiation (above 25 rads) to her pelvis may want to postpone trying to conceive for a month or so after the treatment ends in case the radiation has seriously damaged the DNA of the egg cell preparing to ovulate.

Nutrition. As discussed in Chapter 8, before conception a woman should try to assess her nutrient status (or have a nutritionist, OB/GYN, midwife, or primary care physician do it) in order to determine whether or not she has any vitamin or mineral deficiencies (or excesses). She should try to eat a balanced, diversified diet in the several months prior to pregnancy and should consider taking multivitamin and mineral supplements. For most women trying to conceive, it is probably prudent to take folic acid supplements in order to lower the risk of neural tube defects.

Medical Conditions. As discussed in Chapter 8, if a woman has a medical condition, such as diabetes, that has a significant chance of affecting the nutritional environment of her embryo, she should work with an OB/GYN to get it under control before trying to conceive.

Medications. As discussed in Chapter 10, if a woman takes chronic medication (such as for epilepsy), she should check with a well-informed OB/GYN or a teratogen information service to find out whether or not the medication is risky for embryos. If it is, she should find out whether a less risky medication can be substituted.

Addictions. As discussed in Chapters 8 and 10, if a woman is addicted to alcohol, cocaine, or any other drug that poses a substantial risk to embryos, she should seek treatment before conceiving.

Cats. As discussed in Chapter 11, a woman who has been exposed recently to cats or to soil contaminated by cat feces may want to get tested for toxoplasmosis. If she is infected with the *Toxoplasmosis gondii* parasite, she should postpone conceiving until after treatment.

Dietary Toxins

As discussed in Chapter 3, most natural dietary toxins are cleared from the body fairly rapidly—although trace amounts may persist for a long time—which means that most dietary toxins consumed before pregnancy will not affect the embryo. The natural toxins in potatoes may be exceptions, because they persist in the body for long periods of time and appear to be teratogenic in some mammals. In general, a woman who is planning to conceive probably does not need to worry about eliminating particular foods from her diet (unless it is found that they contain toxins that persist in the body for long periods of time and are likely teratogens).

Occupational Exposures

As discussed in Chapter 10, a woman trying to conceive should take precautions to avoid exposure to large doses of solvents and other occupational chemicals. She may need to ventilate her workspace, wear gloves, don a mask, or wear other protective gear.

Men Planning to Father a Child

To what extent can birth defects be caused by chemicals to which the father was exposed? A drug, occupational chemical, or contaminant that is swallowed, inhaled, or otherwise absorbed by a man often can be detected, at least in trace amounts, in his semen. However, as far as I know, no animal or human study has demonstrated that any birth defect is caused by the transfer of teratogens from semen to the uterus. If a woman has sex after the embryo's cells begin to differentiate, the semen is unlikely to reach her uterus, because it is blocked by cervical mucus, which forms a dense plug at the beginning of pregnancy. Some chemicals in semen could potentially cause birth defects by mutating the DNA of the sperm that subsequently fertilize eggs. But in animal experiments, producing birth defects in this way usually requires very high doses of chemicals that do not reflect normal human exposures. (Certain chemicals that end up in semen, however, can temporarily reduce a man's fertility.)

As discussed in Chapter 8, one substance that appears to damage the DNA of sperm is cigarette smoke. The future father who smokes may be able to mitigate this damage by smoking less and by consuming substantial amounts of vitamin C (roughly 1,000 mg per day) for three months before conception—which spans the time it takes the body to produce a new generation of mature sperm cells. Even nonsmoking men should consider consuming ample amounts of vitamin C (250 mg per day) to try to minimize damage to the DNA of their sperm.

Some occupational chemicals that are able to mutate the DNA of sperm are potential risk factors for birth defects, so a man who is occupationally exposed to high levels of solvents or other chemicals should take precautions to minimize exposure to them, such as by wearing protective gear and ventilating the workspace.

Appendix B

～❦～

Teratogen Information Services

TERATOGEN INFORMATION services are located throughout
North America. Some services operate like hotlines, welcoming
calls from all interested persons, including pregnant women,
their parenting partners, and health care providers. Other services provide information only to physicians and other health
care providers. The North American services are listed below,
categorized by U.S. state or Canadian province. Most U.S. services will accept calls only from residents of their state, because
their funding comes primarily from state taxes. Some services,
however, will accept calls from other states, although they give
priority to callers from their own state. Currently, over half the
states in the United States have a teratogen information service.

A person would call a teratogen information service to seek
information about the teratogenic risks of a certain drug, virus,
radiation procedure, occupational chemical, or other substance.
The teratogen consultant, who is usually a geneticist, dysmorphologist, genetics counselor, or other specialist, is likely to ask
the caller to specify the dose and the timing of exposure to
the substance during pregnancy. Information regarding common drugs often is available immediately over the telephone, but

PREGNANCY SICKNESS

answers to questions about relatively obscure drugs or occupational chemicals may require some research on the part of the teratogen consultant before an assessment of probable risk can be given. A few services even recommend that the caller visit an associated clinic for a more thorough evaluation and consultation. Since many women panic when they realize that they have inadvertently taken a drug or been exposed to a virus during pregnancy, much of what the teratogen information services do is to calm their callers' fears. In general, the services strongly emphasize degree of risk; that is, when they confirm that a certain chemical is a risk factor for birth defects, they put the risk in perspective by comparing it to the background risk of birth defects.

The teratogen information services are run independently. They don't share a central database, but they do use many of the same sources of information, and, as members of the international Organization of Teratogen Information Services (OTIS), they often exchange information at conferences or through newsletters. Although for the most part information about a particular drug or other substance that callers would receive from one service is usually the same as the information that they would receive from another, information can be expected to vary somewhat from service to service due to differences in the background and training of the individual teratogen consultants and in the scientific studies that different services sponsor. Information on the causes of birth defects is accumulating, so estimates about risks of particular substances sometimes change from year to year.

Teratogen Information Services

United States

Arizona

Arizona Teratogen Information Service (ATIP)
University of Arizona Health Sciences Center, Department of
  Pediatrics
Tucson, AZ
1-800-362-0101 (in Arizona only)
602-626-6016 or 602-626-5175
For Arizona residents only

Arkansas

Arkansas Genetics Program Teratogen Counseling Service
University of Arkansas for Medical Sciences
Little Rock, AK
1-800-358-7229 (in Arkansas only)
501-296-1700
For Arkansas residents only

California

California Teratogen Registry (California Teratogen Information
  Service and Clinical Research Project)
UCSD Medical Center, Department of Pediatrics
San Diego, CA
1-800-532-3749 (in California only)
619-294-6084
For California residents only

PREGNANCY SICKNESS

Colorado

Teratogen Information & Education Service (TIES)
University Hospital, Division of Genetics
Denver, CO
1-800-221-6420
303-372-1825
For health care providers of Colorado, Kansas, Nebraska, and
Wyoming only

Connecticut

Connecticut Pregnancy Exposure Information Service (Preg-
nancy Riskline)
Division of Human Genetics, University of Connecticut Health
Center
Farmington, CT
1-800-325-5391 (in Connecticut only)
203-679-1502
For Connecticut residents only
For pregnant women, women planning pregnancy, their part-
ners, and health care providers

District of Columbia

Reproductive Toxicology Center
Columbia Hospital for Women Medical Center
Washington, D.C.
202-293-5137 (for information on how to subscribe)
For subscribers on an annual fee basis
For health care providers only

Teratogen Information Services

Florida

Teratogen Information Service
University of Florida Health Science Center
Gainesville, FL
1-800-392-3050 (in Florida only)
904-392-3050

Teratogen Information Service
Department of Pediatrics, University of South Florida
Tampa, FL
813-975-6905

Indiana

Indiana Teratogen Information Service
Department of Medical and Molecular Genetics, Indiana
  University School of Medicine
Indianapolis, IN
317-274-1071
Open to callers anywhere

Iowa

Iowa Teratogen Information Service
University of Iowa, Hospital and Clinics, Department of
  Pediatrics
Iowa City, IA
319-356-2674
Will accept callers from outside Iowa

PREGNANCY SICKNESS

Kansas

Teratogen Information & Education Service (TIES)
University Hospital, Division of Genetics
Denver, CO
1-800-221-6420
303-372-1825
For health care providers of Kansas, Colorado, Nebraska, and
   Wyoming only

Genetic Services
Wesley Medical Center
Wichita, KS
318-688-2362
For Kansas health care providers only

Massachusetts

Pregnancy Environmental Hotline (Massachusetts Teratogen
   Information Service)
National Birth Defects Center
Waltham, MA
1-800-322-5014 (in Massachusetts only)
617-466-8474
For New England residents and for health care providers
   anywhere

Cambridge Hospital
Occupational and Environmental Health Center
Cambridge, MA
617-498-1580
Open to callers anywhere

Teratogen Information Services

Missouri

Genetics and Environmental Information Service (Genis)
Department of OBGYN, Genetics, Washington University
  School of Medicine
St. Louis, MO
314-454-8172
Primarily for Missouri residents but will accept callers from
  other states

Montana

Pregnancy Riskline
Salt Lake City, UT
1-800-521-2229 (in Montana only)
For Utah and Montana residents only

Nebraska

Nebraska Teratogen Project
University of Nebraska Medical Center, MRI
Omaha, NE
402-559-5071
For Nebraska health care providers only

Teratogen Information & Education Service (TIES)
University Hospital, Division of Genetics
Denver, CO
1-800-221-6420
303-372-1825
For health care providers of Nebraska, Colorado, Kansas, and
  Wyoming

PREGNANCY SICKNESS

New York

Teratology Information Service
Buffalo, NY
1-800-724-2454 (in New York only)
716-874-7328 ext. 137
For New York residents only; outside of western New York
open to health care providers only

North Carolina

Burroughs Wellcome Company
Research Triangle Park, NC
1-800-722-9292 ext. 8465
919-315-8465
Open to callers anywhere regarding drugs manufactured by
Burroughs Wellcome

North Dakota

North Dakota Teratogen Service
Division of Medical Genetics, University of North Dakota
School of Medicine
Grand Forks, ND
1-800-962-0143
701-777-4277
For health care professionals anywhere

Pennsylvania

Pregnancy Safety Hotline
Reproductive Genetics, Western Pennsylvania Hospital
Pittsburgh, PA
412-687-SAFE (7233)
Open to callers anywhere

Teratogen Information Services

Pregnancy Safety Information Line
Department of Genetics, Magee Womens Hospital
Pittsburgh, PA
412-641-4168
Open to callers anywhere

South Dakota

South Dakota Teratogen and Birth Defects Information Project
University of South Dakota Medical School, Birth Defects
    Genetics Center
Vermillion, SD
1-800-962-1642 (SD only)
605-677-5623
For South Dakota residents only

Tennessee

Teratogen Information Service
T.C. Thompson Children's Hospital
Chattanooga, TN
615-778-6112
Open to callers anywhere

Texas

Texas Teratogen Information Service
Texas State Department of Mental Health and Mental
    Retardation
1-800-733-4727 (in TX only)
817-383-3561
For Texas residents only

PREGNANCY SICKNESS

Utah

Pregnancy Riskline
Salt Lake City, UT
801-583-2229
1-800-822-2229 (Utah callers only)
For Utah and Montana residents only

Vermont

Vermont Pregnancy Risk Information Service
Vermont Regional Genetics Center
Burlington, VT
1-800-531-9800 (in Vermont only)
1-800-932-4609 (in New York only)
802-658-4310
For residents of Vermont and the New York counties of
Clinton, Essex, and Franklin

Washington

CARE Northwest
University of Washington, Department of Pediatrics
Seattle, WA
1-800-859-5343
206-543-3373

West Virginia

West Virginia Teratogens in Pregnancy Service (TIPS)
Department of OB/GYN, West Virginia University
Morgantown, WV
304-293-1572
Open to callers anywhere

Teratogen Information Services

Wisconsin

Teratogen Information Service
La Crosse Regional Genetics Services
La Crosse, WI
608-791-6681
Open to callers anywhere

Wisconsin Teratogen Project
University of Wisconsin-Madison
1-800-442-6692
608-262-4719
Open to callers anywhere

Wyoming

Teratogen Information & Education Service (TIES)
University Hospital, Division of Genetics
Denver, CO
1-800-221-6420
303-372-1825
For health care providers of Wyoming, Colorado, Kansas, and
  Nebraska

Canada

British Columbia

Provincial Medical Genetics Programme
British Columbia Children's Hospital
Vancouver, British Columbia
604-875-2157
For physicians from British Columbia only

PREGNANCY SICKNESS

Ontario

Motherisk
Hospital for Sick Children, Division of Clinical Pharmacology
Toronto, Ontario
416-813-6780

Foetal Risk Assessment from Maternal Exposure (FRAME)
   Program
Children's Hospital of Western Ontario, Division of Clinical
   Pharmacology
London, Ontario
519-685-8293

Ottawa Motherisk
Children's Hospital of Eastern Ontario, Poison Information
   Center
Ottawa, Ontario
613-737-2320
For Ontario residents only

Safe-Start Teratogen Project
Chedoke-McMaster Hospital
Hamilton, Ontario
905-521-2100 ext. 6788
For health care providers anywhere

Quebec

Info-Grossesse: The Pregnancy Healthline
McGill University, Department of Epidemiology
Montreal, Quebec
514-933-8776

Appendix C

～∽～

Suggested Further Reading

THIS BIBLIOGRAPHY represents a tiny fraction of the scientific and medical literature that contributed to my research on the function of pregnancy sickness and the prevention of birth defects. The books and articles included below are those that I think would most interest a typical reader of this book. Most are books and review articles that cover some of the main topics of this book; some are specialized research articles that may be of particular interest to certain readers. Readers who would like to delve more deeply into particular topics may want to perform a medical literature search on the database Medline, which provides references to and summaries of several million medical and biological articles. Compiled by the National Library of Medicine, Medline can be accessed free of charge at many university medical and biology libraries as well as on a fee-per-hour basis through some commercial on-line services.

Chapter 1.   Introduction

Function of Pregnancy Sickness

Profet, M. 1992. Pregnancy sickness as adaptation: A deterrent to maternal ingestion of teratogens. In J. Barkow, L. Cosmides,

PREGNANCY SICKNESS

and J. Tooby (editors): *The Adapted Mind* (pp. 327–365). New York: Oxford University Press.

Historical Beliefs About Pregnancy Sickness

O'Brien, B. and Newton, N. 1991. Psyche versus soma: Historical evolution of beliefs about nausea and vomiting during pregnancy. *Journal of Psychosomatic Obstetrics and Gynaecology.* 12:91–120.

Chapter 2.   Natural Toxins and Our Natural Defenses Against Them

Evolutionary Theory

Dawkins, R. 1976. *The Selfish Gene.* New York: Oxford University Press.
Williams, G. C. 1966. *Adaptation and Natural Selection.* Princeton: Princeton University Press.

Natural Plant Toxins and Our Sensory Perception of Them

Duke, J. A. 1985. *Handbook of Medicinal Herbs.* Boca Raton, FL: CRC Press.
Garcia, J. and Hankins, W. G. 1975. The evolution of bitter and the acquisition of toxiphobia. In D. A. Denton and J. P. Coghlan (editors): *Olfaction and Taste* (vol. 5) (pp. 39–45). New York: Academic Press.
Keeler, R. F. and Tu, A. T. (editors). 1983. *Handbook of Natural Toxins: Plant and Fungal Toxins* (vol. 1). New York: Marcel Dekker.
Rosenthal, G. A. and Janzen, D. H. (editors). 1979. *Herbivores: Their Interaction with Secondary Plant Metabolites.* New York: Academic Press.

Suggested Further Reading

Enzyme Defenses Against Toxins

Jacoby, W. B. (editor). 1980. *Enzymatic Basis of Detoxification.* Vol. 1. New York: Academic Press.

Hodgson, E. and Levi, P. E. 1987. *A Textbook of Modern Toxicology.* New York: Elsevier Science Publishing.

Mechanisms of Nausea and Vomiting

Davis, C. J., Lake-Bakaar, G. V., and Grahame-Smith, D. G. (editors). 1986. *Nausea and Vomiting: Mechanisms and Treatments.* New York: Springer-Verlag.

Garcia, J. 1990. Learning without memory. *Journal of Cognitive Neuroscience.* 2:287–305.

Chapter 3.   The Vulnerable Embryo

Normal and Abnormal Development of the Embryo

Moore, K. L. and Persaud, T. V. N. 1993. *The Developing Human: Clinically Oriented Embryology.* 5th Edition. Philadelphia: W. B. Saunders.

Studies on the Abilities of Various Chemicals to Cause Birth Defects

Schardein, J. L. 1993. *Chemically Induced Birth Defects.* 2nd edition. New York: Marcel Dekker.

Birth Defects and Region

Lie, R. T., Wilcox, A. J., and Skjaerven, R. 1994. A population-based study of the risk of recurrence of birth defects. *The New England Journal of Medicine.* 331:1–4.

Pregnancy Sickness
and Low Miscarriage Rates

Weigel, R. M. and Weigel, M.M. 1989. Nausea and vomiting of early pregnancy and pregnancy outcome: A meta-analytical review. *British Journal of Obstetrics and Gynecology.* 96: 1312–1318.

Potatoes and Neural Tube Defects;
Potatoes and Clay-Eating

Renwick, J. H., Claringbold, W. D., Earthy, M. E., Few J. D., and McLean, A. C. 1984. Neural-tube defects produced in Syrian hamsters by potato glycoalkaloids. *Teratology.* 30:371–381.

Nevin, N. C. and Merrett, J. D. 1975. Potato avoidance during pregnancy in women with a previous infant with either anencephaly and/or spina bifida. *British Journal of the Preventive Society of Medicine.* 29:111–115.

Johns, T. 1991. Well-grounded diet—the curious practice of eating clay is rooted in its medicinal value. *Sciences.* 31(Sept–Oct):38–43.

Chapter 4.   How a Woman's Body Defends Her Embryo Against Toxins

Physiological Changes in Women
During the First Trimester

Clapp, J. F. III, Seaward, B. L., Sleamaker, R. H., and Hiser, J. 1988. Maternal physiological adaptations to early human pregnancy. *American Journal of Obstetrics and Gynecology.* 159: 1456–1460.

Hytten, F. E. 1984. Physiological changes in the mother related

Suggested Further Reading

to drug handling. In B. Krauer, F. Krauer, F. E. Hytten, and E. del Pozo (editors): *Drugs and Pregnancy: Maternal Drug Handling—Fetal Drug Exposure* (pp. 7–15). New York: Academic Press.

Chapter 5. Why Pregnancy Sickness Varies So Much in Severity

Pregnancy Sickness in !Kung Hunter-Gatherer Women

Shostak, M. 1981. *Nisa: The Life and Words of a !Kung Woman.* Cambridge, MA: Harvard University Press.

Chapter 6. Preparing for Pregnancy Sickness

Fallacies about Pregnancy Sickness and Coping with Pregnancy

Kasper, A. S. 1980. Nausea of pregnancy: An historical medical prejudice. *Women & Health.* 5:35–44.

Chapter 7. Managing Pregnancy Sickness: Trusting Food Aversions

Natural Toxins in Human Foods

Ames, B. N., Profet, M., and Gold, L. S. 1990. Dietary pesticides (99.99% all natural). *Proceedings of the National Academy of Sciences.* 87:7777–7781.

Ames, B. N., Profet, M., and Gold, L. S. 1990. Nature's chemicals and synthetic chemicals: Comparative toxicology. *Proceedings of the National Academy of Sciences.* 87:7782–7786.

Chapter 8. Balancing Good Nutrition and Pregnancy Sickness

Diet in the Ancestral Hunter-Gatherer Environment

Eaton, S. B., Shostak, M., and Konner, M. 1988. *The Paleolithic Prescription.* New York: Harper and Row.

Reasons Why the Body Sometimes Suppresses Reproduction

Wasser, S. K. and Isenberg, D. Y. 1986. Reproductive failure among women: Pathology or adaptation? *Journal of Psychosomatic Obstetrics and Gynaecology.* 5:153–175.

The Relationship Between Fat and Fertility

Frisch, R. E. 1988. Fatness and fertility. *Scientific American.* March: 88–95.

Nutritional and Other Conflict Between the Mother and Her Embryo/Fetus

Haig, D. 1993. Maternal-fetal conflict in human pregnancy. *The Quarterly Review of Biology.* 68:495–532.

The Woman's Metabolic Rate During Pregnancy

Poppitt, S. D., Prentice, A. M., Jequier, E., Schutz, Y., and Whitehead, R. G. 1993. Evidence of energy sparing in Gambian women during pregnancy: A longitudinal study using whole-body calorimetry. *American Journal of Clinical Nutrition.* 57:353–364.

Folic Acid for the Prevention of Neural Tube Defects

MRC Vitamin Study Research Group. 1991. Prevention of neural tube defects: Results of the medical research council vitamin study. *The Lancet.* 338:131–137.

Suggested Further Reading

Werler, M. M., Shapiro, S., and Mitchell, A. A. 1993. Periconceptional folic acid exposure and risk of occurrent neural tube defects. *Journal of the American Medical Association.* 269:1257–1261.

Vitamin C as a Protection Against Sperm Damage

Fraga, C. G., Motchnik, P. A., Shigenaga, M., Helbuck, H. J., Jacob, R. A., and Ames, B. N. 1991. Ascorbic acid protects against endogenous oxidative DNA damage in human sperm. *Proceedings of the National Academy of Sciences of the United States.* 88:11003–11006.

Iron Withholding as a Defense Against Infectious Microorganisms

Stuart-Macadam, P. and Dent, S. (editors). 1992. *Diet, Demography, and Disease.* New York: Aldine de Gruyter.
Weinberg, E. D. 1989. Cellular recognition of iron assimilation. *The Quarterly Review of Biology.* 64:261–290.

Diabetes and Birth Defects

Kitzmiller, J. L., Gavin, L. A., Gin, G. D., Jovanovic-Peterson, L., Main, E. K., and Zigrang, W. D. 1991. Preconception care of diabetes: Glycemic control prevents congenital anomalies. *Journal of the American Medical Association.* 265:731–736.

Weight Gain During Pregnancy

Johnson, J. W. C., Longmate, J. A., and Frentzen, B. 1992. Excessive maternal weight and pregnancy outcome. *American Journal of Obstetrics and Gynecology.* 167:353–372.
Parker, J. D. and Abrams, B. 1992. Prenatal weight gain advice: An examination of the recent prenatal weight gain recom-

mendations of the Institute of Medicine. *Obstetrics and Gynecology* 79: 664–669.

Chapter 9.   Too Much or Too Little
Pregnancy Sickness and What to Do About It

Treatments for Excessive Pregnancy Sickness

Livingston, E. G. and Hammond, C. B. 1992. Hyperemesis gravidarum: Is it a disease? *Postgraduate Obstetrics and Gynecology.* 12:1–6.

Hyde, E. 1989. Acupressure therapy for morning sickness. *Journal of Nurse-Midwifery.* 34:171–178.

Sahakian, V., Rouse, D., Sipes, S., Rose, N., and Niebyl, J. 1991. Vitamin B6 is effective therapy for nausea and vomiting of pregnancy: A randomized, double-blind placebo-controlled study. *Obstetrics and Gynecology.* 78:33–36.

Chapter 10.   Pregnancy Sickness Does Not Protect
Against All Modern Toxins: Alcohol, Cigarettes,
Medicines, and Pollutants

Studies on the Ability of Various Modern Toxic
Substances to Cause Birth Defects

Friedman, J. M., Little, B. B., Brent, R. L., Cordero, J. F., Hanson, J. W., and Shepard, T. H. 1990. Potential human teratogenicity of frequently prescribed drugs. *Obstetrics and Gynecology.* 75:594–599.

Schardein, J. L. 1993. *Chemically Induced Birth Defects.* 2nd edition. New York: Marcel Dekker.

Suggested Further Reading

Shepard, T. H. 1992. *Catalog of Teratogenic Agents.* 7th edition. Baltimore: Johns Hopkins University Press.

Chapter 11.   Other First-Trimester Hazards to Embryos

Teratogenic Microorganisms

Dickinson, J. and Gonik, B. 1990. Teratogenic viral infections. *Clinical Obstetrics and Gynecology.* 33:242–252.

Kurppa, K., Holmberg, P. C., Kuosma, E., Aro, T., and Saxen, L. 1991. Anencephaly and maternal common cold. *Teratology.* 44:51–55.

Lynberg, M. C., Khoury, M. J., and Cocian, T. 1994. Maternal flu, fever, and the risk of neural tube defects: A population-based case-control study. *American Journal of Epidemiology.* 140:244–255.

Zeichner, S. L. and Plotkin, S. A. 1988. Mechanisms and pathways of congenital infections. *Clinics in Perinatology.* 15:163–188.

Heat and Birth Defects

Milunsky, A., Ulcickas, M., Rothman, K. J., Willett, W., Jick, S. S., and Jick, H. 1992. Maternal heat exposure and neural tube defects. *Journal of the American Medical Association.* 268:882–885.

Travel During the First Trimester

Bia, F. J. 1992. Medical considerations for the pregnant traveler. *Infectious Disease Clinics of North America.* 6:371–388.

PREGNANCY SICKNESS

Radiation During Pregnancy

Bentur, Y., Horlatsch, N., and Koren, G. 1991. Exposure to ionizing radiation during pregnancy: Perception of teratogenic risk and outcome. *Teratology*. 43:109–112.

Brent, R. L. 1980. Radiation teratogenesis. *Teratology*. 21: 281–298.

Spermicide Use Near the Time of Conception

Einarson, T. R., Koren, G., Mattice, D., and Schechter-Tsafriri, O. 1990. Maternal spermicide use and adverse reproductive outcome: A meta-analysis. *American Journal of Obstetrics and Gynecology*. 162:655–660.

Chapter 12. Beyond the First Trimester

Prenatal Diagnosis

D'Alton, M. E. 1994. Prenatal diagnostic procedures. *Seminars in Perinatology*. 18:140–162.

Garmel, S. H. and D'Alton, M. E. 1994. Diagnostic ultrasound in pregnancy: An overview. *Seminars in Perinatology*. 18: 117–132.

Kolker, A. and Burke, B. M. 1994. *Prenatal Testing: A Sociological Perspective*. Westport, CT: Bergin and Garvey.

* * *

The approach to medicine used throughout this book—looking at our evolutionary past to help understand the functions of the various mechanisms in the human body—is often referred to as "evolutionary physiology" or "Darwinian medicine." Two recently published books with this same approach to medicine

Suggested Further Reading

that have major implications for understanding, preventing, and treating diseases are the following:

Ewald, P. W. 1994. *Evolution of Infectious Disease.* New York: Oxford University Press.

Nesse, R. M. and Williams, G. C. 1994. *Why We Get Sick: The New Science of Darwinian Medicine.* New York: Times Books.

INDEX

PREGNANCY SICKNESS